UNDERSTANDING SOCIAL
WELFARE MOVEM

Also available in the series

Understanding the finance of welfare (second edition)
What welfare costs and how to pay for it
Howard Glennerster
"... a total winner ... provides interest and excellence throughout."
SPA News, review of first edition
PB £21.99 (US$36.95) ISBN 978 1 84742 108 1
HB £65.00 (US$99.00) ISBN 978 1 84742 109 8
264 pages February 2009
INSPECTION COPY AVAILABLE

Understanding social security (second edition)
Issues for policy and practice
Edited by Jane Millar
"This updated second edition brings together some of the leading writers in the field to provide a critical analysis of the recent changes to the social security system."
Dr. Liam Foster, Department of Sociological Studies, University of Sheffield
PB £21.99 (US$36.95) ISBN 978 1 84742 186 9
HB £65.00 (US$99.00) ISBN 978 1 84742 187 6
344 pages February 2009
INSPECTION COPY AVAILABLE

Understanding the policy process (second edition)
Analysing welfare policy and practice
John Hudson and Stuart Lowe
"This is an exciting and innovative textbook on welfare policy making... an outstanding text."
British Journal of Social Work, review of 1st edition
PB £21.99 (US$36.95) ISBN 978 1 84742 267 5
HB £65.00 (US$99.00) ISBN 978 1 84742 268 2
352 pages March 2009
INSPECTION COPY AVAILABLE

Understanding equal opportunities and diversity
The social differentiations and intersections of inequality
Barbara Bagilhole
"This a timely and useful text which guides the reader through the conceptual, institutional and legal maze that lies behind 'equal opportunities' and 'diversity'."
Professor Teresa Rees, Pro Vice Chancellor, Research, Cardiff University
PB £21.99 (US$36.95) ISBN 978 1 86134 848 7
HB £65.00 (US$99.00) ISBN 978 1 86134 849 4
272 pages April 2009
INSPECTION COPY AVAILABLE

For a full listing of all titles in the series visit www.policypress.org.uk

www.policypress.org.uk

INSPECTION COPIES AND ORDERS AVAILABLE FROM:
Marston Book Services • PO Box 269 • Abingdon • Oxon OX14 4YN UK
INSPECTION COPIES
Tel: +44 (0) 1235 465500 • Fax: +44 (0) 1235 465556 • Email: inspections@marston.co.uk
ORDERS
Tel: +44 (0) 1235 465500 • Fax: +44 (0) 1235 465556 • Email: direct.orders@marston.co.uk

UNDERSTANDING SOCIAL WELFARE MOVEMENTS

Jason Annetts, Alex Law, Wallace McNeish and Gerry Mooney

First published in Great Britain in 2009 by

The Policy Press
University of Bristol
Fourth Floor, Beacon House
Queen's Road
Bristol BS8 1QU, UK

tel +44 (0)117 331 4054
fax +44 (0)117 331 4093
email tpp-info@bristol.ac.uk
www.policypress.org.uk

North American office:
The Policy Press
c/o International Specialized Books Services
920 NE 58th Avenue, Suite 300
Portland, OR 97213-3786, USA
tel +1 503 287 3093
fax +1 503 280 8832
email info@isbs.com

British Library Cataloguing in Publication Data
A catalogue record for this book is available from the British Library

Library of Congress Cataloging-in-Publication Data
A catalog record for this book has been requested

ISBN 978 1 84742 096 1   paperback
ISBN 978 1 84742 097 8   hardcover

Cover design by Qube Design Associates, Bristol
Front cover: photograph kindly supplied by www.alamy.com
Printed and bound in Great Britain by Hobbs the Printers, Southampton

Contents

Detailed contents

List of abbreviations

AIMS	Association for Improvements in Maternity Services
ALRA	Abortion Law Reform Association
CARE	Christian Action Research and Education
CND	Campaign for Nuclear Disarmament
CPE	*contrat première embauche*
CPGB	Communist Party of Great Britain
EU	European Union
GP	general practitioner
ICT	information and communication technology
IMF	International Monetary Fund
LEA	local education authority
LGBT	lesbian, gay, bisexual and transgendered
LSE	London School of Economics and Political Science
MP	Member of Parliament
MPU	Mental Patients' Union
NAC	National Abortion Campaign
NAFTA	North American Free Trade Agreement
NAMH	National Association for Mental Health
NGO	non-governmental organisations
NHI	National Health Insurance
NHS	National Health Service
NICE	National Institute for Health and Clinical Excellence
NLB	National League of the Blind
NUT	National Union of Teachers
NUWCM	National Unemployed Workers' Committee Movement
NUWM	National Unemployed Workers' Movement
NUWSS	National Union of Women's Suffrage Societies
NVALA	National Viewers' and Listeners' Association
NVDA	non-violent direct action
OECD	Organisation for Economic Co-operation and Development
PAC	Public Assistance Committee
RMT	resource mobilisation theory
SMC	Scottish Medicines Consortium
SML	Scottish Militant Labour
SMO	social movement organisation
SPUC	Society for the Protection of Unborn Children
SSBA	Scottish School Boards Association
SSP	Scottish Socialist Party
STARR	Stop the Ayr Road Route (Alliance)
TUC	Trades Union Congress
UAB	Unemployment Assistance Board
USM	urban social movement
WSPU	Women's Social and Political Union
WTO	World Trade Organization

Acknowledgements

We would like express our appreciation for all the hard work done by Emily Watt, Jessica Hughes, Leila Ebrahimi, Laura Greaves and all at The Policy Press who facilitated the production of this book. We are also grateful to Colin Barker, Magnus Ring, Chris Rootes and Peter Tatchell for kind words in their testimonials and to our anonymous referees at both commissioning and completion stages for constructive criticisms and useful suggestions concerning content and structure. Finally, we would like to thank all those social movement activists who gave their time to inform our various researches, and the wider social movement community which continues to offer political inspiration and hope for the future through word and deed.

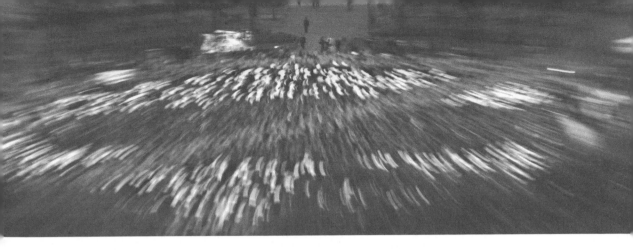

Introduction

'If you sow misery, you harvest anger.' (Slogan of unemployed protesters, France 1998)

'Brush with direct action. Helps to prevent truth decay.' (Slogan of anti-capitalist protesters, Seattle 1999)

'Your actions are pointless if no one notices.' (Graffiti on wall, Dundee 2008)

Just over a decade ago, a new wave of international protest broke out on the streets of Seattle. Between 27 November and 3 December 1999, the world's most powerful leaders were in Seattle to discuss global trade agreements under the auspices of the World Trade Organization (WTO). It was a good place for them to get together to discuss how to organise global markets more profitably. After all, Seattle is home to the great brand success stories of the world we live in – Microsoft, Starbucks and Nike. It is also fairly remote from other North American cities, making a coordinated national or international protest difficult to organise. But something happened at Seattle that no one expected: the meeting of the most powerful people on the planet was abandoned in the teeth of resilient and determined demonstrations. In the event, WTO officials packed their bags to go home full of recrimination against each other that no deal on trade could be brokered. But mostly they fumed about the storm of resistance created by the protesters outside the Convention Center.

On the key intersections of Seattle's streets, thousands of protesters fought and recoiled from the acrid tear gas, percussion grenades and rubber bullets fired at them by armoured police units. Seattle resembled some terrifying science fiction scene, a Robocop–Darth Vader–Judge Dredd cliché come to life to wreak vengeance on the puny bodies of flesh and blood protesters. Astonishingly, against ferocious levels of physical repression, the demonstrators held firm. Anything from 60,000 to 80,000 people protested over the five days. The protests were remarkably organised and coordinated, including an impressive level of participation by local people (Charlton, 2000). Under extreme police provocation, perhaps the biggest surprise of Seattle was the unity displayed in action by many diverse groups, above all between direct action activists and the US trade union movement. Teamsters marched alongside Turtles.[1] Many protesters were seasoned campaigners from past civil rights struggles, anti-war and anti-racism campaigns, and community activism. Newer direct action activists included:

> Earth First!, the Alliance for Sustainable Jobs and the Environment (the new enviro–steelworker alliance), the Ruckus Society (a direct-action training center), Food Not Bombs, Global Exchange and a small contingent of anarchists, dressed in black, with black masks, plus a hefty international contingent including French farmers, Korean greens, Canadian wheat growers and British campaigners against genetically modified foods. (St Clair, 1999, p 88)

These were joined by tens of thousands of rank-and-file trade unionists and labour movement activists determined to resist any further incursions by the WTO into US workers' living standards. When direct-action protesters were violently attacked by the police, shocked rank-and-file trade unionists rushed to their defence.

What has this motley gathering at Seattle in 1999 got to do with social welfare? Like many social movements, Seattle has both a direct and an indirect relationship to social welfare. Directly, the forces assembled to protest against the WTO were concerned with social welfare broadly understood (Danaher and Burbach, 2000). For some, global trade in welfare services was transforming the right to public goods into private commodities available only to those with the ability to pay. For others, global trade creates huge but avoidable diswelfare outcomes for the poorest parts of the developing world. Still others extended what we mean by welfare to embrace the damage being done by industry to the natural environment of our planet, the ultimate source of our subsistence and well-being. More indirectly, Seattle shaped the struggles of the next decade. In one way or another, the 'anti-capitalism' that manifested itself at Seattle informed the prevailing mood for any group that found itself contesting the market-led reorganisation of social welfare and, more pointedly, state welfare.

Brutal Police Action

Seattle became a symbolic model of resistance to the domination of human welfare by corporate interests. As social movement activists put it, 'another world is possible'. European intellectuals like Pierre Bourdieu, Jurgen Habermas and Jacques Derrida issued appeals for a social movement in defence of 'social Europe'. By this, Bourdieu (2003, p 56) meant the development of a new internationalism, or 'universal voluntarism', to defend and extend the non-market bases of social welfare:

> Social history teaches that there is no social policy without a social movement capable of imposing it and that it was not the market, as some would have us believe today, but the labor movement that "civilized" the market economy while greatly contributing to its effectiveness. Consequently, for all those who genuinely wish to oppose a social Europe to the Europe of the banks and money – flanked by a police and penitentiary Europe (which is already far advanced) and a military Europe (a probable consequence of intervention in Kosovo) – the question is how to mobilize the forces capable of achieving the end and which bodies to carry out this work of mobilization.

Post-Seattle, popular resistance to neoliberal capitalism seemed to provide an answer to Bourdieu's question about which forces and bodies would mobilise against the destruction of social welfare through market reforms and warfare. One expression of this was the popular rejection of neoliberal Europe in the 'No' vote in the national European Union (EU) referendum held in France in 2005.

Wherever corporate interests met at G8 or WTO meetings, they were greeted with mass protest. In 2001, brutal police actions against the massive demonstrations that shook the Genoa G8 summit saw a protester, Carlo Giuliani, shot dead by armed police and scores of detainees tortured. The highest point of protest came in February and April 2003 when millions marched against the looming war in Iraq. Another huge demonstration met the 2005 G8 summit held in Gleneagles, although the main event was held 60 miles away in Edinburgh. While it lacked the militant temper of its direct action predecessors, the huge mobilisation in Edinburgh managed to shine a spotlight on the problem of world poverty and third world debt. Meanwhile the direct action in Gleneagles itself became a sideshow.

In some ways, this seemed to mark the ebb tide of the remarkable cycle of protest that emerged so suddenly at Seattle. Yet social movements continue to emerge in the most expansive and unexpected ways. For instance, in 2005, France saw major mobilisations around the 'No' campaign for the EU constitution, riots in the inner-city suburbs, and wide-scale anti-employment reform protest. In October 2006, riots erupted in 274 towns in the Paris region after two immigrant youths were electrocuted at the end of a police chase. In the rundown suburbs, thousands of mainly unemployed youth fought with police and destroyed property (see Sahlins, 2006, for a range of social science analyses). And this was not unique to France.

Similar uprisings of dispossessed young people occurred in protests at police oppression in the US black ghettoes in the 1960s and 1970s and Los Angeles in 1992, and in Britain in 1981 in the inner-city slums of Brixton, Toxteth and Handsworth. In each case, an event occurs that concentrates in a single symbolic moment the profound sense of injustice and years of resentment, grievance and alienation that such communities suffer at the hands of the authorities. In December 2008, Greece saw a similar convulsion that shook society to its core (Pittas, 2009). Again, the trigger was the police killing of a young person. Within hours, riots exploded in Athens. The next day, a mass demonstration at the central police station demanded justice and was met by police tear gas. Students occupied schools and universities. Thousands of supporters of the insurgent youth marched to join a demonstration outside Parliament on the day that millions of workers participated in a general strike against neoliberal policies.

In the French case, new protests followed in March and April 2006 in the urban centres against the First Employment Contract (*contrat première embauche* or CPE). The CPE was designed to create a more flexible and docile workforce and represented a deterioration in employment conditions for people under the age of 26. This time, youth in education, especially those active against fascism and racism, acted as a lightning rod for the deep currents of French society (Kouvelakis, 2006). Millions demonstrated, rioting was renewed, mass strikes took place and students occupied university buildings. All this disorder forced the government to withdraw the legislation and gave the social movements their first national success in a decade.

This new wave of struggle coincided with the crisis of the world economy and neoliberal ideology, worsening environmental degradation, and endemic warfare (see the concluding chapter). Some, like Davis (2009), view Athens as potentially opening up new vistas of popular protest:

> Athens is being widely envisioned as the answer to the question, 'After Seattle, then what?' The anti-WTO demonstrations and the 'Battle of Seattle' in 1999 opened a new era of non-violent protest and grassroots activism. Now an entire cycle has come to an end just as the Wall Street boiler room of global capitalism has exploded, leaving in its wake both more radical problems and new opportunities for radicalism.

Of course, as Davis notes, the significance of Athens for the expansion of social movement activity will only become clear with the benefit of hindsight. Nevertheless, it seems clear that divisions within national governments about how to deal with the crisis of neoliberal legitimation and geopolitical domination will stimulate social movement mobilisations. In January 2009, anti-war demonstrators across the globe protested against the Israeli attack on Gaza in their tens and hundreds of thousands in Athens, Baghdad, Barcelona, Cairo, London and Tel Aviv.

The 'miracle' of social movements

> The unemployed movement, i.e. the simultaneous initiation of a collective organization and the chain reactions that had led to it and that it contributed to producing: from isolation, depression, individual resentment and vindictiveness towards scapegoats, to collective mobilization; and from resignation, passivity, withdrawal and silence, to making oneself heard; from depression to revolt, from the isolated unemployed individual to the collective of unemployed, from misery to anger. This is how the slogan of the demonstrators became true: 'If you sow misery, you harvest anger'. (Bourdieu, 2008, p 294)

Many social movements when they first appear often have something of the character of a surprise about them. In this sense, social movements are quite literally astonishing. Dull, tedious reality is enlivened and energised by mobilisations and protest. Social movements stand out from the banal background of everyday life. The plain excitement of being with others in public displays of collective togetherness temporarily tears a hole in the fabric of the taken-for-granted, atomised nature of reality. This is what made Seattle appear for many as a spontaneous manifestation. From the outside, it seemed to arrive, without warning, out of nowhere. From the inside, for long-standing activists worn down by years of fruitless campaigns or defeats, the sudden appearance of newly energised movements seems to defy the laws of gravity. Hence, it is important to understand that social movements do not spring out of nowhere fully formed. Instead, they always have a specific 'pre-history' of unspectacular, unseen, patient, molecular, frustrating, routine, face-to-face relationships (Charlton, 2003).

Seattle was no freak of nature. It was not a one-off, accidental or spontaneous event without antecedents. Throughout the 1990s, protest was already stirring against market reforms. Despite the presidential election of Nicolas Sarkozy in 2007, committed to the 'modernisation' of the French welfare state and an expressed commitment to destroy 'the heritage of May 1968', social movements have, perhaps more than elsewhere in Europe, defended the welfare state in France with greater success through recurrent forms of popular mobilisation. In November 1995, a French transport workers' strike to resist pension reform presaged the wider social movement of December 1995. Two million public sector workers brought France to a standstill in protest against the 'Juppé Plan' for reforming the social security system. Although traduced by professional sociologists as a narrow corporatist defence of sectional interests that stood in the way of welfare modernisation, in the December movement labour activists drew connections with a diverse range of other activists among students, gay people, immigrants and unemployed people. This heralded a wave of protest where each movement learned to adapt tactics and forms of struggles mutually from each other. In January 1998, unemployed workers thus used the tactic of occupying prominent buildings from the *sans-papiers* (immigrants denied 'legal' status) whose 1996 occupation of a church and eviction by riot police became a national *cause célèbre*. Similarly, a protest by workers against redundancies at a factory in Mamers took the form of a 'die-in', emulating the form of protest adopted by AIDS activists ACT UP.

The 1998 unemployed workers' movement showed remarkable organisational skills in demanding adequate increases to recover some of the devalued social security payments. For Bourdieu (1998), the collective mobilisation of the unemployed is something of a 'social miracle'. What seemed so 'miraculous' to Bourdieu was that the unemployed appear to be the most vulnerable group in society, possessing little in the way of structural strength or material resources. In the past, the unemployed have been susceptible to reactionary appeals, for instance that immigrants are to blame for the lack of jobs and that authoritarian political solutions, including fascist ones, are necessary. More usually, the unemployed are seen as a lazy, apathetic, demoralised, welfare-dependent and criminalised 'underclass'. In the case of the French movement, the mobilisation of the unemployed challenged all these preconceptions, including the idea of the lazy, feckless unemployed scrounger who refuses to get out of bed to do an honest day's work.

In fact, as the chapters of this book testify, there is nothing 'miraculous' about dispossessed and oppressed groups organising themselves to demand improvements in welfare services or benefits. From its earliest days, capitalism created a class of wage labourers, some of which were unable to find paid employment, became dependent on charity or, worse, were exposed to absolute destitution. In a capitalist society, nearly all social and personal needs are met through the payment of money wages, which are then exchanged for the goods and services essential to life itself. From the beginning, social movements have contested and challenged market-based inequalities and suffering, resorting to direct action, demonstrations, petitions, mass meetings, hunger marches, occupations of buildings, vandalism of machinery, and political campaigning. Such movements typically make demands for citizenship rights to ensure that adequate welfare measures like unemployment benefits, national insurance and social security are put in place by government action.

For some scholars and politicians, social movements of ordinary people fighting for material improvements to their lives represent the past. They are rather nostalgic, old-fashioned reminders of a time before the creation of the welfare state largely resolved the age-old problem of distributing the most basic material necessities, housing, education and healthcare to those most in need. Since the Second World War, it is often assumed, the welfare state has taken care of these more elementary needs. The 'new' social movements that have emerged since the 1960s are concerned with more elevated, symbolic or even spiritual needs such as identity, nature, sexuality, justice, peace, faith or cultural beliefs rather than the crude physical necessities of yesteryear (Williams, 1989). And the nature of what a social movement actually is has been transformed from mass organisations of the working class, largely male and exclusively white, and organised from the top down, to much more diverse, highly educated, tactically daring, inclusive and participatory groups (Bagguley, 1992).

While this dichotomous picture of *old* and *new* social movements is particularly marked in some social movements' scholarship, it has barely resonated within social policy as a discipline (Martin, 2001). It is a key aim of this book to redress both the simplistic division of old and new social movements through the prism of social welfare and the absence of social movements in much social policy. A rigid division of social movements into old and new forms will fail to do justice to the struggles over welfare of the past couple of centuries, let alone the past few years. In one sense, these were clearly a politics of the belly, struggles for material improvements. But, at the same time, they were also demands for dignity, respect, recognition, equality and democracy, attributes that are said to characterise more recent movements (Melucci, 1989). Neither were they always or even usually mass movements of the majority, as the frozen picture of a homogenous, largely male and white working class suggests.

What are social movements?

Social movements are heterogeneous, dynamic, constantly evolving social collectivities. By their very nature they make any attempt at hard-and-fast definition, categorisation or classification a rather foolhardy exercise. Social movement scholars endlessly agonise over what exactly distinguishes a social movement from other forms of collective action, such as interest groups, 'single-issue' campaigns, protests, coalitions or political parties. Definitional hair-splitting is not a very productive pastime (Crossley, 2002). Nevertheless, some rudimentary sense of what constitutes a social movement allows us to isolate certain characteristic features. For Tilly (2004, p 3), social movements constitute a distinctive form of 'contentious politics' – 'contentious' because the claims that are made will come into conflict with the interests of some other group; 'politics' because some appeal is made to or role is expected of government. Hence, the contentious politics of 'social welfare' are translated into the policy process of 'state welfare'. In making claims around state welfare, social movements respond to, struggle against or bring into play the institutions of the modern state.

This has not always been the case. Social movements are a quintessentially modern political phenomenon. Developed in the West from around the mid-18th century, social movements embodied three key elements (Tilly, 2004). First, social movements conduct *campaigns* as organised and sustained collective claim-making on authorities, usually the state. Second, they perform distinctive *repertoires of contention* through combining different forms of political activity, communication and voluntary association such as public meetings, processions, rallies, demonstrations, petitions, media relations and propaganda. Third, they are compelled to display the social movement virtues of '*worthiness, unity, numbers and commitment*' on behalf of themselves or their constituencies.

Likewise, Della Porta and Diani (2006, p 20) propose a loose three-point definition that conceives of social movements as a 'distinct social process'. Social movement actors, first, enter into conflict with clearly identified opponents; second, actors are linked by dense informal networks; and third, they share a distinct collective identity. In this definition there is a similar emphasis on conflict but without the state necessarily being central to the field of conflict. Instead, there is an emphasis on the structure of actors' interaction and the bonds that tie movement activists together. From a social welfare perspective, making a claim on the state at some level is of crucial importance. So while both of these definitions are useful, in the case of welfare movements more than networks and interaction is needed. An emphasis on the state apparatus is vital.

Clearly, social movements seem to suggest something quite different from conventional, mainstream political parties. Again, a hard-and-fast definition is not advisable, not least because there is not a clear line dividing 'conventional' from 'unconventional' politics. Rather, as Byrne (1997, pp 24-5) suggests, the most meaningful way to conceive of social movements is as part of a 'continuum of political action' located in a 'grey area' where conventional and unconventional blur, and where 'ideology, tactics and organisation may become rather different'. Forming part of this continuum are other groupings and organisations that have also challenged the prevailing social order in one way or another. However, Byrne (1997) argues that a distinction needs to be drawn in order to isolate what are genuine social movements from more limited and short-lived campaigns and groups. First, 'protest campaigns' are confined to limited, single-issue, short-term campaigns. Examples would include the Anti-Poll Tax campaigns of the late 1980s and user and self-help campaigns in health and social care. Second, broader 'protest movements' may contain a wide variety of organisations, oriented towards a broad area of government policy, which endure over time, and aim to change public values. Examples here would include CND and Greenpeace. Finally, genuine 'social movements' for Byrne are longlasting movements, conceived in the broadest sense to be striving for fundamental social change. These contain within themselves a wide variety of organisations and groups, such as protest campaigns and protest movements. Examples of such are the peace movement, the environmental movement and the women's movement.

Byrne provides a useful typology of protest groups. Criteria such as the timeframe of campaigns, the breadth of their ideology and the depth of their ultimate goals help to differentiate between all sorts of campaigns and organisations. However, for our purposes we adopt a looser vocabulary in this book. Each of the campaigns covered in subsequent chapters can be considered as part of an overall social movement pressing for the reform of state welfare in some way or another. So while we resist absolutely fixed approaches to defining or categorising the protests around social welfare, it is important at the outset to bear in mind that campaigns, protest events, organisations and social movements may all refer to different moments of the same process. One aim of this book is to encourage an understanding of social movements as a part of a wider totality involving not only far-reaching movement goals but also more immediate interventions by local activists, leaders, actions, events, interaction with the state, the media, political parties and so on. While individual chapters deal with particular campaigns and events, they are not understood by us as wholly localised and isolated examples and case studies of protest, removed from the wider political culture desiring welfare reform.

These form part of what we might identify as a broader 'social welfare movement'. Like social movements more generally, 'social welfare movements' can be defined in various ways. Oppositional collective action at the point of service delivery is one way of delineating a social welfare movement. For Harrison and Reeve (2002, p 757), the term refers to 'a connected series of conscious actions, interactions and interrelationships constituting collective action focused or organised around the consumption and/or control of important services, and/or the meeting of individual, household or group needs and aspirations, outside the sphere of direct wages'. At some level this involves a challenge to the welfare or regulatory politics of the state. Enduring, organised, contentious interaction of rank-and-file activism with state welfare characterises social welfare movements. But despite specific studies of particular sites of struggle in health, education, housing, social care, social security and so on, there has been little development of an overall approach to the social welfare–state institutions–social movement nexus. While a continuum can be charted from direct action protest through advocacy and user groups to incorporation with managerial structures, a focus on contentious politics reserves our understanding of social movements to conflictual politics that resist assimilation to authority structures and the dilution of a culture of challenge.

Such a movement was integral to the making of the British welfare state in the years 1942 to 1948. A loose coalition of social movement networks from within and around the labour movement campaigned for progressive reform of education, a free modern healthcare system, a fair system of social security and benefit entitlements, and improved housing stock. This agitation contributed directly to the radical political mood during the war years and the landslide Labour victory in the General Election of 1945. The welfare state today remains a child of this moment of social reform – a spoiled child, a political compromise, a constantly contested terrain. As such, the idea of a welfare consensus does not quite capture the sometimes ideologically fraught and practically disputed nature of state welfare: it is always a zone of 'contentious politics'. Welfare contention was heightened through the combined shocks of the end of the long post-war economic boom in the late 1960s and the advent of new 'social welfare movements'.

'New welfare movements' comprise a variety of groups that come together to express specific demands collectively, from HIV+ to reproductive rights groups, but who are united as a social movement by a concern with the fundamental demand for empowerment, representation, and ensuring the quality and accountability of user-centred provision (Williams, 1992; Martin, 2001, p 374). As such, *new* welfare movements differ from the welfare movements of previous generations in the UK. They operate in and around an already established welfare state system to preserve, extend, deepen and improve service delivery. They form part of what has been called a 'culture of challenge' where expert authority is increasingly contested (Scrambler and Kelleher, 2006). In the contemporary era when neoliberal antipathy to state welfare has been central to government social policy making, these movements have mobilised to defend the very principle of social welfare itself and to defend the institutions and jobs associated with that principle.

In the 21st century, social movements are increasingly operating at a transnational or global level because the interests that they have mobilised around – whether it be environmental justice, human rights or economic exploitation – are recognised as being insoluble at a national level and require coordinated international action. The negative side-effects of globalised capitalism require global solutions. Naomi Klein (2001, p 84) argues that:

> around the world, activists are piggy-backing on the ready-made infrastructures supplied by global corporations. This can mean cross border unionization, but also cross sector organizing – among workers, environmentalists, consumers, even prisoners, who may all have different relationships to one multinational.

Transnational social movement networks (often facilitated by a combination of information technology and international non-governmental organisations) link activists together in a loose, ever-shifting community of interlinked interests, which shares resources (information, organisation, personnel, finance and so on) to stand in opposition to the dominant neoliberal version of globalisation – built, Naomi Klein (2001, p 88) argues, 'on the back of human welfare'. These networks emerged dramatically into the open for the first time at Seattle. In one sense, corporate institutions and their allies in right-wing think-tanks, mainstream political parties, academia, corporation boards, banks and trading floors, and the media may be likened to a 'social movement from above', in conflict with the coalition of 'welfare movements from below', whose abiding concern is to forge an alternative world of a welfare-centred globalisation. These issues are explored in Chapter Eleven.

Welfare movements in context

In modernity an intimate relationship has been established between social welfare and social movements. As the democratic ideal took hold in the 19th century, the idea was born that all men and, somewhat belatedly, all women were created equal. It can therefore look as if the welfare state is merely the last step on the long historical march of liberal democratic societies, the culmination of an innate civilising process. A further aim of this book is to restore the active agency of social movements to social policy. State welfare can be understood as a process of contentious politics and not simply as a product of expert stakeholders.

A single book cannot possibly do justice to the many facets of welfare movements. We therefore recognise at the outset that many important welfare movements are barely discussed. Much, much more can been said, for instance, about the direct-action campaigns of mental health and disabled activists. An important book, *Contesting Psychiatry*, by social movement scholar Crossley (2006), analyses psychiatry and mental health as a complex and shifting 'field of contention'. Crossley identifies historical waves of mental health and anti-psychiatry activism. Founded in 1946, the mainstream organisation, the National Association for Mental Health (NAMH), rejected criticisms of psychiatric practices based on an ideology of 'mental hygiene'. As this model came under attack from the anti-psychiatry movements of the 1960s and 1960s, a radicalised NAMH transmogrified into MIND in the 1970s to reflect a newlyfound voice for modern patient rights. This coincided with the formation of a patient's movement, the Mental Patients' Union (MPU). By the 1980s, a 'second-wave' anti-psychiatry movement emerged through groups, alongside radical survivor movements. In the 1990s, such groups as Mad Pride and Reclaim Bedlam drew on the tactics and style of the wider direct-action movement engaged in anti-corporate and environmental protest.

Disability rights activists reject institutional practices of dependency and incapacity that deny effective civil rights to disabled people (Oliver, 1990; Shakespeare, 1993). Some disabled people have actively organised to resist disablement as a form of discrimination and prejudice (Oliver, 1990; Shakespeare, 1993; Dowse, 2001; Barnes, 2007). The Disablement Incomes Group was set up in 1965 by two disabled women, leading to the formation of the Disability Alliance. A demand for recognition for disabled rights broader than benefits lobbying lay behind the founding of the Union of the Physically Impaired Against Segregation. By 1981, the British Council of Organisations of Disabled People brought together 130 organisations claiming to represent 400,000 disabled people. Disability rights confront similar dilemmas to other social movements such as the alternative of direct action or institutional incorporation (Barnes et al, 2007). Incorporation has been posed ever more sharply with the setting up by the government of the Office of Disability Issues, which has had the effect of further blurring the boundaries between movements 'of' and organisations 'for' disabled people (Barnes, 2007). One indication of how incorporation can erode the ability of social movements to act independently was the cancellation of the Disabled People's Rights and Freedoms march from Birmingham to London in 2004 organised by the group Our Rights Now (Cook, I., 2004). Self-consciously modelled after the unemployed marches of the 1930s, ironically themselves modelled after earlier disabled people's marches (see Chapter Four), a coordinated march in support of the Disabled People's Rights Charter had to be abandoned in light of the difficulty of raising the necessary finance.

We have not selected empirical examples to bolster a preconceived affinity with one or other theory of social movements. Nor are we claiming that the historical and contemporary movements covered in the book necessarily represent the only or the most significant shapers of state welfare. In this sense, the book represents a genuine collaboration across research interests and political commitments. In any case, this was how we initially conceived the book; it is down to others to judge how successfully it has been realised.

Structure of the book

We have attempted to convey the heterogeneous character of welfare movements and some of the specific qualities of different movements covered in individual chapters. To prevent this from becoming too unwieldy, the book has been organised around a clear structure that arranges the narrative into three parts. Part One sets out the historical, ideological and theoretical context for what follows. Part Two charts the interrelationship of welfare movements and social welfare in the founding and development of the classical Beveridgean welfare state in the period following the Second World War. Part Three analyses the impact on social welfare of the new social movements that emerged in the 1960s and after.

In order to counter the sometimes excessive emphasis that social policy as a discipline places on the role of politicians, professional bodies and state administrators in the creation of state welfare, Chapter One analyses the role attributed to social movements in the immediate post-war phase, at the height of what is sometimes thought of as the 'golden age' of the welfare state. The chapter compares one of the most influential accounts of the rise of the welfare state, T.H. Marshall's (1950) 'Social class and citizenship', to the classical Marxist analysis of the welfare state, John Saville's (1957-58) essay 'The welfare state: an historical approach'. Chapter Two develops this approach further by looking at the relationship of social welfare and social movements in a much longer historical timeframe. It situates the emerging popular struggles over civil, political and social rights in the 19th and 20th centuries in specific local and institutional cultures. Chapter Three shifts the emphasis from historical analysis to the theoretical analysis of welfare movements. It establishes the main lines of debate in recent social movement scholarship, whether to characterise movements according to how they mobilise the resources at their disposal or according to the values and ideologies that animate them.

Part Two addresses the part played by social movements in the founding politics of and later developments in the classic Beveridgean welfare state. This part is roughly organised around the 'five giants' identified by Beveridge: idleness (unemployment), want (poverty), sickness (health), squalor (housing) and ignorance (education). Almost 70 years later, Beveridge's giants remain central to the politics of state welfare. Chapter Four focuses on how the unemployed struggles of the inter-war years shaped subsequent thinking on social security and employment policy. Against considerable hostility and Red scares, a national unemployed movement was built by rank-and-file activists in the pit of the economic depression of 1930s to resist benefit cuts and demand dignity for the unemployed. Chapter Five moves from the early politics of the National Health Service to consider the later challenge to the founding assumptions of medical experts by the women's movement. Here, distinctions between social movements and self-help groups, user groups or voluntary providers have become somewhat blurred in practice. Chapter Six deals with the politics of contention stimulated by urban social movements. Struggles around housing, from the Glasgow rent strikes of 1915 to contemporary campaigns against housing stock transfers, have thrown into especially sharp relief the 'politics of place' as an essential component of social welfare. Chapter Seven maps the long, difficult struggle for comprehensive education. Given the central role accorded education as a panacea for social ills and personal improvement, a variety of antagonistic interests historically contested around educational institutions and values.

Part Three examines the impact on social welfare of what are often called 'new' social movements. This refers to the advent of radical, direct action campaigns that emerged out of the political tremors of the 1960s. Chapter Eight indicates something of the transition that has taken place in British society in the past few decades by considering one of the ideological bedrocks of the welfare state – family policy. As the family structure was being reshaped by a range of social forces, a conservative counter-movement emerged in an effort to influence social policy to restore or salvage an idealised notion of the 'traditional' nuclear family. This involved framing as 'deviant' other family forms such as single parents or civil partnerships, one to be corrected by state welfare programmes, moral regulation and legislation. Chapter Nine considers how an equally cherished ideal, that of civil rights, long regarded as a firmly established progressive element of state welfare citizenship entitlement, became the focus for struggle in a range of post-war civil rights movements. The chapter highlights the past 50 years of anti-racist struggle, paying close attention to the Asian youth movement. Anti-racism and multicultural politics continually tread a fine line of being co-opted and resistance dissipated by authorised community leaders and partnerships.

Chapter Ten extends our understanding of welfare movements further by drawing attention to the environmental movement, a diverse assemblage of activists that has welfare values at the core of its philosophy and action. What might be called 'eco-welfarism' has successfully placed sustainability, both social and natural, firmly on the political agenda, so much so that 'sustainability' has become the small change of public policy discourse. As the chapter shows through a case study of anti-road protests, eco-welfarism exposes some of the basic faultlines between sustainable communities, especially deprived ones, and infrastructural development. Chapter Eleven takes us full circle back to our starting point: Seattle. It establishes the relevance for social welfare of the so-called 'anti-globalisation' movement' or, more accurately, the 'global social justice movement'. Troubling questions are raised by the social justice movement about social welfare as a universal claim of right as against the specific struggles of particular groups. As neoliberal capitalism plunges deeper into crisis as we write, this chapter has a pointed relevance about how local, regional and national movements mediate global forces and processes. This movement has also opened out the debate about which values ought to govern our shared fate on this planet.

Note

[1] Teamsters is the name for the US truck drivers' trade union. Turtles refers to the hundreds of environmental activists who wore sea turtle costumes at Seattle. This was in protest against WTO efforts to repeal the US Endangered Species Act as an unfair barrier to market trade.

Part One

*Social movements and welfare:
ideology, history and theory*

one

Protest and principle in state welfare

Introduction

What part did social movements play in the formation of state welfare? Many accounts relegate social movements to a footnote in the development of state welfare while emphasising the role played by politicians, professional bodies and state administrators. Yet more was involved than the benevolent actions of a few elite individuals and groups. This chapter examines the prehistory of state welfare and explores the role attributed to social movements from competing social scientific perspectives. In order to do so, we compare perhaps the most influential account of the rise of the welfare state as expressing social rights, namely T.H. Marshall's (1950) lecture and essay 'Social class and citizenship', to 'one of the earliest and finest Marxist analyses of the welfare state' (Mishra, 1981, p 75), that of John Saville's essay 'The welfare state: an historical approach' (1957-58). Both accounts appeared at a precise historical moment, that of the post-war, high watermark for the egalitarian hopes that were placed in state welfare in Britain. Since this moment is often viewed in retrospect as a 'golden age' for state welfare, revisiting the analyses of leading British social scientists and historians of that age provides us with a measure of how they accounted for the role played by social movements from below.

Both Marshall and Saville locate state welfare within a wider sociohistorical trajectory in the development of British social policy. The major faultline that this chapter focuses on is the debate between idealist and materialist approaches to the history of welfare. Marshall tends to picture this as a smooth line in the almost inevitable development of the *ideal* of social rights while Saville tends to emphasise the *material* social conditions that lie behind the discontinuous and contingent nature of social rights. This allows us to compare their respective accounts according to the sociological precept that people make history in conditions that they do not choose. Social reform therefore occurs in a historical conjuncture that contains the following elements:

- constraints and possibilities imposed by objective institutional structures;
- some combination of historical continuities and discontinuities represented by a crisis such as war or social upheaval;
- the role played by values, ideas and principles; and
- a willingness of broad masses of people to undertake popular mobilisation from below.

In contrast to the hegemony of the top-down social administration school represented by Marshall and others, we are at pains in this book to restore the bottom-up element in the contested and contentious politics of state welfare. More reflection of the role played by social movements and direct action provides a long overdue antidote to what E.P. Thompson (1970) called 'the condescension of posterity' in the erasure of struggles from below in many accounts of the establishment of social policy.

Citizenship rights: a Whig history

Perhaps the most famous sociological account of the rise of state welfare was penned some 60 years ago by T.H. Marshall (1950) in his celebrated essay 'Citizenship and social class'. Marshall was Professor of Sociology at the London School of Economics and Political Science (LSE), which was founded in 1883 by the Fabian socialists Sidney and Beatrice Webb. A social reformist colouration was stamped on sociology at the LSE with the overlap between Fabian socialism and the 'new liberalism' of the late 19th and early 20th centuries (Halsey, 2004). This social-reformist confluence, known as 'Lib-Labism' after its peculiar mixture of Liberalism and Labourism, resulted in the dominance at the LSE of the tradition of social scientific investigation known as 'social administration'. Social administration emphasised empirical research as essential to underpin pragmatic, practical solutions to social problems from the top downwards, a tradition that is alive and well in the dominant approach of today's 'evidence-based social policy'. Social administration sat within a distinctively British intellectual approach to distinctively British social problems and the assumed civilising mission of Britain at home and abroad. Its intellectual underpinning – British idealism

– appealed to the rational mind, or social conscience, that the empirical evidence for reform was compelling and that the reforms themselves required careful management by qualified experts in social administration, objective bureaucracy and welfare professionalism.

New liberalism advocated an interventionist role for the state to ensure that all citizens in the national community are able to exercise the positive freedom to participate fully in its political and cultural life. In 1907, a leading New Liberal, L.T. Hobhouse, was appointed by the LSE to the UK's first professorship in the relatively new discipline of sociology (Halsey, 2004). In his major work *The Elements of Social Justice* (1922), Hobhouse rooted the case for citizenship-based welfare reform within a tradition of idealist social philosophy. Idealism in this context assumes that social reform can be achieved by appeals to rational dialogue and moral sentiment, leading to a change in the minds of doubters and sceptics. British idealism influenced the development of sociology in Britain through Hobhouse's evolutionary approach to a 'social mentality', which holds communities together through shared social norms. Communities evolve most efficiently where individuals have the capacity and opportunity to develop as freely interacting, equal personalities, adapting social norms in the process. Therefore state intervention is permitted to create equal opportunities for personal growth and remove unnecessary constraints on interpersonal development such as poverty, ignorance, sickness and destitution. As Marshall (1950, p 16) expressed it:

> The duty to improve and civilize oneself is therefore a social duty, and not merely a personal one, because the social health of a society depends upon the civilization of its members. And a community that enforces this duty has begun to realize that its culture is an organic unity and its civilization a national heritage.

Class antagonisms were to be mitigated by a nationalist pride in imperial British values, a racially based sense of superiority, and the subordination of women through an ideology of motherhood to the role of efficient procreation for the nation (Williams, 1989). This tradition culminated in the Beveridge Report of 1942, whose attack on the 'five evils' of disease, want, squalor, ignorance and idleness aimed to raise the status of (male) British citizens through addressing material deficiencies in ways that were thought compatible with a market economy, the British empire and the patriarchal family structure.

Within this tradition, Marshall set out his classical approach to citizenship in the immediate post-war period (1949) just when it appeared that the inequalities of social class might be ameliorated – although certainly not abolished – by the equal rights conferred by full citizenship of a national community. Indeed, Marshall (1950, p 7) argued that equal rights helped to legitimate class inequalities, 'so much so that citizenship has itself become, in certain respects, the architect of legitimate social inequality'. Overall, however, market-based inequalities were thought by Marshall to be lessening under the impact of state-led equalities of citizenship. 'The urge forward along the path thus plotted is an urge towards a fuller measure of equality, an enrichment of the stuff of which status is made and an increase in the number of those on whom status is bestowed' (Marshall, 1950, p 18). Social-democratic principles of equality through the rights conferred by citizenship at last seemed in the 'golden age' of state welfare to be emerging triumphant over the previously dominant liberal principles of unequal competition between individual agents in the free market.

In its insistence on gradual, peaceful reform, social democracy was credited by Marshall, among others, as creating the welfare state from above as the culminating point of the long march of civilised progress of the British nation by far-sighted individuals committed to high-minded ideals such as equality, social justice and national unity. Marshall's form of social democracy told its own story of the triumph of social evolution as represented by the welfare state: 'the modern drive towards social equality is, I believe the latest phase of an evolution of citizenship which has been in continuous progress for some 250 years' (Marshall, 1950, p 7). Until then, feudal society made any claim to social justice a rather arbitrary affair based on the *status* enjoyed (or not) by social position rather than citizenship *rights* in the modern sense. Social relations under feudalism ensured that there was no such thing as separate rights available equally to every member of society. It is only fairly recently that any such thing could be conceived and, indeed, for Marshall (1950, p x) it was 'only in the present [20th] century, in fact I might say only within the last few months' that modern citizenship rights were finally granted. This evolutionary story situates Marshall, like social democracy more generally, in the Whig tradition of historical understanding. Whig history constructs a linear narrative to arrange the past according to the expediency of pressing ideological needs in the present (Butterfield, 1932).[1]

Social-democratic Whiggery is forcefully advanced by Marshall as he unfurls a story of the steady progress of equality over the years until he reaches the summit of evolution in the months immediately before he gave his lecture. Class is made by Marshall to conform to an evolutionary ideal where the worst inequalities are erased through the rights and duties of comprehensive citizenship whose entitlements emerge from simply belonging to an increasingly just and orderly national community. This is perhaps understandable from Marshall's idealist perspective of creating an orderly and more equal society. In 1949, he stood at the opening up of what many consider the 'golden age' of the welfare state and corporatist state management of the capitalist economy (Harris, 1972). From these heights, rational social and political change could seem very much like a top-down affair, something that has an impact on lower classes and other social groups but that they themselves play little part in making.

Famously, for Marshall full citizenship depended on the progressive capture of three kinds of rights: civil rights, political rights and social rights. Each of these elements of citizenship corresponded to certain institutions at definite stages in historical evolution. According to Marshall (1950, p 10), by the early 19th century, *civil rights* were established bearing 'in most essentials, the appearance that they have today'. Civil rights are those necessary for individual liberty, freedom of speech, the right to justice and, especially important for the emerging society, premised on a legally enforceable exchange between capital and waged labour in 'the right to own property and to conclude valid contracts' (Marshall, 1950, p 8). Civil rights were won above all by the courts of justice, whose steady work was only disturbed by popular movements animated by the French revolution:

> This eighteenth-century achievement, interrupted by the French revolution and completed after it, was in large measure the work of the courts, both in their daily practice and also in a series of famous cases in some of which they were fighting against parliament in defence of individual liberty. (Marshall, 1950, p 10)

Above all, the individual right was won for adult males to freely choose an employer rather than being tied for life as an indentured serf or servile peasant.

Indeed, while Marshall (1950, p 11) grants the courts the main role in establishing civil rights, he also concedes that the courts were merely ratifying the new reality of free wage labour: 'The Common Law is largely a matter of common sense'. In other words, 'the generally accepted way of life' mentioned by Marshall was already in the throes of change well before the courts and Common Law formalised the new civil right to become free wage labourers. Moreover, by emphasising the role played by lawmakers, Marshall seriously understates the symbolic use of the language of civil rights in the plebeian culture of 'free-born Englishmen' to legitimately raise a protest against meagre Poor Law administration in times of want and to force concessions from the gentry (see Chapter Two). As Thompson (1991, p 74) summarised the reciprocal nature of 18th-century rights: 'The plebs were aware that a ruling-class that rested its claim to legitimacy upon prescription and law had little authority to over-rule their own customs and rights'.

Political rights took longer to be granted and initially depended on the successful exercise of civil rights to acquire property. Nineteenth-century reforms, principally the 1832 Reform Act, extended the franchise to very limited sections of society, that of freehold property owners. Not until the 1918 Representation of the People Act was the franchise widened on the democratic basis of equal political rights – albeit limited to 'manhood' suffrage only – rather than on the exclusive basis of property ownership. Nevertheless, full political rights, even when formally granted as in the right to vote or stand for election, remained restricted where class prejudice was perpetuated by a deferential attitude among the working class to 'the elites who were born, bred and educated for leadership' (Marshall, 1950, p 22). Gradually, in Marshall's narrative, the working class established a political identity independent of elite groups. As they did so, political rights became entwined with the demand for social rights. Universal suffrage was therefore sought by the working class less as an end in itself, as some immanent idealist unfolding of the democratic principle of equality, than as a means to redress immediate social grievances.

As new civil rights progressed alongside the free market in wage labour, a conflict ensued with traditional *social rights* to protection through local wage regulation and Poor Law support. This reflected the shift from a society arranged by *status* to one organised by *contract*. Status conferred by membership of a local community came into conflict with the contract struck between independent individuals in the marketplace. Attempts to regulate the market through the Speenhamland system of a guaranteed wage and family support were doomed to failure under the new spirit of capitalist individualism (Polanyi, 1944).[2] By the time of the 1834 Poor Law Act, traditional social rights were forced to retreat more completely under the claims made by free market competition. Forced into the workhouse, and thus into a dependent, non-market relationship, the poor and the destitute were denied any scrap of civil or political rights.

By 1950, for Marshall, *social rights* were enshrined in the equal status afforded by institutions of the welfare state, overturning the domination of life by the *laissez-faire* contractual bargaining between individuals. 'Social rights in their modern form imply an invasion of contract by status, the subordination of market price to social justice, the replacement of the free bargain by the declaration of rights' (Marshall, 1950, p 40). However, Marshall provides little sense of the social forces that brought the universal franchise or social rights into existence. He emphasises a clash of incompatible *principles* rather than a clash of social class *interests* when he claims that 'the impact of citizenship on social class takes the form of a conflict between opposing principles' (Marshall, 1950, p 18). By focusing on principles and ideals, Marshall's Whig history tends to impose an idealist teleology on the history of welfare and downplay material constraints and opportunities. Political reforms therefore appear as the idealist demi-urge of an evolutionary principle of equality rather than an unceasing, now open/now hidden struggle between antagonistic social groups. Hence, for Marshall the *principles* of equality embodied in citizenship rights are 'at war' with the *principles* of inequality embodied in the capitalist class system. Such principles animated the emerging package of social rights – 'from the right to a modicum of economic welfare and security to the right to share to the full in the social heritage and to live the life of a civilised being according to the standards prevailing in the society' (Marshall, 1950, p 8). Status therefore depends on principles while contract depends on interests. Attempts to establish an 'equality of status' rather than an equalisation of incomes indicates that conflicts over the wage contract are essentially something secondary, as Marshall notes in his discussion of trade unionism.

It is only outside of formal political citizenship that Marshall recognises an alternative source of social power. In the trade unions' creation of a parallel system of 'industrial citizenship', the working class used their combined civil rights as free wage labour to demand social rights. 'These civil rights became, for the workers, an instrument for raising their social and economic status, that is to say, for establishing the claim that they, as citizens, were entitled to certain social rights' (Marshall, 1950, p 26). This demand by trade unions for social rights was heard, Marshall notes, during the industrial militancy of the Great Unrest (1910-14) that swept across Britain in the years before the First World War. By 1950, trade unions could defend social rights by working collaboratively within government, whereas 'in the past trade unionism had to assert social rights by attacks delivered from outside the system in which power resided' (Marshall, 1950, p 41). For Marshall, this means that trade union leaders must respect 'the duties of citizenship', above all political stability and social order, and take 'responsibility' for the wider welfare of the national community. Unofficial action by the trade union rank and file represents a repudiation of responsibility, acting in their own narrow self-interest as a throwback to an earlier phase in the evolution of social rights. Since this is one of the few times that Marshall (1950, p 41) considers in any detail the role played by subjective agency from below, it is worth quoting his thought in full:

> Trade union leaders in general accept this [responsibility], but this is not true of all members of the rank and file. The

traditions built up at a time when trade unions were fighting for their existence, and when conditions of employment depended wholly on the outcome of unequal bargaining, make its acceptance very difficult. Unofficial strikes have become very frequent, and it is clear that one important element in industrial disputes is discord between trade union leaders and certain sections of trade union members. Now duties can derive either from status or from contract. Leaders of unofficial strikes are liable to reject both. The strikes usually involve breach of contract or the repudiation of agreements. Appeal is made to some allegedly higher principle – in reality, though this may not be expressly asserted, to the status rights of industrial citizenship.... In some recent unofficial strikes an attempt has, I think, been made to claim the rights both of status and of contract while repudiating the duties under both these heads.

Rank-and-file union members show scant regard for the formal duties of citizenship and insist on the informal democracy of unofficial action in defence of their contractual rights. Such action placed strikes and other forms of what became known as 'extra-parliamentary action' outside the terms of national citizenship. Workers taking industrial action in their own interest were consigned to the status of irrational Others, acting on the fringes of reason and responsibility.

Marshall's formal sociology of citizenship tidies away the haphazardly strewn historical material of class struggle and social movements. Absent is any consideration of the role of the urban bourgeoisie in mobilising the apparently natural claim of civil rights in its conflict with the feudal rights of the *ancien régime*. Neither is there much recognition of the role played in the struggle for political rights by the emergent working-class movements like the Chartists (Thompson, 1984). Finally, while there is some mention of trade unionism in the struggle for social rights, the wider context of the labour movement and the proximity of a revolutionary threat, and the dangers of wartime mobilisation in the development of state welfare, is overlooked. Outside of antagonistic social interests, Marshall's 'principles' of equality arise *deus ex machina* from a 'social conscience' that wishes to alleviate the worst extremes of class suffering, or what Marshall called 'class abatement'. From the idealist heights of social administration, Marshall naturalises class inequalities by comparing them to environmental 'nuisances' like the acrid smoke belching from factory chimneys:

> And so in time, as the social conscience stirs to life, class-abatement, like smoke-abatement, becomes a desirable aim to

be pursued as far as is compatible with the continued efficiency of the social machine. (Marshall, 1950, p 20)

As Bottomore (1992, p 73) summed up the limits to Marshall's teleological history of citizenship rights:

> Specific social groups were involved in the struggle to extend or restrict such rights, and in these conflicts social classes have played a major part. Marshall recognised that a measure of conflict existed but he expressed it as a clash between opposing principles rather than between classes, and his discussion of class was primarily concerned, as he said, with the impact of citizenship on social class, not with the ways in which the historical development of classes had itself generated new conceptions of citizenship and movements to expand the rights of citizens.

Marshall was always at pains to champion social justice and equal opportunity within a social-democratic framework. Later when a new wave of social movements made themselves felt in the 1960s and 1970s, Marshall (1972) turned his attention to what he called the 'value-problems of welfare-capitalism'. Unless the value demands of the protest movements are accommodated within the social framework of representative government, the mixed economy and the welfare state, Marshall (1972, p 32) argued, the alternative would be some variant of totalitarian rule:

> The transformation sought by the more purposeful and less destructive sections of those voicing our present discontents is one of attitudes and values rather than of basic structure, though institutional change changes are sought as a means to this end, as is also the protection of the environment.

Marshall could not foresee at this stage that the alternative was not one between the value-rationality of deepening social democracy or the bureaucratic rationality of Stalinism but a neoliberal refashioning of the relationship between state and market.

It may be that Marshall was simply proposing an ideal-type evolutionary schema as a heuristic device for understanding his trinity of rights. While his essay depends on this kind of purchase from idealist reductionism, he is also concerned throughout to appeal to the empirical basis for the emergence of social rights. His essay can be seen as both a guide to thinking about rights and an historical interpretation of the specific case of England (rather than Britain). Be that as it may, an idealist commitment to evolutionary Whiggery prevented Marshall from registering that the onset of crisis and the emerging ideology of the New Right would herald a neoliberal attack on the values of welfare capitalism for an entire generation. It is the concern of the rest of this chapter to outline the contested, non-teleological development of welfare rights, understood not merely as the clash of competing principles but also as the clash of antagonistic social forces. This will, arguably, demarcate the ground on which both the rise of new social movements and the neoliberal counter-assault were prepared.

The New Left, reform and protest

An alternative sociohistorical framework for understanding the rise of state welfare emerged within 10 years of Marshall's account. In the second half of the 1950s, a generation of politically engaged historians and intellectuals of the British New Left challenged some of the political assumptions of the times (Chun, 1995; Kenny, 1995). Disillusioned with Stalinist dogma and the orthodoxy of the Communist Party of Great Britain, and revolted by its uncritical support for the Soviet repression of the Hungarian Uprising in 1956, a number of talented socialist intellectuals attempted to create a new, independent social and political movement through the critical rejuvenation of Marxist ideas. Out of this milieu, a sociohistorical approach to the welfare state was given a particularly sharp expression by the Marxist historian John Saville (1957-58). Almost as a detailed rejoinder to Marshall, in his 1957 essay for the New Left journal *The New Reasoner*, Saville challenges the idea that the welfare state represents a staging post in the inevitable path to socialism and equality. Instead, Saville (1957-58, pp 5-6) argues, the welfare state emerged thanks to the interaction of three underlying dimensions:

> (1) the struggle of the working class against their exploitation;
> (2) the requirements of industrial capitalism (a convenient abstraction) for a more efficient environment in which to operate and in particular the need for highly productive labour force; (3) recognition by the property owners of the price that has to be paid for political security.

It is not only class struggle that determined the shape of state welfare. Social policy also became a functional precondition for the further accumulation of capital and the political concessions granted under the framework of liberal-democratic institutions provided the best shell for channelling social antagonism away from more incendiary forms of protest and struggle.

In his claim that 'it is not the middle class or any group of property owners who have been the prime mover in social change', Saville (1957–58, p 9) does not attempt to minimise the role played by the challenge from below of the labour movement. His point is that the more thoughtful and enlightened sections of the ruling class began to converge with the demands of working-class socialism around the need for a more thorough programme of radical reform. In this way, fundamental disputes between the classes about property rights might be avoided or mitigated in the interests of economic efficiency and political stability. This has some echoes with Marshall's claims about class abatement, as well as a longer tradition of radical New Liberal thought and middle-class reformism like the Fabianism of the Webbs. However, Saville (1957–58, p 9) departs radically from Marshall's claim that 'social conscience' animated by higher values and collective principles of citizenship was the bedrock cause of social reform:

> Social conscience, except in the hearts and minds of a small minority among the middle class, is a frail instrument of social policy, and conscience normally requires the support of some powerful 'interest' before it is translated into practice.

As a Marxist, Saville (1957–58, p 10) instead holds that social reform is the product of class struggle, where the shape, organisation and determination of working-class pressure from below conditions the evolution of state welfare, and that the ruling class only concede reforms reluctantly and grudgingly:

> Only the massive development of the working class movement and the recourse to methods of direct action have been able to shift the mountains of unreason that have built themselves upon the foundations of private property.

After the shock to bourgeois values represented by Chartism and the state repression that followed the 1848 mass mobilisation, the working class became ever more firmly locked outside the formal politics of parliamentary democracy (Saville, 1990). In this void, workers developed their own defensive organisations in the form of trade unions created by and for skilled craftsmen. At the height of its mobilisations in 1839, 1842 and 1848, Chartism threatened to overturn existing property relations so dangerous was the demand for basic democratic rights in those years (Charlton, 1997). The 'six points' of the Charter – universal suffrage, equal representation, removal of property qualifications, annual parliaments, payment for Members of Parliament (MPs), and use of the ballot – provided a focus for the formation of a truly national working-class movement across the length and breadth of Britain (Thompson, 1984). This was far from the evolutionary course of events plotted by British Whig history where reason would sooner or (more usually) later prevail over the militant hotheads making utopian demands for democracy and social justice in the here and now. Both the 1832 Reform Act and the 1834 Poor Law Amendment Act decisively excluded the working class from participation in the official political culture of British democracy, setting the context for the mass movement that grew up in support of the Charter mobilisations in the late 1830s and the 1840s. As Charlton (1997, p 84) puts it:

> If there was any hint that the Charter might have been a means for the middle class to siphon off working class fury over the New Poor Law it was blown apart by the belligerent mass meetings in the North in 1839, the South Wales Rising and the partial uncovering of insurrectionary plotting in several parts of the country.

The franchise was only gradually extended to the working class in the period from 1867 until 1918, and 1927 for working-class women. But where Marshall might see this as part of the natural evolutionary course in the typically British tradition of slow but sure political reform, Saville views it as a stalling game by the ruling class to deflect the potential political power represented by the numerical superiority of proletarian voters. Delay in the introduction of basic political rights for the working class by a few decades allowed the Tories and the Liberals to occupy more favourable ground than their previous defence of an exclusive right to property might suggest. Saville (1957-58, p 14) quotes the Radical Liberal Joseph Chamberlain from an 1885 speech advocating an early blueprint of the welfare state: 'what ransom will property pay for the security which it enjoys?' In the conflict between the civil rights of contract and the social rights of status, far-sighted Liberals made judgements about how to cope with the democratic 'ransom' that the working class would inevitably demand. Which outcome overall would best maintain political stability and existing property relations became a pressing matter of elite reflection. A judicious approach to reform from above represents the obverse side of elite fears of radical working-class mobilisation from below. Saville notes that this tactic also had the effect of delaying the emergence of a mass-membership socialist party in Britain and, it might be added, clouded the reception of Marxism within the British labour movement (Hobsbawm, 2007).

When the Labour Party finally emerged, it immediately came under the influence of liberal reformism, 'Lib-Labism', and initially refused to let itself be known as a 'socialist party' (Miliband, 1972). Here the influence of the Fabian Society proved decisive in defining the ideological terrain of state welfare, building on the ideals represented by the New Liberalism. Fabianism stressed the practical and pragmatic nature of reform where the 19th-century state was already compelled by efficiency claims, as much as by the claims of social justice, to intervene in market relations to alleviate widespread hardship. For leading Fabians like Sidney and Beatrice Webb, 'practical men' oblivious of or hostile to any collectivist ideology had by the turn of the 20th century already come to depend on the 'unconscious socialism' of municipal planning and public health legislation (Briggs, 1962). Crucial here was the idea that once 'the facts' of social degradation were exposed before a well-meaning middle class public, their social conscience would be stirred into action and such rational minds would be compelled to accept the tide of collective provision rather than fight against it. More radical working-class demands for the full franchise and a more comprehensive transformation of the social structure could thereby be stilled by judicious elite action. As Sidney Webb complained in 1896, 'The difficulty in England is not to secure more political power for the people, but to persuade them to make any sensible use of the power they already have' (cited in Bruce, 1968, p 161).

Having established the constellation of conditions – class struggle, economic efficiency and political stability – that precipitated greater state intervention for the collective provision of welfare, Saville (1957-58, pp 16-17) identifies the three phases of reform in the first half of the 20th century. First, the wave of Liberal reforms of 1906 to 1914 included:

- 1906: meals for deprived school children;
- 1907: medial inspection for school children;
- 1908: first old-age pensions;
- 1909: introduction of a minimum wage for selected industries;
- 1911: the beginning of national health and unemployment insurance.

Second, Saville gives the example of how the ruling class rode out the high point of working-class militancy in 1919 through delay, evasion and concession, while Lloyd George cleverly outflanked the tamely inept leadership of the Labour Party and the trade unions. Hence, the reforms of the inter-war Conservative and Labour governments were piecemeal reflections of an emerging 'middle way':

- 1918: Maternity and Child Welfare Act;
- 1919: Housing and Town Planning Act;
- 1920: Unemployment Insurance Act;
- 1926: Haddow Report on education;
- 1927: Widows, Orphans and Old Age Contributory Pensions Act;
- 1934: Unemployment Act.

Finally, the 1945-50 Labour government introduced what became the modern welfare state. Standing so close in time to Labour's welfare reforms Saville (1957-58, pp 17) is careful to indicate that the welfare state was not as radical as has since been portrayed in many 'golden age' accounts but represented a minimum programme of reform acceptable to the Conservative opposition: 'It was a modest programme, and a couple of decades overdue by the standards of the previous half century and its achievement was followed by a partial retreat in 1950 with the imposition of charges for certain health services'. In some respects, the welfare state must be considered a success for those who opposed any 'socialist measures' that threatened to interfere with the workings of the free market, including the market in wage labour.

> Since the welfare state in Britain developed within a mature capitalist society, with a ruling class long experienced and much skilled in the handling of public affairs, its growth and development has been slow and controlled; and the central interests of property have never seriously been challenged. (Saville, 1957-58, p 24)

The radicalisation of British society provoked by wartime measures led to a mainstream consensus across the Labour and Conservative parties that managed reform was preferable to unchecked grievances from below (Calder, 1969). As the Conservative Quentin Hogg (later Lord Hailsham) put it in a debate in the House of Commons in 1943: 'If you do not give the people social reforms they are going to give you social revolution' (Hansard, 17 February 1943). After decades of winning at best piecemeal reforms, the labour movement came to regard the welfare state as its lasting achievement, a valedictory lesson for the futility of more radical protest movements led by the Communist Party and the Independent Labour Party, which in the past they claimed had made unrealistic demands for the socialist transformation of society.

> The struggle for any particular reform has always in this country aroused so much opposition that when it is achieved it is at least

understandable that those who have spent half a lifetime on its behalf too easily believe that with its enactment a new period of social history is beginning. (Saville, 1957-58, p 17)

This was true for at least the more reformist sections of the New Left, who argued that state welfare combined with the Labour government's programme of nationalisation represented a 'transition to socialism'. In the debate in the pages of *The New Reasoner* that followed Saville's essay, Thompson (1958) contended that the British welfare state was 'profoundly anti-capitalist' because services are provided on the basis of need rather than ability to pay. By reducing social reforms to mere 'palliatives' that the ruling class were prepared to concede anyway, Saville had minimised the role played by the 'mass pressure' of the working class:

> It had to be fought for at every stage, and although the leaders of individual campaigns – such as those for family allowances or free school meals – may have appeared to be isolated humanitarians, their support has always come from the organised labour movement – as well, of course, as from humanitarians in all parts of society. What is more, the opposition has always come from the spokesmen of property, and it is significant that the first move made by Conservative chancellors when a reduction in government expenditure is called for has been towards these same services. This is not only because the government itself hates them, but because the whole political philosophy of those who support such governments is against the conception of need as a criterion of service. (Thompson, 1958, pp 127-8)

For Thompson, working-class organisation and values, the objective function of public sector welfare workers, the growing scale of the capitalist enterprise, and the internal divisions of the ruling class all indicated that capitalism is incubating the future socialist society in the womb of the existing society. State welfare represented a material victory for working-class movements and values, what Marx called 'the political economy of the working class', of 'social responsibility and human dignity' prevailing over exchange and profit. In their commitment to public service rather than private profit, teachers, doctors and health workers constitute 'an objectively anti-capitalist force in society' (Thompson, 1958, p 129). Social reform is less a demonstration of the impregnable unity of the ruling class in their ability to delay, fudge and deflect state welfare, so emphasised by Saville, than an indication of the deep divisions within their ranks, which, in their mutual antipathy and competition with each other, sometimes breaks out into open civil war. State welfare is only possible where an ideological or political crisis exposes such divisions as they emerge from the internal competition among capitalists, with the larger, more efficient producer consuming the weaker, less efficient one, ultimately precipitating a crisis of the entire system of private property. 'The combined demands for social services and higher wages put forward by the working class will continue to drive out the less efficient capitalist, and to tax the national productive capacity, perhaps to breaking point' (Thompson, 1958, p 129). Attempts would indeed be made to resolve imbalances between tax revenues and social welfare benefits but in ways that would reverse any supposed line of evolution towards socialism.

This optimistic, evolutionary prognosis was widely held by the labour movement and social-democratic intellectuals at the time. It was also widely felt that there would be continuous forward movement towards equality, something that was rudely discounted by Saville's prescient internationalist insight that the decline of British imperialism would place added strains on the British economy to continue to deliver welfare improvements:

> When therefore we accept, and rightly, the achievement of the Welfare state as the product of working class agitation and struggle, we should also be clear that a part, at least, of the flexibility and maneuverability of the ruling class has been derived from the possession of the world's largest Empire. (Saville, 1957-58, p 24)

Only later would it become clear that this view of state welfare as a supposedly privileged site for the 'organic national unity' of white male Britons was also rapidly becoming untenable with immigration from Asia and the West Indies, not least to occupy the lowest rungs of the welfare state hierarchy (Williams, 1989). Saville was also concerned that the very success represented by the welfare state and large-scale political trade union organisation had become 'social and political shock absorbers', demobilising struggles from below by confusing a more comprehensive socialist programme with improved living standards and levels of security that were contingent on the post-war economic boom. In such ways, the labour movement became tied up in ideological knots:

> On the one hand since they are the result of struggle, the labour movement has grown stronger with success; on the other, since so far social and economic reforms have easily been absorbed into the economic system, there is an immense confusion of

ideas as to what exactly has been achieved. (Saville, 1957-58, p 24)

As the mythical national consensus around 'fair shares for all' and British 'fair play' began to breakdown in the 1960s, the kind of critique raised by Saville against Marshallian approaches to British citizenship became more widely shared by an emerging generation of activists and intellectuals. Hence, by the mid-1960s, Wedderburn (1965, p 143) could echo Saville's emphasis on the need 'to focus attention on the demands of the working class for social justice and upon an analysis of the political strength of the working class; and its success in winning allies from particular pressure and interest groups'. By then, new social movements, student radicalism, anti-racist struggles, second-wave feminism and working-class struggles were beginning to emerge to redefine the terrain on which state welfare would be contested over the next decade and beyond. And, waiting in the wings, a counter-assault would emerge to selectively assimilate previously marginal agendas of the new social movements while attempting to roll back the seemingly unassailable gains of state welfare and the forces that made them.

Conclusion

People do not make history in conditions that they themselves have freely chosen. This sociological axiom illuminates our understanding of the formation, development and reproduction of the institutions of the welfare state. According to this axiom, a number of interrelated elements have been forefronted in this chapter that are often neglected or downplayed in the study of social policy. Conflicting understandings of the historical making of the welfare state emerged from the post-war debate represented by Marshall and Saville. It is clear that the relationship between social movements and social policy is always a multifaceted one. We want to highlight five core elements from this chapter:

- the subjective role of collective agency;
- the limits and possibilities of objective institutional structures;
- historical continuities and discontinuities;
- the role played by values, ideas and principles; and
- popular mobilisation from below.

First, the Marshall–Saville debate in this chapter helped re-establish the importance of subjective *agency* in historically shaping the contours of state welfare. For Marshall, agency is bound up with those elite institutions that support civil, political and social rights; for Saville, agency concerns the contending sides in the struggle between the classes.

Second, the historical preconditions are both *constraining* – people encounter objectively given conditions, which place limits on what they can realistically do – and *permissible* – these conditions permit and support, as well as prohibit, social actions of various kinds. Through the collective agency of social movements, objectively given conditions are themselves altered in the process. A centrally important discovery of the chapter is that institutional structures not only inhibit social action, they also make social action possible in the first place. While Saville is alive to the power of ruling groups to frustrate, reduce and delay reform as an objective constraint on working-class demands, Marshall presents us with a vision of British historical evolution as an expression of the civilised values that unifies the national community. The result is an abstract form of agency without a subject.

Third, history is punctuated by *discontinuous* moments of change. The history of the welfare state is not simply an evolutionary, 'upwards and onwards' steady march of progress as Marshall would have it. State welfare has equally been shaped by dramatic moments of conflict and contention, as well as more mundane forms of resistance and passive acquiescence. As Saville explained, the history of social policy has therefore been marked by sharp discontinuities in the ideological legitimation and institutional politics of welfare. On the other hand, systemic *continuities* are represented by the survival of private property, although this can sometimes be muffled by the ideological contention over the meaning and significance of state reforms and public provision.

Fourth, agency is not an exclusively top-down prerogative. In many influential accounts, state welfare appears as if it was the creation of far-sighted and benevolent elite institutions and individuals sharing in a national *value consensus*. As we have seen, for Marshall and Fabian reformism, a social conscience is stimulated by rational arguments conducted at the apex of representative interest groups and qualified experts. Persuasive appeals are made to ethical values, the empirical evidence and a pragmatic approach to social reform. Both Marshall and Saville share a concern to establish the important role played by far-sighted elite groups introducing reform from above, managing and controlling its extent and nature. On the other hand, Saville's historical materialism registers the different facets of welfare reform in the structures of divergent class interests within capitalism, whereas Marshall invokes the growing convergence of principles in a value consensus spread across class society.

Finally, as Saville demonstrates, the structure of society at any point in time sets definite limits and constraints on the kind of social action that is possible. But, conversely, *social action* through popular *mobilisation* has an effect, directly or indirectly, on the very nature of the social structure. In other words, *agency from below* cannot be consigned to a political or social vacuum by the wiliness of ruling class stratagems. The next chapter selectively examines concrete historical examples of protest and principle in the making and deflection of social reform. It also centrally explores the contribution that social movements make to our understanding of state welfare.

Note

[1] The Whigs were an elite political party between the early 18th century and mid-19th century who defended parliamentary rule against absolutist heredity monarchical rule. A mythical Whig narrative developed around the theme of natural British progress towards liberal democracy against inherited privileges of political power. The origin of the term 'Whig' is somewhat obscure. It seems to derive from the 17th-century social movement of Scottish radical Presbyterians belonging to the 'Kirk Party' who marched on Edinburgh in their thousands with widespread popular support in 1648 to resist Charles 1. This became known derisively as the 'Whiggamore Raid' after the lowly status of the 'whiggamor' marchers, the Gaelic term for drivers of horse or cattle.

[2] For Karl Polanyi (1944), the Speenhamland system was an early expression of the contradiction between a guaranteed minimum of welfare and the priorities of a society increasingly based on market relations (see Block and Somers [2003] for a careful reassessment of Polanyi's claims). Speenhamland offered relief to the poor, including the 'able-bodied', through a kind of basic income calculated against the cost of bread and the number of dependent children. Its name derives from the village of Speenhamland in Berkshire, England. In May 1795 local magistrates recognised that the Poor Law did not allow families to meet basic needs due to a combination of bad harvests, rising population and the inflationary impact that war with France had on food prices. There were also fears that the food riots of that year might turn into a revolutionary upheaval such as that recently seen in France. Like later critics of welfare benefits, Speenhamland was viewed by free market critics as creating disincentives to work for a market-based rate of pay and for creating an unsustainable burden of poor relief on local parish elites. As the danger of revolt passed, the Speenhamland principle was abandoned and the ability of the local state to interfere in self-regulating labour markets was curtailed by the 1834 Poor Law.

Further reading

There is no better starting point than T.H. Marshall's original essay, 'Citizenship and social class' (Pluto Press, 1950).

Current research on citizenship is reported in the journal *Citizenship Studies*.

See the debate about evolutionary thought and historical materialism in the book *Historical Materialism and Social Evolution* edited by Paul Blackledge and Graeme Kirkpatrick (Palgrave Macmillan, 2002).

John Saville's analysis of the origins of the welfare state 'The welfare state: an historical approach' appears in a number of edited collections and can be found at the following website: www.amielandmelburn.org.uk/collections/nr/index_frame. htm

Customs in Common by E.P. Thompson (Merlin Press, 1991) is an important collection of essays about popular protest in 18th-century England.

A useful history of the New Left of which Saville and Thompson were integral parts is *The First New Left: British Intellectuals after Stalin* by Michael Kenny (Lawrence & Wishart, 1995).

two

The making of modern social welfare movements

Introduction

As Chapter One suggested, agency from below must be allowed its own specific gravity in shaping the forces underlying the historical development of state welfare. We have already alluded in Chapter One to the significance of Chartism and the Great Unrest of 1910-14 in the demands from below for and resistance from above to progressive welfare reform. To this we could add a whole series of popular protest movements that fell well short of structural or institutional transformation but nevertheless have had either an enervating effect or a stiffening effect on the resistance of ruling groups to welfare reform. As it developed in England, the new social relations of capitalism were met repeatedly with innovative forms of protest, from deferential appeals to insurrectionary movements. They also encountered ferocious opposition from ruling groups combined with unfavourable political conditions that often made even the smallest concession for minor social reform seem like a utopian impossibility.

This chapter further develops the explanatory parameters set by the competing 'golden age' frameworks of Marshall and Saville. Although the ideas of Marshall introduced in Chapter One are often subject to criticism by historians of the welfare state, there has been a general acceptance, one that stubbornly persists, of 'evolutionary pluralism' – underlying assumptions about the gradual, peaceable and responsive nature of state welfare. Here we more firmly situate the emerging popular struggles over civil, political and social rights in the 19th and 20th centuries in the context of market capitalism. Historically, popular struggles were fought over traditional rights based on paternalist ideas of custom – or 'customary rights'. Put as a crude historical schema, a shift is registered leading from, first, struggles over *informal customary rights* of the 18th century to, second, struggles over more *formal legal rights* in the 19th century, culminating, third, in the struggles for *universal rights* to welfare by the middle of the 20th century and, finally, a proliferation of *particular group rights* (on the basis of gender, sexuality, ethnicity, disability) by the end of the 20th century. As such, recent protest has returned to a grassroots tradition deeply embedded in specific local and institutional cultures. Such cultures help to shape the form of protest through the kind of claims and actions that they sanction and legitimise, what Tilly (1995, pp 49-51) referred to as 'repertoires of contention'. Here we consider particularly useful Thompson's (1991) idea of the 'moral economy of the crowd' in the 18th century and how this notion has been updated to account for welfare struggles, for example in Scott's (1990) idea of 'public transcripts' and 'hidden transcripts'. This leads on to a consideration of the relationship between the mobilisation of 'poor people's movements' and the transient character of mass mobilisations. Some, like Piven and Cloward (1979), consider formal organisations to be obstructive of popular protest from below, a judgement that we consider far too brusque to account for the relationship between organisational structure and mobilisations. Finally, we consider some of the ways that Marshall's legacy has been updated by the proliferation of rights more recently demanded by the new social movements. This leaves us at the threshold of Chapter Three, which provides a more nuanced conceptualisation of new social movements, social reform and popular struggle.

Customary rights and popular struggle

From the 16th century through to the 19th century, revolt and unrest in agricultural districts were responses to an emerging system of subsistence through the sale of waged labour, periodic unemployment, overwork and poverty wages. During this earlier period, what Marx (1976) called the 'primitive accumulation of capital' witnessed peasants being forcibly driven from the land and hurled into the free market, in the process transformed into 'free and rightless proletarians' divorced from the means of production. Whig historians like Marshall emphasise how this freedom is realised as a 'civil right' but at the cost of traditional 'social rights'. Missing here is the immense (and most uncivil) human suffering and degradation that centuries of primitive accumulation imposed on 'free labour'. This represented a change in 'the form of servitude' rather than its abolition. As Marx (1976, p 875) argued:

The historical movement which changes the producers into wage-labourers appears, on the one hand, as their emancipation from serfdom and from the fetters of the guilds, and it is this aspect of the movement which alone exists for our bourgeois historians. But, on the other hand, these newly freed men became sellers of themselves only after they had been robbed of all their own means of production, and all the guarantees of existence afforded by the old feudal arrangements.

In such unpropitious conditions, the emerging working class fought to retain the customary rights that capital set out to abolish. This can be seen in the extent and intensity of popular opposition to the 1834 Poor Law (Knott, 1986). By the 19th century, the principle of formally free, but substantively unfree wage labour was consolidated by the 1834 Poor Law Amendment Act. Capitalist social relations, premised on the divorce of wage labour from the means of subsistence, appeared now as a firmly established fact of life that would not be easily dislodged. Failure to comply with the new boom–slump employment cycle and harsh factory discipline meant destitution, vagrancy, prostitution or, worse, the workhouse or the debtor's prison.

The context of the 1834 Poor Law was the threat to order posed by the 'Swing riots' of 1830 in the agricultural districts of East and South England (Hobsbawm and Rude, 1969). Impoverished agricultural labourers felt the severity of rural depression with desperately low wages and further wage cuts, unemployment and the replacement of labour by machinery. There were few methods of protest open to this vulnerable class of rural labourers. These included:

- protest against wage cuts or demand higher wages;
- demand the right to parish relief;
- resort to the 'crimes' of theft, poaching or smuggling;
- threaten farmer employers with the destruction of property; or
- destroy the machinery that displaced labour from agrarian work.

A complete lack of political rights made futile any resort to formal political devices like petitioning. Instead, a millennial hope for a 'new state of things to enrich and elevate the Poor' could be found in 'obscure poor men's discontent' (Hobsbawm and Rude, 1969, p 86).

Large-scale riots, attacks on property and machine-wrecking were legitimated by the rural insurgents as socially just actions: 'they believed in "natural right" – the right to work and to earn a living wage – and refused to accept that machines, which robbed them of this right, should receive the protection of the law' (Hobsbawm and Rude, 1969, p 249). Ferocious repression followed the rural insurgency as the rebels were hunted down by the authorities, executed, transported or, in one case, publicly whipped. In the aftermath, a terrible price was paid by the British working class that would limit popular mobilisations until the emergence of Chartism and trade union organisation. Abandoned by customary social rights and excluded from political citizenship, the subaltern classes developed their own instruments of resistance at subterranean depths of low-intensity class war and ideological subversion:

> The New Poor Law of 1834 knocked the last nails into the coffin the ancient belief that social inequality could be combined with the recognition of human rights. After 1830, and especially after 1834, the labourers knew that they had to fight alone (or at all events without rural allies) or not at all. For another twenty years or so they waged a silent, embittered, vengeful campaign of poaching, burning and rural terror – which erupted into epidemics of incendiarism and cattle-maiming at moments of acute distress, notably in 1843-4. The majority remained inert and passive until the rise of the agricultural workers' trade unions in the 1870s. (Hobsbawm and Rude, 1969, p 17)

This capacity for resistance and protest was evident in the previous century with the plebeian appeal to 'custom' to defend social rights, above all to be fed, coming under threat or needing extended.

The moral economy of protest

Food riots are concerned with satisfying a basic need – hunger. But rioting as a popular form of protest is always sanctioned by culture and custom under the specific conditions of actual or threatened crisis. The 'politics of the belly' is always at the same time a 'politics of the head'. Although Marshall and others discuss the loss of traditional 'social rights' to 'civil rights' in the 18th century, the modern idea of social rights needs to be distinguished from more customary practices, social norms and 'common rights'. A common right might be appealed to as the right to resist and destroy the enclosure of common land as capitalist agriculture parcelled up the remaining open land in England. Custom and common right can also appear as rather conservative claims for an exclusive and privileged entitlement to share in the local resources of a subsistence economy. But when these come under threat their defence can excite popular mobilisation and direct action. Thompson (1991, p 188) famously termed this the 'moral economy of the poor':

> a consistent traditional view of social norms and obligations, of the proper economic functions of several parties within the community which, taken together, can be said to constitute the moral economy of the poor. An outrage to these moral assumptions, quite as much as actual deprivation, was the usual occasion for direct action.

At times of hunger and distress, the labouring poor attempted to impose traditional paternalist obligations on their masters who, in the course of transforming themselves more fully into efficient capitalists, increasingly resisted extra-market obligations.

Against the pejorative connotations of the term 'riot' to describe popular protests, Thompson (1991) discusses the frequent recourse to insurrection, often led by poor women – in 1740, 1756, 1766, 1795 and 1800 – in response to the scarcity and high price of bread. Rather than physical attacks on bakers and granaries, the real locus of political action was to force bread sellers to set a 'reasonable price' through a customary appeal that market prices ought to be regulated in periods of dearth and that the 'civil rights' of profit making be placed outside acceptable social conventions for the duration of distress.

> What is remarkable about these 'insurrections' is, first, their discipline, and, second, the fact that they exhibit a pattern of behaviour for whose origin we must look back several hundreds of years; which becomes more, rather than less, sophisticated in the eighteenth century; which repeats itself, seemingly spontaneously, in different parts of the country and after the passage of many quiet years. (Thompson, 1991, p 224)

While riots proved to be a costly 'social calamity' and often failed in their immediate objectives, direct action or its rumoured threat may still have contributed generally to a more modest setting of food prices based on the moral obligation imposed by the common weal of the English crowd. The moral economy of the crowd exists as an arena of extra-market bargaining. As if to reinforce Saville's claim about the management of protest by ruling elites, the authorities did appear to respond by becoming more competent in handling or, more usually, deflecting the threat of disturbances by moral appeal, veiled or open threat, and concession.

Nevertheless, with the deepening development of capitalist markets, the tissue of custom and social norms of paternalist obligation became increasingly usurped by the impersonal social relations of equal exchange. In some ways, a moral economy only becomes apparent when its underlying assumptions are challenged directly and the tacit nature of the bargain between ruler and ruled is reformulated in more explicit tones. Some 60 years after the Captain Swing riots in England, as Davis (2001) shows in his book *Late Victorian Holocausts*, millenarian movements emerged in the context of drought and famine in the colonised world of the 1890s – in the Chinese Boxer Rebellion, in Korea, in the Philippines, in parts of Africa and in Brazil – drawing popular support for incendiary forms of protest from local, regional and national eschatological traditions. For instance, failure to provide famine relief in North China during 1897 and 1901 fuelled an uprising led by the Boxer movement of poor peasants, rural labourers and unemployed bargemen, drawing on martial arts cultures and traditions of social banditry to shape the insurrectionary nature of the rebellion. A worldwide struggle for social justice had already been set in train by imperialist expansion and disdain for native cultures.

In other ways the tactics of these incendiary movements belonged to more traditional forms of protest. By the 19th century, these were being replaced by increasingly routine forms of protest. As the leading historian of social movements has shown (Tilly, 1995), protest in Britain had by the 1830s turned resolutely away from localised outbursts of discontent informed by a parochial outlook aimed at targets immediately close to hand such as the local gentry or grain merchants during bread riots. These began to be replaced by generalised forms of collective action through loose alliances of spatially and socially diffuse social groups around a shared grievance, culminating in the nationalisation of protest. With the formation of large-scale national organisations like the Chartists, a universalistic outlook was adopted that made explicit claims about rights, especially after Thomas Paine's (1791) famous appeal for the *The Rights of Man*. National reform movements were made possible by the growing literacy of the urban proletariat, the spread of print-capitalism and more regularised forms of public association. As the state unified populations within a defined territory, standardised the language and claimed for itself an exclusive right to the legitimate use of violence, physical conflict with the forces of authority raised the stakes of the game dramatically. Short of this, protest could be effective using regularised forms other than desperate acts of violent conflict. This is what Tilly (1995) calls the 'generic' tactics of 'modular' movements that could be adapted to many different campaign movements, in different places and at different times. For instance, public petitions become a popular tool of protest in reform movements campaigning against slavery or for the People's Charter. These are specifically modern 'repertoires of contention', by which Tilly refers to the regular, learned and self-conscious choice of tactics that are available to collective movements as part of their cultural understanding of what is possible and realistic (see the examples in *Table 2.1*).

Table 2.1: Repertoires of contention

Old	New
Festival	Election rally
Rough music	Public meeting
Seizure of grain	Strike
Armed turnout	Demonstration

Not that physical conflict was entirely displaced. Tilly's point is that urban insurrection when it occurred adopted the language of rights, where 'the people' claimed the sovereign right to physically force concessions at a national level from their rulers or even overthrow them altogether. This new unification of protest created alliances not just based on narrow occupational or corporate identities but also across more diverse populations. Wider identities of class extended beyond immediate locality or occupation. Such common identities and modular forms of collective action were further enhanced by the spread of print media in the form of pamphlets, books and, above all, newspapers. By appearing alongside each other on the printed page, print media equalised the status of ruler and ruled, further eroding unthinking deference to traditional forms of hierarchical authority (Anderson, 1991). The political press became what Lenin (1903) called the 'scaffolding' that kept activists in touch with ideas and events up and down the length of the country. Newspaper-based democratic alliances increasingly identified the centralised state as the object of protest, either as a body to be appealed to in the name of the nation or opposed in the name of freedom. Modern 'repertoires of contention' take the centralised state for granted as the focus for its demands for reform and the object of its resistance. The centralised bureaucracy of the state displaced the role of direct violent action, which it always threatened to meet with ferocious repression. Once repression subsided, laws were typically enacted to restrict the political space for collective action and the hand of the police was strengthened and extended. State elites could also overreact, for instance, in response to an insurrection abroad, mistaking reformist social movements at home as seditious revolutionaries and in the process compelling them to adopt more radical demands and militant tactics. This was not the smooth space of evolution rights envisaged by Marshall but an uneven and incomplete process of contentious politics. As Tarrow (1994, p 66) summarises the extension of political rights by Western nation–states:

> In a very real sense citizenship emerged through a rough dialectic between movements – actual and feared – and the national state. From the post-revolutionary suffrage reforms to the British factory legislation of the 1840s to the unemployment and health reforms of imperial Germany and the factory inspectors instituted in the French third Republic, state reforms were either direct responses to social movements or attempts to preempt their development.

In such ways, the state became a frame for collective action, shaping both the nature of demands for rights and how this demand might be prosecuted.

The tactics of poor people's movements

For now we want to draw attention to the way that Thompson's notion of a moral economy has entered into our understanding of the repertoires of social movements. This concept was further extended by Scott (1977) to account for peasant conceptions of social justice, rights and reciprocity in Lower Burma and Vietnam. Unlike English rural labourers, peasant subsistence is more directly related to land use for production rather than consumption through setting market prices. Scott developed his conception of the moral economy of social movements in his well-known books *Weapons of the Weak* (1985) and *Domination and the Arts of Resistance* (1990). All manner of tactics and manoeuvres are deployed by the weak and the poor as everyday forms of resistance to domination by more powerful groups and individuals. These include a range of petty refusals, sanctions and forms of insubordination that place definite limits on the effective action of the powerful, who are expected to at least make a show of acting in line with customary ideals and precedents. Subordinate groups have the power to hold the powerful to their own ideals, inscribed in what Scott (1990) calls shared but biased 'public transcripts'. Subordinate groups can take advantage of the licensed claims made in public transcripts that the interests of everyone are being looked after to legitimate acts of resistance. As part of the 'art of resistance' the weak are also able to draw on their own 'hidden transcripts' of a dissonant culture concealed from the purview of dominant groups.

Clearly, the public transcript of equal citizenship rights to welfare services affords subordinate groups avenues for legitimating their deeply held grievances about actually existing inequalities of resources and power. In his approach to movements of the weak, Scott's argument about the dialogical basis of legitimate protest and subvention of dominant mores therefore provides a useful frame for reflecting on the subterranean depths of any social movement's prehistory, operating below the shallows of overt social mobilisation and fully enunciated political programmes. However, a major problem with this shift to discursive transcripts is that every trivial gripe and gesture raised by subordinate groups can be couched as evidence of proto-resistance. Indeed, this has been a marked feature of a certain strain of cultural studies where mundane acts of consumption are raised into counter-hegemonic tactics to defy the powerful (de Certeau, 1984). When everything becomes resistance, the term loses its power to name the specific nature of contentious, oppositional politics of protest movements.

Subsequent chapters will develop more detailed conceptual frameworks for analysing the empirical cases of historically concrete, unequal relations of power as they contend around state welfare. For now, we want to register the need to look beyond formal political organisations like the Labour Party and the trade unions to the self-activity of rank-and-file campaigners and their vexed relationship to organisational structures. Much contemporary discussion of 'new' social movements places great significance on their assumed middle-class composition. Of course, in one sense this all depends on what is meant by 'middle class', a debate that we cannot enter into here. It also reflects a bias against the idea that poor people are capable of mobilising in their own interests. In their critically acclaimed book *Poor People's Movements: Why they Succeed, How they Fail*, Piven and Cloward (1979) attempt to understand the institutional structuring of working-class movements in the US during the 1930s through to the 1960s outside of the straitjacket of abstract models of how mobilisations from below ought to be behave. In so doing they examine in historical detail the unemployed workers' movement of the 1930s' Depression, the unionisation drives and agitation of the 1930s, the civil rights activists around Martin Luther King, and the National Welfare Rights Organization of the 1960s. Their focus is on 'collective defiance as the key and distinguishing feature of a protest movement' (Piven and Cloward, 1979, p 5). Interest in mass defiance, Piven and Cloward argue, tends to be neglected behind an unwarranted focus on the formal organisations that are built out of social insurgency. Too much social movement theory abounds with evidence of the social origins of protesters, the forms of leadership styles and problems of organisational reproduction:

> Protest seems to be wondered about mainly for the many and
> fascinating aspects of social life which it exposes, but least of all
> for its chief significance: namely, that it is the means by which
> the least privileged seek to wrest concessions from their rulers.
> (Piven and Cloward, 1979, p 23)

Piven and Cloward resist collapsing their understanding of social
mobilisation into that of formal organisations. Instead, they view mass
membership organisations as signalling the death-knell for radical protest
since they too often evolve into conservative bureaucratic oligarchies,
which attempt to control the rank and file through demobilisation and
elite appeasement. For them the political influence of the poor is mobilised,
not organised.

Active mass movements represent a transformation in the socially
enabling power of previously quiescent groups to overcome the sense
of shame internalised by a culture that blames the poor for their own
plight. Social insurgency therefore involves a transvaluation of the usual
terms of social arrangements, as inscribed in Scott's 'public transcripts'
and on which everyday life is conducted. In breaking with quiescence,
mass action is precipitated by a profound sense of social dislocation: 'For
a protest movement to arise out of the traumas of daily life, people have
to perceive the deprivation and disorganization they experience as both
wrong and subject to redress' (Piven and Cloward, 1979, p 12). Protests
can only win what social conditions have already made possible for ruling
groups to concede:

> Driven by turmoil, political leaders proposed reforms that were
> in a sense prefigured by institutional arrangements that already
> existed, that were drawn from a repertoire provided by existing
> traditions. And an aroused people responded by demanding
> simply what political leaders had said they should have. (Piven
> and Cloward, 1979, p 33)

Everyday life for the impoverished working class is experienced through a
series of emergencies as coercive disenfranchisement. When widespread talk
about rights co-exists with their substantive denial in conditions of social
dislocation, collective defiance is sanctioned as both morally just and socially
appropriate. Rights are no longer abstract trans-historical values. They
are invoked to give sense to what is experienced locally and concretely:
'People on relief experience the shabby waiting rooms, the overseer or the
caseworker or the dole. They do not experience American social welfare
policy' (Piven and Cloward, 1979, p 20). Revolt by the poor tends to issue

in the immediate institutional object of their oppression rather than against systemic causes. Concessions by the powerful may be withdrawn when the poor no longer threaten defiance and disruption. But some reforms endure even when the movement has subsided. This has been the case with state welfare. Saville argued (see Chapter One) that this occurred because the reforms have their radical edge blunted, they are conceded only after the mass movement loses momentum or is repressed and, most importantly, such reform is compatible and perhaps even functional for the continued domination by the ruling interest.

The antipathy of Piven and Cloward towards formal organisation has to be set in the context of their own experiences during the 1960s in the US welfare rights movement. Yet the historical cases that they rely on are of qualitatively different kinds. In one case, the unemployed of the 1930s and the welfare activists of the 1960s, involved specific claims by structurally weak agents for welfare relief. In the other two cases, the 1930s' unionisation struggles and the 1960s' civil rights struggles, these were nationally significant movements and, more importantly, were ones where the agents themselves were strategically placed, as organised workers and black electors, to transform the political ground on which they stood. Piven and Cloward recognise this distinction as reflecting the wider cultural values of American society. On the one hand, the civil rights struggle was conferred widespread legitimacy beyond its opponents because it appealed to the dominant values of self-reliance and democratic rights. On the other hand, the welfare rights movement offended against such values and, as such, remained the 'movement of paupers, of a pariah class' (1979, p 320). Their focus on 'movements' of 'paupers and pariahs' also indicates a shift from a specific focus on working-class movements. From an examination of *organisations* of the working *class* to that of the rather more amorphous categories of 'poor people' and 'movements', Piven and Cloward reflect a more general disenchantment with the organised working class that followed the upturn of the 1960s mobilisations (see Chapter Three). This often celebrates in a rather one-sided way an attachment to seemingly spontaneous or disorganised expressions of revolt (see, above all, Hardt and Negri, 2004). Piven and Cloward at least have the merit of serious orientation on genuine mass movements and concrete reforms unlike the misformed voluntarism of some direct action movements that tend to celebrate 'the politics of the deed' and the myth of physical confrontation for its own sake. However, their failure to disentangle the unstructured poor from the organised working class ignores the fact that organisational forms that endure over time like mass trade unionism continue to exist because of the ongoing benefits that even routinised bargaining can often deliver. Formal organisations do not simply collect dues from members as a rigid bureaucratic structure. Enduring formal organisations also exist to defend and even extend the gains won at the high-tide mark of mobilisation. In contrast, groups that lack the continuity, discipline and structure of organisational necessity may well rise up like a rocket but are just as likely to fall to earth like a stone. As Hobsbawm (1984, pp 291-2) remarks in his critique of Piven and Cloward:

> [A]ttempts to build permanent mass organisations out of unorganized constituencies ('the unemployed', draft resisters, consumers, or even such more existentially cohesive groups like blacks and women) have almost universally failed. Such organizations, generally feeble and fluctuating, are either groups of leaders whose aim is to mobilize essentially unorganized masses for action, or more likely stage armies marching about making a noise like real armies and, with luck, being accepted as the representatives and interlocutors of their constituencies, because under certain circumstances the institutional system requires someone to fill this role.

It is precisely the mobilisation of 'unorganised constituencies' that is celebrated more often than critically analysed in certain strains of 'new social movements' theory (see Chapter Three). But to the extent that the poor are no longer subject to the condescension of history it is because we have learned of them through the traces that have come down to us of their attempts to organise and endure. As Saville and many others have noted, it is the traditional aim of dominant groups to attempt in various ways to disorganise mass movements from below precisely in order to confuse and disorient them. In reversing the relationship between organisation and political efficacy, Piven and Cloward turn a necessity into a virtue.

Conclusion

Is it always or usually the case, as Marshall, Saville and Piven and Cloward argue in their different ways, that in granting social reforms, ruling elites always know precisely what to concede, when and how? Social dislocation and political or economic crisis can disorientate dominant groups as well as subordinate movements (Gramsci, 1971). A crisis can induce miscalculations about the balance of forces, especially if this is gleaned by dominant groups mainly from the empirical facts of visible contention over the public transcript. Ruling groups may also begin to accept unthinkingly their own Panglossian promotional culture that all is well in this best of possible worlds. Ideological rhetoric about value-consensus and social equipoise may induce myopia about the depth of unrest and resentment over welfare reforms. This rarely registers in accounts of state welfare that are committed to some form of evolutionary or pluralist explanation.

Some historians of state welfare, such as Thane (1982), attribute to Marshall the idea that citizenship reflects the need by the state to respond to and assimilate the demands of the organised working class. In so doing, Thane (1982, pp 290-2) claims to advance a more rounded account of the relationship between class and welfare than Marshall managed. For Thane, while there is some truth in the claim that organised labour forced concessions from the state, the reality was more complex. First, the most vulnerable groups in society such as women and the poor were unlikely to benefit directly from industrial militancy since 'those in greatest need, were usually not the most organised and politically influential section of the working class, and neither organised workers nor the state necessarily put their interests first' (Thane, 1982, p 290). Sometimes the organised working class resisted the incursions of state welfare as resistance to the 'policing' function of the centralised bureaucratic apparatus, preferring to rely on their own collectively organised industrial strength to generate high levels of employment and high wages. Typically, the working class were internally divided by gender, ethnicity, skill or job security. Finally, the state may itself be constrained from granting concessions to the organised working class; indeed, the state may be driven to curtail or even repress working-class organisation.

Accounts such as Thane's and Marshall's emphasise Britain as being an exceptional case among nation-states in the more or less peaceable, harmonious and orderly national transition to state welfare. Unlike other parts of Europe, this traded on a willingness for compromise and consensus across British society, especially of a give-and-take attitude between the leaders of business and labour. From such perspectives, Britain provides an exemplary instance of a pluralist society where there is no single centre of power. Instead, all interest groups are represented in the negotiations and compromises that help to constitute state welfare: 'One effect of the growth of state welfare has been to maintain a *remarkably stable* distribution of material rewards and power' (Thane, 1982, p 300, emphasis added). The accent on the uniquely British traditions of stability and consensus, 'remarkable' or otherwise, recurs in many such accounts of state welfare. Fraser (1984, p 226), in his standard history *The Evolution of the British Welfare State*, claims that:

> Because social policy comprises the community's response to the practical needs of society as whole, the Welfare State is subject to those same evolutionary forces which were its ancestor. The

Welfare State was thus not a final heroic victory after centuries of struggle, but the welfare complex of a particular period adapting itself to the needs of the next generation.

Others from the social administration tradition accept that the line of evolution of the welfare state may not have been a straight one in the manner of Marshall's schema. Still, it has been a 'romantic' journey all the same, emerging as a confusion of pluralistic demands caught between the principles of individualism and collectivism:

> The whole process of development, at least until the present, has been one of evolution, of uneven response to problems, of unexpected twists and turns of policy, of responsiveness to many pressures and indifference to others, of compromise, of political accident, of chance. There has been nothing inevitable about it, except in so far as a concern for the well-being of the population and an increase in the power of the State, growing *pari passu*, were bound eventually to produce some system of social welfare. (Bruce, 1968, p 332)

Yet the evolutionary perspective has proven unable to stand the test of time. More recent critics of Marshallian notions of citizenship have noted its distinct lack of relevance to contemporary Britain. Marshall and many others assumed a more or less ethnically and nationally homogenous, white, male, Christian, British society where the main division was that of social class. This has been overtaken, it is claimed, by the development of a more diverse, multicultural Britain, the growth of national identity among the constituent nations of the UK, and the widening of activity by women in the public sphere (Parekh, 2000). This has given rise to a whole series of claims for rights based on collective identity such as national rights, ethnic rights, religious rights and cultural rights of various kinds. Such demands for an expansive set of citizenship rights have emerged alongside the rise of new social movements. Many of these will be considered in detail in the case studies of later chapters. At this point, we merely wish to signal the changing conceptions of citizenship and social movements.

Today, social movements demand that citizenship rights be extended far beyond Marshall's narrow conception of civil, political and social rights as part of a project for the amelioration of class conflict. Indeed, there has been a proliferation of rights discourses and mobilisation, few of which any longer use the language of class. Partly as a result of the women's movement and the gay liberation movement, existing rights should be further extended or even supplanted by *sexual rights* (Richardson, 2000). Similarly, with the emergence of the environmental or Green movement and the dire warning of impending ecological catastrophe, demands have been made that the nation-state and transnational institutions should recognise *ecological rights* (Cahill, 2002). Part of the same shift in the values of rights has been the social mobilisation and discourses around *animal rights* (Regan, 2004). And perhaps most widespread of all is the idea of *human rights* as an essential attribute of a flourishing human being (Turner, 1993).

These various demands for rights represent in a perverse way the latest stage of evolutionary pluralism, even though some social movement discourses consider themselves to be 'post-citizenship' or 'post-national'. After all, any appeal for rights needs to correspond to an institutional apparatus to uphold and confer protection and entitlements. Marshall identified the courts with civil rights, Parliament with political rights and the welfare state with social rights. It is less clear which institutions will enshrine the new evolutionary pluralism of rights. While the 1948 United Nations Declaration on Human Rights is often taken as a model, some such as Parekh (2000, p 134) object that it is unable to claim universal validity based as it is on liberal values and a state form that are not universally shared across cultures. Such cultural relativism tends to characterise 'post-materialist' demands for rights based on values rather than on interests, although we have previously noted that by the early 1970s Marshall had cause to evaluate how welfare capitalism might respond positively the value frameworks posed by the emerging social movements. Much 'post-materialism' depends on a notion of value autonomy based around self-enclosed claims about rights and identity divorced from the substantive interests of classes in society. Agency risks being reduced to a reified, closed community of specific values and group claims, with at best a tenuous connection to capitalist political economy and the nation-state. These issues will be addressed more fully in later chapters (see especially Chapter Three). For now the point raised by the contemporary proliferation of rights forces us to move beyond evolutionary pluralism to account more adequately for the role played by collective action in the creation, reproduction and reform of state welfare. In this way we may be in a better position to examine critically the more recent proliferation of rights and their meaning for social welfare in later chapters of this book.

Further reading

The important study of *Poor People's Movements: Why they Succeed, How they Fail* by Frances Fox Piven and Richard A. Cloward (Pantheon Books, 1979) remains in print and is readily available.

The Evolution of the British Welfare State by Derek Fraser (is a standard top-down history and is also still in print in an updated edition (Macmillan, 1984). Similarly, *The Five Giants: A Biography of the Welfare State* by Nicholas Timmins (HarperCollins, 1995) is a hugely readable account of the history of the welfare state.

Other valuable histories include *The Foundations of the Welfare State* by Pat Thane (Longman, 1982) and *The Origins of the British Welfare State: Society, State and Social Welfare in England and Wales, 1800-1945* by Bernard Harris (Palgrave, 2004). A particular version of this history is offered by the MP Frank Field on the BBC website: www.bbc.co.uk/history/british/modern/field_01.shtml

On social movement theory, which was introduced in this chapter, lively accounts can be found in *Power in Movement: Social Movements, Collective Action and Politics* by Sidney Tarrow (Cambridge University Press, 1994) and *Social Movements 1768-2004* by Charles Tilly (Paradigm Publishers, 2004).

three

Theorising social movements and social welfare

Introduction

Social movements constitute the most vigorous modes by which modern societies put accumulated social knowledge about themselves into practice to alter their social, reproductive and developmental trajectories. Traditionally, sociology and related disciplines within the social sciences focused on the labour movement and movements associated with religious and political ideologies. As the previous chapters have shown, these movements shaped the key institutions of the modern British nation-state and created the political pressure necessary for the gradual accession of the civil, political and social rights that are associated with citizenship. Since the 1970s, however, a large body of social research and sociological theory has grown to focus on the significance of what have come to be labelled the 'new social movements', a (contested) generic term, which has come to denote the wide array of oppositional social, political and cultural groupings, currents and organisations that grew out of the flowering of New Left radicalism, student rebellion and 'counter-culture' in the late 1960s. For these new social movements – the most salient being women's, peace, environmental, student and minority rights – the citizenship rights won by previous generations were too limited and did not properly address issues such as identity, lifestyle, equality, democratic inclusion and ecology.

In the UK context, the 'new' social movements attacked the post-war social and political consensus on all fronts and in doing so created debate within the 'old' movements themselves around the question of how to engage with the appearance of the new social actors and the issues that they raised. The welfare system became a key area of contestation with new social welfare movements (Williams, 1992; Martin, 2001) emerging to challenge the state (local, regional and national) around issues pertaining to collective consumption (Castells, 1977a) (for example, public housing, health, education, transport, amenity and so on) and the exclusionary hierarchies and controlling rigidities of its bureaucratic administration. Equally, the very conception of 'welfare' that had been institutionalised within the welfare system was subject to radical critique and redefinition in new ways that were concomitant to the wider issues raised by the new movements (environment, gender, sexuality, ethnicity, disability and so on).

Although the ardour of the 1960s' political militancy was short-lived, its impact in the advanced liberal democracies has been highly significant in terms of both the theory and practice of politics. In terms of theory, it revitalised dormant participatory ideologies such as anarchism, political ecology and revolutionary socialism; while at the same time politicising personal, cultural and moral issues (for example, sexuality, gender and family roles) that were hitherto considered apolitical. In terms of practice, it facilitated the development of non-institutionalised and unconventional modes of political action (petitions, boycotts, occupations, wildcat strikes, demonstrations, direct action and so on), and their normalisation as forms of political participation (Norris, 2002; or what Tarrow, 1994, calls the 'repertoire of contention'). During the contemporary era, social movements have increasingly challenged the parties, institutions and traditional decision-making processes of representative democracy as adequate vehicles of governance. In the early 2000s, the sociocultural prominence of the environmental, human rights, fair trade and anti-capitalist movements, coupled with the protest movement against the ongoing wars in Iraq and elsewhere, and the myriad of shorter-lived protest campaigns that have emerged around the defence of public and welfare services from market encroachment, are currently the most visible manifestations of the new post-1960s mode of 'doing politics'.

This chapter aims to show how the body of scholarship that is associated with social movement theory can be utilised as an interpretive framework to define and analyse movements that have mobilised in the British context around the broad contested terrain of social welfare. As the Introduction indicates, the task of defining what a social movement is is in itself contested – this chapter does not attempt to offer a definitive answer – rather it will provide a broad explanatory account of the main European and North American empirical and theoretical traditions in the field and in doing so point to the main points of theoretical and conceptual contention. This account will then be drawn on to identify themes and foci, which will be used in subsequent chapters to define welfare movements, understand their mobilisation and to conceptualise their organisation, tactics and strategy.

The Atlantic divide: social movements theory in the US and Europe

Definitional questions surrounding social movements (see the Introduction) are compounded by the divergent development of European and American sociological research traditions within the field of social movements scholarship. Indeed, since the 1970s, the separation has become so acute that what can be described as an 'Atlantic divide' has opened up, whereby the resource mobilisation theory (RMT) perspective dominant in the US and the new social movements perspective dominant in Europe have become synonymous with their geographical locations (Ryan, 2006). For American RMT, social movements are held to constitute another expression of the 'normal' political processes that give rise to various competing social entities within an open pluralist democracy. Hence, Cohen (1985, p 675) has described the American view of social movements as 'Clausewitzian'; that is, 'the continuation of orderly politics by other (disorderly) means'.

European new social movements theorists, on the other hand, view social movements as constituting historically specific modes of collective action that are discontinuous with the remit of 'normal' politics in that unconventional tactics and strategies are employed outside established political institutions with the goal of bringing about social change through the spheres of civil society and culture and/or through the transformation of the state. Moreover, in their application, American RM theories tend to operate on the micro and meso levels dealing with the how of social movement mobilisation and organisation, whereas European theories address macro-structural questions of why social movements should arise as collective actors at particular historical junctures (Melucci, 1980). The cleavage that exists between the Americans and Europeans is no mere accident of geography, but rather stems from a variety of interrelated sociopolitical sources – partly from the differences in the ideological and political nature of the social movements that rose to prominence on either side of the Atlantic in the 1960s and 1970s; partly from the differences that have developed historically between the two political cultures; but perhaps most significantly as explored below, partly from the different ideological and theoretical perspectives that have been salient in the respective social scientific academies in the course of their uneven historical development.

American perspectives 1: strain theories of collective behaviour

During the 1950s and 1960s, social scientific approaches to the study of social movements in the US were dominated by variants of the 'science of collective behaviour'. Key representations of this approach are embodied in the Parsonian structural functionalism of Smelser (1962), the relative deprivation theories of Gurr (1970) and the theories of mass society developed by Kornhauser (1959) and Gusfield (1963). Each of these theoretical approaches share a common Durkheimian focus on the psychology of anomic social disconnectedness and malintegration produced by the structural strains of a rapidly modernising social system. Internalisation of social strain and related grievance amplification is held to be the primary motivating factor behind participation in modes of unconventional norm-breaking forms of collective activity. Politics in this conception is solely of the institutionalised party political/lobby group variety and therefore collective movement activities that do not follow this pattern are held to fall outside the remit of what constitutes normal political processes. Thus, all forms of unconventional modes of collective behaviour including social movements, protests, riots and rebellions fall within the same typological and explanatory framework.

Collective behaviour approaches perceive the individual as being caught up in the 'hysteria' of the crowd (Le Bon, 1995), which is understood to move in the manner of a contagious disease via rumour, innuendo and solidifying counter-norm ideologies (for example, fascism and communism) in a transitory life cycle from spontaneous collective rebellion to the constitution of unstable social entities, which flourish for short periods until the system (if directed effectively) subsumes them to once again return to an integrated equilibrium. Mayer (1995), in her critical commentary, points to the two central underlying philosophical and political assumptions that underpin strain theories of collective behaviour. First, because modernisation will in due course benefit all sections of society, collective resistance to that process is doomed to failure if elites properly manage the modernisation process; and second, resistance is necessarily irrational and ultimately irrelevant to the developmental trajectory of modern society because the political system approximates the pluralist ideal of an open democratic polity. Therefore, according to American theories of collective behaviour, 'extra-institutional forms of action can only be a matter of marginal, deprivileged groups who lack the cognitive or temporal resources to use the access' (Mayer, 1995, p 170). The dominance of the collective behaviour theoretical paradigm in the 1950s and early 1960s illustrates the widespread influence that Bell's (1960) 'end of ideology' thesis enjoyed in social scientific academia and the conservative cold-war mentality of much of the American mainstream sociology of the period (as embodied in Parsonian structural functionalism) whose main concern it would appear was to defend the social and political status quo.

The social upheavals and conflicts of the 1960s were to radically challenge and expose the frailties of theories of collective behaviour and to engender no less than a paradigmatic shift in social scientific approaches to the study of social movements in the US. With the advent of the black civil rights movement in the early 1960s, and more importantly with the rapid growth of the New left, student and anti-Vietnam war movements across the Western world in the later 1960s, it became increasingly apparent to a new generation of American sociologists, many of whom were themselves movement activists, that collective behaviour approaches to understanding social movements were deeply flawed.

There were three mains strands of critique. First, by the second half of the decade, it had become clear that many of the actors participating in social movement activities could hardly be labelled anomic misfits and deviants. Rather, the activists were often (although not always) the young, highly educated sons and daughters of the middle classes. Second, the notion of social grievance as the prime motivating factor was deemed inadequate because clearly grievances have existed in all societies across time and space. Therefore, the question of the timing of the emergence of social movements, and in particular the movements of the 1960s at a time of historically unprecedented material affluence, needed to be addressed. Third, and related to the latter point, was the fact that collective behaviour theories in deeming social movements irrational could not properly account for their sustainable organisational structures, strategic choice of tactics or their ultimate, often very rationally defined objectives. With the dawn of the 1970s came the advent of yet more social movements in advanced Western societies such as the US and the UK – the women's and environmental movements being the most prominent – and these merely served to further compound the inadequacies of theories of collective behaviour.

American perspectives 2: resource mobilisation theory

The reaction that began in the 1960s against the classical collective behaviour paradigm took the form of the development of what has come to be termed 'resource mobilisation theory' (RMT). Zald (1992, pp 330-1), one of the chief exponents of this approach, neatly summarises the core components as follows:

> First, behaviour entails costs, therefore grievances or deprivation do not automatically or easily translate into social movement activity, especially high risk social movement activity. The weighing of costs and benefits, no matter how primitive, implies choice and rationality at some level.... Second, mobilisation of resources may occur from within the aggrieved group but also from many other sources. Third, resources are mobilised and organised; thus organising activity is critical. Fourth, the costs of participating may be raised or lowered by state and societal supports or repression. And fifth ... there is no direct or one to one correspondence between amount of mobilisation and movement success.

Here there is a clear break with the collective behaviour stress on psychosocial processes, feelings of deprivation or grievance incurred by social strain, and the deviant irrationality of collective behaviour. Instead, grievances are held to be a common and constant feature of all societies – therefore acting on them through social movement activities is dependent on strategic decision making that implies the rational consideration of possible negative costs and positive benefits of participation.

A cost/benefit conception of rationality lies at heart of all theories operating within the parameters of the resource mobilisation paradigm. This conception is derived from Olson's (1965) original application of rational actor theory to the dynamics of 'the logic of collective action' as displayed in the economic interest groups he was researching at the time. Olson's starting point is a utilitarian model of rationality, which assumes that the instrumental maximisation of an individual's self-interest will always take priority in the process of decision making. In relation to collective or group activities it will only be rational for an individual to participate if benefits can be accrued that outweigh the costs and, importantly, if those benefits can only be attained by participation. This type of benefit Olson termed 'selective' and stands in contrast to 'collective' benefits that are public goods that can be accrued as a result of group activities whether or not the individual concerned actually participates. The carrot of collective benefits is therefore not enough on its own to persuade individuals to participate, rather selective benefits must be on offer if the individual is not to 'free-ride' and attempt to benefit without contributing (Olsen, 1965). Olson's theory constituted an important cornerstone in the development of the resource mobilisation approach because it created a foundational basis on which to emphasise the rationality of participation in social movement activities. Moreover, as Zald (1991, p 350) points out, Olson alerted resource mobilisation theorists to the 'wide disparity between the distribution of beliefs in favour of a given collective condition, and the number of people who acted on those beliefs', and he also stimulated thinking 'about interests, group identification and value preferences'. In short, then, Olson provided much of the stimulus for the shift to the meso level of organisational analysis that is so central to the resource mobilisation approach.

Resource mobilisation theory and the body of empirical research that it has inspired centres on the effectiveness of the way in which social movement organisations (SMOs) accumulate, maintain, structure, employ and deploy their resources (McCarthy and Zald, 1973). Canel (1992, p 40) describes resources as taking both material and non-material forms and 'include money, organisational facilities, labour, means of communication ... legitimacy, loyalty, authority, moral commitment, solidarity'; while mobilisation 'is the process by which a group assembles resources and places them under collective control and ... [are] employed for the purpose of pursuing group goals'. For RMT, society is perceived a priori as consisting of a plurality of grievance-defined aggregated groups that approximate latent social movements. However, only when these groups are stimulated by contact with organisational resources do they become active social movements. Hence, RMT conceives of social movements in almost purely organisational terms because no matter how loose or rudimentary that organisation is, it is nevertheless the pivotal feature of social movement mobilisations without which they could not take place.

Leaders, or 'movement entrepreneurs' (McCarthy and Zald, 1977), also hold an important place within RMT. This is because they possess the special qualities and experience required to properly utilise resources and hence make the most of opportunities that allow the formation of social movements from the ever-present pool of social grievances. Leaders are usually established community figures prior to mobilisation, tend to be the founding members of SMOs and are the prime movers in driving a mobilisation towards its goals. In the contemporary era, leaders are often drawn from the new middle class because it is this class that possesses the resource skills (education, public speaking, journalism, presentation acumen, management experience and so on) most pertinent to operating within the channels of dialogue that are concomitant to the 'information society' (Castells, 2000).

Movement goals are conceived by RMT as being expressly political in form because mobilisations necessarily involve a contest over the exercise of power with other mobilised groups. They are also political because such contests are primarily orientated towards gaining access to, or acceptance within, the state and established social institutions where power over the distribution of resources is concentrated. Social movement mobilisations occur because social groupings with specific grievances have been blocked or excluded from making use of the usual channels of dialogue between state and civil society to seek redress. Instead, they rationally make use of whatever organisational resources become available to make their demands heard – conversely, if there are no such resources then a mobilisation will not take place. In RMT, because social movements are merely aiming for inclusion so as to participate more fully in social-directional decision making, they are not conceived to pose a challenge to the legitimacy of the liberal-democratic political system, rather they constitute a reformist safety valve that ensures its continued existence. Success in this conception is generally judged on the criteria of how professionally a movement's core SMO or SMOs are managed, the size and quality of its activist resource base and how much influence it has with political elites in gaining desired policy changes and access to increased resources.

American perspectives 3: the political process model

Over time a number of more sophisticated theoretical variants have developed within the resource mobilisation paradigm of which the historically orientated political process model associated with McAdam (1982, 1996), McAdam et al (1988), Tilly (1978, 2004) and Tarrow (1989, 1994) is the most significant. Unlike the original RMT model, which tends to emphasise the necessity of (and reliance on) the appropriation of organisational and political resources that are largely under the external control of elite social groups for social movement mobilisation, the political process model argues that indigenous internal organisational resources and mobilising structures must also exist if a successful mobilisation is to occur. Such resources are held to take the form of prior existing institutions as in McAdam's (1982) arguments concerning the importance of indigenous black organisations (for example, churches, colleges and pressure groups) for the mobilisation of the black civil rights movement in the 1960s. Or they may also be constituted by the more mundane aspects of bureaucratic organisation like the creation of a formal constitution, authoritative office bearers/leaders and a membership list that Gamson's (1975) research on 53 'challenger' SMOs in US history between 1800 and 1945 found was a prerequisite for groups to initiate themselves prior to mobilisation, if success is to be achieved.

According to political process perspectives, the individual comes into contact with organisational resources within 'micro-mobilisation contexts' (McAdam et al, 1988) or 'mobilising structures' (Tarrow, 1994). These are settings or situations where interactions take place with members or leaders of a given SMO, for example a trade union meeting in relation to the labour movement. Micro-mobilisation contexts can therefore be defined both as a key source of organisational resources – that is, movement activists and their related skills and material assets – and as constituting 'a communication network or infrastructure'. Indeed, as McAdam et al (1988, p 718) argue, it is 'the strength and breadth' of these micro-mobilisation contexts 'which largely determine the pattern, speed and extent of movement expansion'.

Frame theory develops the notion of micro-mobilisation contexts to point to the ways that social movements portray an issue in a particular way to a specific audience in order to gain membership and support. Framing recognises that events and situations need to be interpreted and that social movements cannot assume that its potential constituents' interpretation of events will be 'congruent and complimentary' with the SMO. The discussion of frames and framing is an important part of the humanising of RMT that hitherto had failed to account for micro-mobilisation processes, in part due to its strong aversion to earlier social psychological explanations of collective behaviour (see Klandermans, 1984). Snow et al (1986, p 464) define a frame as a 'schemata of interpretation' that enables individuals to 'locate, perceive, identify, and label' occurrences within their life space and the world at large. More simply, a frame can be defined as a framework through which we interpret the world by attributing meaning to actions and phenomena. In this way, frames are important since they make experiences meaningful thereby organising and guiding our actions.

Gamson (1995) argues that social movements not only need to define a particular issue as a social problem; they also need to frame that problem as injustice. The construction of an 'injustice frame' is a major part of mobilising social movement activists since if potential constituents do not see an issue as an injustice they will be less likely to participate in the movement. Gamson's work ties in with McAdam's (1982) argument that a successful social movement mobilisation is dependent on a process of 'cognitive liberation' whereby an individual or group not only designates an issue as a social problem but they also come to believe that something can and should be done about it – a change in political perception is required. This is clearly important in explaining why individuals mobilise but this does not properly explain the linkage between the SMO and the individual. Here, Snow et al (1986, p 464) are instructive when they argue that SMOs have to engage in frame alignment; that is, 'the linkage of individual and SMO interpretative orientations, such that some set of individual interests, values beliefs and SMO activities, goals and ideology are congruent and complementary'. Frame alignment cannot be taken for granted – the individual may not see an issue in the same way as an organisation or the individual may disagree with the tactics adopted by the organisation or even the other activities in which an organisation engages – it involves a process of negotiation.

Snow et al (1986) outline four frame alignment processes:

- *frame bridging*, where the SMO seeks to organise a pre-existing but unorganised sentiment among a particular group;
- *frame amplification*, where a value or belief already held by an individual is sharpened or strengthened, for example by demonstrating the urgency of solving a particular problem or explaining how a particular issue ties into the core beliefs of an individual;
- *frame extension*, where a frame is extended to include other issues, for example environmental organisations linking their struggle with class and community struggles for social justice;
- *frame transformation*, where the values and beliefs of the target audience must be completely transformed in order to fit with the SMO's understanding of a particular issue.

Frames have also been used to explain the way in which different social movements use the same frame to make sense of their movement. For example, since the American black civil rights movement, many social movements have used a civil rights frame to garner support for their cause. This is what Snow and Benford (1992) termed a 'master frame'. Feminism, socialism, Christianity, human rights among others have operated and indeed continue to operate as such master frames.

The other significant innovation of the political process model is in its stress on the need for favourable 'political opportunity structures' to be in place if a mobilisation is to be successful. These structures can be defined as the 'consistent – but not necessarily formal, permanent or national – dimensions of the political environment which either encourage or discourage people from using collective action' (Tarrow, 1994, p 18). Shifting political biases within the state and within key administrative decision-making institutions have an important role to play in this encouraging and discouraging process because at certain historical junctures they may be more open or more closed to particular types of social movement demand than to others. Hence, social movements go through historical 'cycles of protest', which may wax and wane depending on the nature of the political opportunity structure. Tarrow (2002, in Macdonald, 2006, p 27) has suggested that in the current period the global institutions of neoliberal capitalism 'not only provide an opportunity structure for contention, but provide unifying themes and identities for those who oppose them'. In recent years, the theory of political opportunity structures has been extended to incorporate 'cultural opportunity structures' and 'economic opportunity structures' in order to offer a more multidimensional analytical framework (Wahlstrom and Peterson, 2006).

Tilly (1986) has used a similar model to show how historically the 'action repertoire' of collective actions and political protests have altered with political modernisation, the growth of civil society and the concomitant shifting structures of political opportunity. Thus, contemporary repertoires of collective action (for example, strikes, demonstrations, electoral rallies and public meetings) differ markedly in form (but not their rational content) from the food riots, tax rebellions and appeals to paternal authority that defined the early modern pre-democratic era. Equally, Tarrow (1994) has illustrated how the most successful types of innovative collective action employed within a given 'cycle of protest' solidify over time into just such a repertoire of action that is used again and again by the social actors engaging in movement and protest activities.

American perspectives: a critical evaluation

The contribution of RMT to understanding social movements has generally been rejected by European social movements theorists because although it importantly directs attention to the organisational and strategic difficulties that social movements face when mobilising, and indeed to the power of motivating factors involving self-interest, its methodological individualist assumptions underpin a one-dimensional (utilitarian) and impoverished conception of human nature/human rationality. Grievance is rejected as a mobilising factor, something that empties social movement mobilisations of any meaning or content at the subjective level (Bagguley, 1992; Crossley, 2003). At a more analytical level, this move also rules out other uncomfortable questions of ideology, values, identity, class, structure, agency, culture and history. Cost/benefit instrumental rationality means that, as Scott (1990) points out, RMT conceives of SMOs as operating under four specific restraints and imperatives:

- The necessity of providing divisible private benefits as well as indivisible collective ones places high organisational costs on collective bodies.
- The search for resources such as external funding becomes a major organisational preoccupation.
- The organisation is restricted in the demands and sacrifices it can realistically expect of its members.
- Occasional low-cost/low-risk tactics ought to be preferable to frequent high-cost/high-risk activities (see Scott, 1990, p 112).

The implication is that all social movements must inevitably follow a trajectory of 'maturation' leading to eventual professionalisation, institutionalisation and ultimately to deradicalisation if they are to acquire the resources to survive, let alone succeed in their aims. These imperatives also mean that social movements will tend to be homogenous centralising bodies that have a predilection to concentration on single issues and the forging of alliances with mainstream political forces, as opposed to the more risky strategy of taking on a wider remit or seeking wider social transformation. For RMT, realism as opposed idealism, and reform as opposed to revolution, are therefore the watchwords of all SMOs because they must follow the same narrow logic of the maximisation of self-interest as the individuals who join them do.

While some SMOs may indeed conform to the logic of RMT (mainstream environmental organisations, trade unions and so on), this logic is far from universal or inevitable. Byrne (1997), in his commentary on social movements in the British context, shows that there are a variety of SMOs and groupings that simply do not 'fit the mould' of the cost/ benefit RMT model. Good examples here are radical feminists (of even the first-wave variety), the Campaign for Nuclear Disarmament (CND), the radical direct-action wing of the Green movement and even the more mainstream Green Party, none of which have compromised their values, moved away from participation in 'high-risk' direct-action campaigns or abandoned their loose networking style of organisation in order to gain access to, or acceptance within, the political mainstream (Byrne, 1997, pp 165-9). In fact, these groupings, according to RMT, should have folded long ago because they have not followed the rational pattern demanded by the realist imperatives of collective action in a pluralist democratic society. Where European theorists have found most in common with American theory is in relation to the more historically oriented and more loosely defined political process model where there has been notable trans-Atlantic convergence around the significance of political opportunity structures, cycles of protest, micro-mobilisation contexts, repertoires of contention and the framing of collective action (for example, Klandermans et al, 1988; Eyerman and Jamison, 1991; Byrne, 1997).

European approaches: theories of the new social movements

In European sociology, Marxism had always been a significant but subordinate bedfellow to Durkheimian- and Weberian-influenced theory and research, but with the generalised 1960s radicalisation, which saw the flourishing of new oppositional movements, and in particular the revolutionary events of May 1968 in France and the upturn in industrial conflict that occurred in its wake throughout Europe in the early 1970s, it went through a process of revitalisation that secured a strong position in sociological academia, the wider social scientific/cultural academic community and importantly within the contemporary social movements themselves. This renewal was aided by the exploration of new and exciting theoretical and critical avenues, which stood in various degrees of opposition to the Stalinised formulaic dogma that had deformed and debilitated the development of Marxism's engagement with the vagaries of the capitalist world since the 1930s. Equally, it also often involved an unabashed engagement with, or indeed appropriation of, ideas from philosophical, scientific, psychological, anthropological and social theories, which were ostensibly located within the realm of bourgeois thought and science. Most notable among these new avenues were those opened up by New left theorists like Marcuse and other members of the Frankfurt School whose neo-Marxist-inspired critical theory was 'rediscovered', Sartre's innovative if unhappy marriage of Marxism and existentialism, Althusser's development of 'scientific' structural Marxism, and in Britain, the eclectic and often groundbreaking socioeconomic, cultural and political criticism of the leftist intellectual coterie surrounding the New Left Review and Socialist Register journals.

These theoretical developments naturally stimulated the field of sociological social movements scholarship, which until the late 1960s had been limited to the concerns central to the classical schools of sociology. The new variants of Marxism and New Left thinking thus became a guiding light in the genesis of a body of theory and research for which the social movements active in the contemporary period became a benchmark. European sociologists began to look at the new social conflicts within the context of the contradictions of capitalism. Focus was directed to questions relating to changes in the structure of post-war capitalism and the relationship therein between those changes and the timing of the emergence of the 'new' movements of the 1960s and 1970s, and the re-emergence of the 'old' labour movement as a militant oppositional force.

By the late 1970s, however, the revolutionary hopes of the previous decade had begun to fade as Western capitalist states and their ruling classes first retrenched and then under the guidance of Conservative governments went on the offensive with the introduction of neoliberal economic policies and the cultivation of hedonistic consumerism in the 1980s. Concomitant to this 'carnival of reaction' came the fragmentation and deradicalisation of the social movements, both 'old' and 'new', in which so many activists, intellectuals and workers had placed their faith. Identity and difference replaced equality and solidarity as the movements' buzzwords while the brief flowering of Marxism wilted (in particular its Althusserian incarnation) under the glare of the interrelated critiques developed by post-structuralist philosophy and post-modern social and cultural theory, which especially to large numbers of those working in cultural and social–scientific academia seemed to capture the contemporary mood of pessimism and cynicism more accurately.

In the early 2000s, the heterogeneous corpus of European social movements scholarship in all its contradictions and internal debates amply reflects the changes in cultural mood, political tempo and social-theoretic fashion that have occurred since the 1960s. Today's theory and research is broadly divided between thinkers who are influenced to varying degrees by Marxism, neo-Weberianism, post-modernism and second-generation Frankfurt School critical theory. While these divisions run deep and particularly in terms of arguments surrounding class, modernity and the basis on which to build an emancipatory politics, European approaches can nevertheless be bracketed together because of a shared disposition towards understanding the 'new' social movements as historical actors that have been brought into being by structural alterations in the nature of advanced capitalism. Although their conclusions may differ, and may differ significantly depending on their ideological position, European theoreticians and researchers of social movements share a common starting point in their focus on macro-structural change. This is change that is increasingly understood as operating across national boundaries in the context of globalised capitalism and the transnational social movements, which contest its economic and political structures (Khagram et al 2002; MacDonald, 2006).

Marxist theory: Castells and urban social movements

Marxism's engagement with the new social movements forms the centrepiece around which much of subsequent European theorising and critical debate in this area of scholarship revolves, whether it be in the reception, adaption, reconstruction or rejection of Marxist ideas. It is necessary therefore to give Marxist theory due consideration before moving on to look at the contributions of other rival perspectives. With the appearance of the new social movements in the 1960s and 1970s, Marxism was posed the serious problem of how to reconcile class politics with new conflicts that did not fit the classic pattern or profile of working-class struggle. For some on the Marxist Left, the response was to dismiss the new movements as a mere petty bourgeois phenomenon that was ultimately irrelevant to the outcome of the class struggle. The alternative non-workerist response, which was to find particular favour among Marxists working in social-scientific academia, was to view the appearance of the new movements as adding new dimensions to the class struggles over distribution and ownership that have animated capitalism since its inception.

Castells' research and theoretical work of the mid to late 1970s is probably the most systematic and best known of Marxist analyses to take an inclusive approach to understanding the nature of the new movements. Castells' starting point is 'the urban question', which he defines as 'the organisation of the means of collective consumption at the basis of the daily life of all social groups: housing, education, health, culture, commerce, transport etc' (Castells, 1978, p 3). Castells argues that the key contradiction that lies at the heart of the urban situation arises out of the inbuilt tension between the allocation of resources to the needs of the productive and profitable industrial sector of the economy and to the needs of the non-productive and hence non-profitable sector of collective consumption. The state's main source of finance is taxation and lending but because both are subject to restraints and limits, fiscal crisis is endemic to the system. The state is forced to constantly cut public spending because, although both sectors are vital to the system, the productive sector must take priority due to its profitability and is therefore able to siphon off resources whenever economic needs dictate. This causes conflicts to arise in the urban environment where over time the needs of both sectors have intensified and where the local state's administration of collective needs has been increasingly subject to the battle for democratic accountability. Castells (1977b, p 43) advances the argument like this: 'Public consumption ... becomes simultaneously an indispensable element for the functioning of the system, a permanent objective of workers demands and a deficit sector of the capitalist economy'. A further contradiction arises from the individual's private pursuit of better standards of living and quality of life and the collective manner in which this process is actually administered. Because the means of collective consumption are managed by public authorities, the entire urban arena becomes politicised since the organisation of schools, hospitals, housing and transportation and so on are fundamental determinants of everyday life.

Urban contradictions do not necessarily result in forms of working-class struggle – this depends entirely on the issue at stake and certain issues may even draw sections of the middle class into conflict with the local state. Because urban social movements do not develop at the point of production, they may therefore develop more easily as broad alliances of anti-capitalist forces rather than through the working class on its own. Such 'collective consumption trade unionism', Castells argues, can involve the great majority of people in the struggle to gain progressive reforms under capitalism. Conflicts that focus on issues of collective assumption alone constitute 'phases and skirmishes' within the 'general process of change', which may 'alter, in an unstable and partial way, the general logic of urban organisation' (Castells, 1977b, p 45). Here the influence of the Euro-communist strategy of the broad democratic alliance (itself a throwback to the popular frontism of the 1930s), which was adopted by many mainland European Communist Parties in the 1970s, is clearly apparent. Also evident is Castells' employment of the Althusserian notion of 'relative autonomy' whereby conflicts in the political and cultural spheres can develop autonomously from conflicts in the economic sphere through their own internal logics. Despite their weaknesses stemming from a tendency to a narrow focus on consumption issues, urban social movements are nevertheless politically significant for Castells because they open up possibilities of both new fronts in the class struggle and new class alliances. We return to explore these and related issues more fully in Chapter Six.

Neo-Weberianism, new social movements and the impact of values

Research on new social movements, such as that carried out by Inglehart (1977, 1990), has been particularly influential in challenging orthodox Marxian notions of the structural/class determination of political processes such as those identified by Castells in his early work. Using cross-national comparisons of quantitative data, Inglehart has shown that new movement membership is primarily drawn from the new middle class in combination with such economically marginalised groups as students and welfare recipients. He argues in a Weberian manner that motivation for participation in the new politics is not directly related to class position, but is rather a product of an orientation towards specific issues that arise in the public sphere from the congruence of dissatisfaction with the state's dysfunctions and the shift towards new post-materialist values in the post-war generation. This generation is unlike those that existed previously because it does not have to constantly strive to attain the material essentials of life and can therefore concentrate on aspects of personal development and the enjoyment of a new-found freedom (from Beveridge's 'five giants'). The new movements personify the new values of this generation in that they stress the importance of rights, identity, quality of life and political participation over the instrumental materialism that took precedence in the previous era. In a parallel with Bourdieu's (1984) notion of the formation of habitus, Ingelhart argues that because these values are inculcated at early stages in life, they persist even when economic conditions deteriorate and affluence is threatened. For Inglehart, the generational nature of the new movements cuts across class and calls into question the ideological division between Left and Right (see also Parkin, 1968; Giddens, 1987).

In the late 1970s, the growing recognition within sociology of middle-class involvement with movement politics sparked a wide-ranging debate concerning the political nature of the middle classes. The American 'new class' thesis, for example, attempted to account for the middle-class radicalism of the previous two decades through the theorisation of a newly formed highly educated professional-managerial class, which contained potentially revolutionary currents (for example, Gouldner, 1979). In Britain, Goldthorpe's (1982) theorisation of a growing 'service class' of professionals and managers who have used the new social movements as instruments of inter- and intra-class politics, has proven to be highly influential. Goldthorpe's arguments tie in well with social movement theorists who have challenged the view that new middle-class involvement in social movements involves strictly altruistic motives, and who suggest instead (echoing RMT) that varying degrees of self-interested instrumentalism are involved. These modes of self-interest range from participation aimed at securing representation in key decision-making institutions through to the attempt to attain hegemony within those same institutions (see Cotgrove and Duff, 1980; Cotgrove, 1982). In this critical vein, Frankel (1987) argues that the influx of 'new class' members who were active in both social movements and the traditional leftist political parties of countries of the Organisation for Economic Co-operation and Development (OECD) has led to their deradicalisation and the replacement of socialist politics with a form of technocratic pragmatism (for instance as with New Labour's 'third way' project) that favours the furtherance of their interests.

New social movements and politics of post-modernity

While Weberians have critiqued the orthodox Marxist position by asserting the relative autonomy of values from class, post-modernist thinkers have taken this argument to its extreme in the development of a 'radical decoupling' thesis whereby there is no longer any rationale for linking political and cultural phenomena to any fixed social base (Crook et al, 1992; Pakulski, 1995). Influenced by the anti-foundationalist epistemology espoused by post-structuralist philosophers like Derrida, Foucault and Baudrillard, post-modern social theorists argue that referent categories such as class, income, status or occupational group no longer have any meaning in a fragmented post-modern world that is heterogeneous, rhizomic and devoid of any discernible structure. Dalton et al (1990) express this view in relation to the 'new politics' when they propose that the:

> new social movements signify a shift from group based political cleavages to value and issue based cleavages that identify only communities of like minded people. The lack of a firm and well defined social base also means that membership tends to be very fluid, with participants joining in and then disengaging as

the political context and their personal circumstances change.
(1990, p 12; see also Maffesoli, 1996)

For post-modernists, the present age is one of delegitimation and narrative
crisis where, as Lyotard (1984, p 3) famously argued, 'the grand narrative has
lost its credibility, regardless of what mode of unification it uses, regardless
of whether it is a speculative narrative or a narrative of emancipation'.
For Lyotard, meta-narratives were responsible for Auschwitz and the
Gulags and have brought the earth to the brink of ecological catastrophe;
it is therefore necessary to wage war on totality and to prize instead the
pluralistic politics, art and science of a post-modern, post-industrial society.
In post-modern social theory, because power in society is held to be diffuse
and indeterminate as opposed to being embodied in a class or group, then
resistance to it must also be of a fractured nature, operating locally through
such 'communities of like minded people' employing oppositional practices
that cannot easily be assimilated by what Foucault (1979) has termed 'the
power network'.

Aside from its use of 'outmoded categories', post-modern social theorists
deem Marxian class theory an inadequate base on which to build an
emancipatory political movement because its concentration on the sectional
interests of the working class does not address the multiple forms of
power/oppression that exist in contemporary society (Laclau and Mouffe,
1985). Socialist class politics are perceived as an irretrievably monocentric
suppression of the radical 'difference' that is necessary for pluralism and
real democracy to exist, and it therefore must be jettisoned in favour of the
particularist concerns of the new social movements. Deleuze (1973: 149)
spells out what this means in practical political terms when he says that:

> [T]he problem for revolutionaries today is to unite within the
> purpose of a particular struggle without falling into the despotic
> and bureaucratic organisation of the party or state machine.
> We seek a kind of war machine that will not recreate a state
> apparatus, a nomadic unit related to the outside that will not
> revive an internal despotic unity.

In a post-modern world, identities – gender, sexuality, ethnicity and so on
– assume a new significance and the concomitant development of identity
politics signifies a further break with the old politics of nation, tradition
or class (Touraine, 1977; Melucci, 1988). Moreover, regarding welfare,
modernisation, as Chapter Two argues, involved a shift from customary
rights to citizenship rights; post-modernisation involves a further shift
towards identity rights.

The ditching of class politics by certain sections of the 'intellectual' Left has on a more theoretical level been complemented by the replacement of Marx by Nietzsche as the philosophical basis for the construction of an emancipatory politics centred on the new movements. This is a development that owes much to the work of Foucault, Deleuze and their followers who credit the latter with being the 'nomadic thinker' par excellence, a philosopher who instigated a new form of politics whose aim is to break all systems asunder, to resist assimilation and to defy the prevailing codes and norms of the day. If a similar project of liberation is to be pursued in the present period, then as Deleuze (1973, p 143) says, we must ask ourselves 'who are our nomads today, who are our real Nietzscheans?'. For thinkers influenced by post-structuralism, the new social movements are practitioners of this type of resistance, whereby the struggle for particular goals takes place at a localised or regional level, outside of established political institutions and using unconventional means, but with no such dangerous utopian intention of capturing state power or altering socioeconomic conditions in any fundamental manner (Melucci, 1989). Foucault (1977, p 231) argues that the system must be engaged 'on all fronts – the university, the prisons, and the domain of psychiatry – one after another, since our forces are not strong enough for a simultaneous attack'. Resistance must, however, avoid the use of any totalising theory, because 'the need for theory is still part of the system we reject'. Hardt and Negri's (2000) theorisation of the amorphous 'multitude' that stands in opposition to 'Empire' is the latest version of this theory for the 21st century and the worldwide anti-globalisation movement (see also Chesters and Welsh, 2006).

Habermas's critical theory: new social movements and the project of modernity

The thesis of a new post-industrial stage in capitalism is also central to the work of Habermas who has advanced a theory of legitimation crisis in order to explain the new struggles that characterise the present historical juncture (1976, 1981, 1987b). Habermas's crisis theory is premised on the inbuilt contradictions that exist between the economic, administrative political and sociocultural subsystems of advanced capitalist societies. In the contemporary era, the growing disparity between public expectations of these subsystems and the state's ability to satisfy both these expectations and the acute demands of economic restructuring has created a crisis of legitimation, which defines the new political paradigm of late as opposed to liberal capitalism (see also the more empirically grounded work of Offe, 1985). The political and economic system requires a mass input of loyalty in order to sustain it but because of its inability to deliver ever-multiplying demands, individual motivations for participation are increasingly coming to be questioned. Habermas argues that in order to offset this crisis the state has attempted to extend its authority through the incremental extension of public policy into previously autonomous actions spheres – a process that he terms 'inner colonisation'.

This strategy has, however, had something of a paradoxical effect for although the state's regulatory functions have increased and thus its formal authority has been extended, at a deeper and more substantive level that authority has been subverted through its own striving for inclusiveness. As the scope of political authority grows, it politicises its own non-political underpinnings and in doing so negates the very source of its original legitimation. In essence, then, the bureaucratic intervention of the state into spheres that were previously autonomous and associated with the private concerns of morality, the family and the community has turned them into public and hence political issues. Work is no longer the sole source of oppression in late capitalist society, rather the growth of state regulatory authority in the lifeworld is removing autonomy in the social and cultural spheres, and eroding civil society. On the one hand, this process has created 'new social pathologies' (for example, racism and extreme nationalism); on the other hand, the new movements constitute modes of resistance to 'the System's colonisation of the lifeworld' (Habermas, 1987b, p 394; see also similarities to Touraine, 1974).

According to Habermas's theory, the new conflicts articulated by the new social movements 'are manifest in sub-institutional, or at least extra-parliamentary forms of protest ... ignited by questions having to do with the grammar of forms of life' (Habermas, 1981, p 33). The new movements represent a shift away from the institutionalised parties and representative democracy that characterised the 'old politics', and are motivated instead by problems centring on the quality of life, individual self-realisation, norms, values and human rights. The new movements respond to specific problem situations that arise when the organic foundations of the lifeworld are under attack and the quality of life is threatened. These conflict situations emanate from a variety of sources: first, 'green problems', for example, urban and environmental destruction, pollution and health hazards; second, problems of excessive complexity, for example, risk and the fear of military potentials for destruction, nuclear waste and nuclear power; and third, an overburdening of the communicative infrastructure, which results in a cultural impoverishment that in turn engenders the growth of particularistic communities based on gender, age, skin colour, neighbourhood, locality or religious affiliation. What unites most of these diverse groups is that they all are critical in one way or another to the System imperatives of unmitigated economic expansion and increasing bureaucratic rationality (see also Habermas, 1981).

While critical of the dangers of particularism, Habermas takes a positive view of the latent emancipatory political potential that the new social movements possess. He argues that this potential stems from their disposition to create alternative institutions and to employ practices that run counter to those that are organised according to the dictates of the 'steering media', that is, state and capital. The new movements encourage experimental forms of participatory democracy that are vital for the revival of communicative reason in society while their alternative institutions and counter-practices defend the lifeworld from System intrusion. Finally, the new social movements, in carrying out these functions, provide examples and prototype models for the possible birth of a new society that for Habermas embodies 'the project of modernity'. This is a society predicated on equality, universal rights and radical democracy while bringing hitherto submerged issues and grievances into the public arena and opening them up to public debate. As Hewitt (1993, p 63) states in his commentary, 'a defence of specific identities and needs provides the grounds for raising more universalistic concerns'.

European theories of the new social movements: a critical evaluation

While there are significant divergencies between the different perspectives to which the label 'new social movements' theory can be applied, each is nevertheless premised on the notion that the key social movements active in the contemporary period are marked by a radical discontinuity with both the social movements of a previous era and with the realm of 'normal' institutional politics. In the European conception, social movements seek to bring about fundamental change as opposed to the American conception whereby they are merely seeking inclusion within the polity to achieve reform. These radical aims are also reflected in the movements' organisational structure whereby they do not necessarily adhere to the formal structural and bureaucratic hierarchies associated with the 'old' politics and instead adopt decentralised participatory forms that are characterised by informal networks of interaction. The new movements propose through their form, ideological content and actions an alternative framework of development to the dominant ethic of unmitigated economic growth and narrow instrumental materialism that impoverishes the realms of culture, politics and the environment (Eder, 1993).

The discontinuity thesis does, however, suffer from a number of problems. First, from the perspective of the dominant schools of American theory as embodied in RMT and political process models, the European account of the origins of social movements does not properly address the instrumental or strategic aspects of collective action whereby the expressive dimension of movement politics is mediated by the organisational imperatives of mobilising resources and the mobilising imperative of self-interest. It also tends to ignore the political dimensions of social movement mobilisations, for example the structure of political opportunities and the interplay between 'formal' institutionalised politics and the 'informal' politics of movement networks. The broad European focus on changing socioeconomic structure, class, values, ideology and identity therefore needs to be supplemented by the more micro and meso concerns of American theory.

Second, perhaps the key problem for new social movement perspectives is in relation to the implied dichotomy between old and new movements. Many of the social movements to which the adjective 'new' has been applied, for example feminism and black civil rights, have their roots in traditions of struggle, which reach back at least as far as the early 19th century (D'Anieri et al, 1990; Calhoun, 1993). The adjective 'new' also carries with it the connotation that the movements to which it has been applied have somehow replaced the 'old' movements or that the old movements are no longer active. It is essentially a term that has often been used to critique the Marxist emphasis on the working class and the labour movement. While some of this critique is merited and especially so in terms of some of Marxism's more dogmatic workerist incarnations, new movement theorists have often failed to recognise that the insurgency of the 'new' social movements in the late 1960s/early 1970s was very much accompanied by a concomitant upsurge in working-class radicalism that was expressed in a new militancy within the labour movement. Equally, by the 1980s, when the labour movement had adopted the much more compliant policies associated with the so-called 'new realism' (and even then in the UK there was the Great Miners Strike of 1984-85), many of the new movements had also adopted much less militant postures.

What this would appear to indicate is that even though society is indeed criss-crossed by diverse conflicts, there is nevertheless a relationship between the radicalisation of different social sectors and social groupings. It also implies that the labour movement and class conflict is far from dead, rather it, like the 'new' movements, goes through cycles of upturn and downturn in struggle as the political process model suggests in relation to movements in general. For these reasons it is suggested that for analytical clarity the adjective 'contemporary' is used where possible throughout this book in place of the word 'new' to describe movements active in the current period.

Conclusion: theorising social welfare movements

Both American and European theoretical perspectives prompt different types of analytical question that lie at the heart of their broad frameworks of interpretation of what social movements are and do. A selection of these questions is set out below as a loose guide to the types of theme that will be covered in the subsequent chapters on social welfare movements.

Analytical questions prompted by American theoretical approaches.

(1)   How much is self-interest a mobilising factor for participants engaging in the activities associated with the social movement?
(2)   What is the role of organisation and resources in the social movement?
(3)   How has the social movement concerned engaged with government institutions in order to achieve its aims?
(4)   What are the key micro-mobilisation contexts where individuals are recruited to the movement's cause?
(5)   Can the social movement be viewed as responding to a favourable political opportunity structure?
(6)   How has the social movement framed its discourse(s) of opposition?
(7)   Has a distinctive tactical repertoire of collective action associated with the social movement developed? What forms has this repertoire taken?
(8)   Has the movement gone through cycles of protest?

Analytical questions prompted by European theoretical approaches:

(1)   Who are the social movement actors in sociodemographic terms?
(2)   Is there a relationship between the social movement actors' class nature and their activism?
(3)   What type of values do the social movement actors hold? In what ways do these values impact on their social movement activities?
(4)   What type(s) of identity have been engendered by participation in social movement activity?
(5)   What is the relationship between the social movement and the interests of the 'old' labour movement?
(6)   How can the movement be understood in relation to structural contradictions within capitalist socioeconomic organisation?

(7)   What are the social movement actors' orientations towards the realm of institutional politics? How far can their politics be deemed 'cultural'?

(8)   Does the network of actors concerned constitute a social movement, protest movement or protest campaign? If one of the latter forms of collective action, then how does it relate to the wider social movement ?

Further reading

There are three key introductory texts to the contested field of social movements theory: *Making Sense of Social Movements* by Nick Crossley (Open University Press, 2002), *Social Movements: An Introduction by Donatella Della Porta and Mario Diani* (Blackwell, 2006) and *Social Movements in Britain* by Paul Byrne (Routledge, 1997).

The Social Movements Reader: Cases and Concepts edited by Jeff Goodwin and James M. Jasper (Blackwell, 2003) provides a variety of useful extracts from classic readings on all aspects of social movement activity, from mobilisation, membership, organisation and development through to strategy, tactics, impacts and decline.

Power in Movement: Social Movements and Contentious Politics by Sidney Tarrow (Cambridge University Press, 1994) and *Social Movements: 1768-2004* by Charles Tilly (Paradigm Publishers, 2004) provide very readable historical overviews of the development of social movements from within the political process perspective.

'New social movements' by Jurgen Habermas (*Telos*, 1981) remains a much-debated article while *Empire* by Michael Hardt and Antonio Negri (Harvard University Press, 2000) is worth exploring for a post-modern take on contemporary global movements.

The journal *Mobilization* is another useful source for articles on social movements theory – its website can be found at www.mobilization.sdsu.edu/

Part Two

*Social movements and the
classical welfare state*

Fighting idleness and want: movements of the unemployed

Introduction

The most famous image of the unemployed is that of a black and white photograph from the 1930s showing an unemployed man on a rainy street corner, head bowed in a dejected posture, dressed in ragged work clothes, clogs, cloth cap and muffler. However, such images of abjection and a 'grin and bear it' attitude on the part of the unemployed can be misleading. The central question that this chapter addresses is: what role, if any, did the unemployed in Britain play in shifting the national priorities of social policy in the inter-war years? Its focus therefore is on how unemployed struggles in the inter-war period shaped the post-war welfare state.

First, we establish that far-reaching reforms in social policy and economic policy were enacted that, at least in part, answered some of the grievances framed by unemployed protests. Second, we consider the nature of unemployment and some of the dilemmas of organising a social movement among the unemployed. We do this through a brief history of the National Unemployed Workers' Movement (NUWM) in Britain. Finally, we conclude this chapter by reflecting on what light social movement theory sheds on the case of the NUWM.

Reforming the scourge of idleness and want

Sir William Beveridge, in his famous 1942 report *Social Insurance and Allied Services*, placed 'want' (poverty) and 'idleness' (unemployment) among the 'first and most urgent needs' of the 'five giants' requiring urgent action

(Timmins, 1995). In the years before the outbreak of the Second World War in 1939, widespread poverty and unemployment stalked Britain. Almost from the end of the First World War to the start of the Second World War, economic instability and dislocation created massive, although fluctuating, levels of unemployment. Later named the 'distressed areas', whole communities were laid waste as local industries such as shipbuilding, coalmining and textiles were forced to reduce their size or close altogether (Ward, 1988). Economic recession polarised society. Particularly harsh treatment was meted out by the authorities to the unemployed and their families. This affected huge swathes of society; around half of the British workforce found themselves unemployed at some time during the 1930s.

'Want' on such a scale, the Beveridge Report (1942, para 445) argued, 'was a needless scandal due to not taking the trouble to prevent it'. Beveridge therefore proposed a system of social security that would provide a 'national minimum' level of subsistence for those unable to work. Such proposals would have been unthinkable just a few years beforehand. Suddenly, with the need for national unity in wartime and growing sympathy for the Soviet Union after the 1941 Nazi invasion, such reforms seemed to make perfect common sense (Calder, 1969). As Beveridge put it, 'Social Security is not a political question at all. It is neither Socialist nor Capitalist. It is simply common sense' (cited in Bruce, 1968, p 26). The political establishment had begun to adopt what the future Conservative Prime Minister Harold Macmillan called a 'middle way' between capitalism and socialism. Even *The Times*, newspaper of the establishment, embraced the need for progressive reform.

However, Beveridge represented no revolution from above. His proposals were not quite 'halfway to Moscow' as he claimed. Although they ran counter to the arbitrary confusion of the hated Means Test, Beveridge's proposals were pitched at a basic level of flat-rate insurance to take care of 'physical want' so that incentives would not be removed for individuals to accept their 'personal responsibilities' and make additional insurance provision for themselves. As Beveridge (1942, para 455) put it: 'The plan is not one for giving everybody something for nothing'.[1] In return for National Insurance contributions, benefits would be granted to ensure a basic income standard. Importantly, this would become the bedrock of T.H. Marshall's (1950) 'social right', a universal entitlement rather than a selective payment 'doled' out according to the Means Test. Family allowances were also proposed to subsidise the poverty wages paid to many workers and in explicit recognition of the 'vital unpaid service' contributed by women.

Social insurance was only one plank of the post-war strategy for dealing with unemployment and poverty. In 1944, the White Paper on employment policy (Ministry of Reconstruction, 1944) recognised the revolution in economic thought associated with the name of John Maynard Keynes. In his *General Theory of Employment Interest and Money*, Keynes (1936) turned traditional economic thinking on its head by insisting that the overriding purpose of the economy should be full employment rather than private profit. Keynes assumed that if left unchecked by state intervention, capitalism possessed an inbuilt tendency to crisis, with resulting widespread unemployment. 'Demand management', positive state intervention in the form of monetary and fiscal instruments, was necessary to regulate consumption in the overall interest of securing full employment. Public spending would 'pump-prime' the economy at the first sight of recession by investing in the public sector, locating industry in 'distressed areas', assisting with labour mobility and organising retraining for new industries.

Full employment during the wartime economy showed in practice that the state could control and direct the economy towards definite ends. If full employment could be achieved in wartime then why not in peacetime? Unemployment would no longer be a political problem but one that could be solved through state-directed economic measures. Such thinking, shared by Beveridge, assumed that, unlike the 'hungry Thirties', more or less full employment would become 'normal' while long-term unemployment would become 'abnormal'. No more than 3% of the workforce would unemployed at any one time compared to the 20% or more that had been acceptable during the inter-war years. These aims were set out in the 1944 White Paper, although it fell somewhat short of a full endorsement of Keynesian interventionism, and in this was much less radical than Beveridge's (1944) own book published later that year, *Full Employment in a Free Society* (Deacon, 1981). Beveridge certainly reflected the political mood of the country for radical change but he did not create it.

Unemployment and the unemployed

Before we examine the NUWM of the 1930s, it is necessary to consider briefly the concept of unemployment. Unemployment is a relatively recent category that emerged from the early 19th-century labour movement demand for the 'right to work'. It only really entered general usage in English in the 1890s (Flanagan, 1991). Before then, worklessness was seen as an individual condition of self-imposed 'idleness' or 'pauperism' (Garraty, 1978). In the mid-19th century, Marx analysed capitalism's need for a permanent 'reserve army of labour', while later Victorian reformers viewed 'unemploy*ed*' individuals as the problem rather than 'unemploy*ment*' as a cyclical feature of capitalist society.

Unemployment as a structural condition is inseparable from the experience of being unemployed in a society that places special ideological value on working for wages. As Perry (2000, p 2) argues, 'Unemployment is not simply a convention of sociologists, a metaphor of limited use, an ideal-type or an invention that draws together a mixture of heterogeneous experiences'. Although it has become fashionable in recent years to treat unemployment as a rational, self-interested choice to remain outside of a wage contract, unemployment can be better understood as an involuntary and often unwanted condition. It is in this sense that the sociologist Mills (1959) famously identified unemployment as one of the key examples of how biography, history and social structure intersect to transform the 'personal troubles' of immediate milieu into 'public issues' of national importance.

Traditionally, the unemployed have been studied in social-psychological terms as a homogenous group suffering the same feelings of hopelessness, isolation and despondency. This perspective was established in the 1930s by the famous Marienthal study carried out by a group of behavioural social scientists (Jahoda et al, 2002). Marienthal was an Austrian textile town that suffered acute levels of unemployment in the 1930s, which the behaviourists attempted to understand by ethnographic methods of investigation. Behaviourism explains political apathy and acquiescence as a condition of the immediate environment of the unemployed. By imposing their own ideological meanings onto the unemployed, Jahoda and her colleagues reduced the unemployed to a single category of people characterised by passivity, isolation and an apathetic disinterest in politics (Cole, 2007).

A more sociological version of this approach is the 'relative deprivation thesis'. This suggests that since large sections of the community find themselves in a similar situation – poor and unemployed – they lack examples of less deprived people – the well-off or employed – to measure themselves against. They lower their expectations to the level of the people around them. In the absence of a contrasting 'reference group' against which to measure their plight, the unemployed are unable to formulate a collective grievance that things should be better (Merton, 1957). According to Runciman (1966), in his classic study *Relative Deprivation and Social Justice*, it is only when classes experience their deprived situation as falling below their own higher expectations or the example of other reference groups that they are moved to do something about it by framing their condition as socially unjust (Gurr, 1971).

Isolated communities suffering more or less uniform types of deprivation like the unemployed will tend to resign themselves to their fate since everyone seems to be in the same boat. As Runciman (1966, p 60) saw it: 'The Depression reduced rather than heightened the magnitude and intensity of relative deprivation because few of its victims felt it to be obviously avoidable'. Only in exceptional conditions of 'extreme injustice' where 'severe anomalies in the often haphazard welfare provisions introduced or amended by successive governments' provoked grievances of 'relative deprivation' were the unemployed mobilised into political action in their own interests. More usually, the unemployed thought of themselves as 'victims of misfortune rather than injustice'. Unemployment appears as a natural calamity rather than the result of a certain way of organising the economy.

A similar sort of relative deprivation perspective informed George Orwell's (1937) essay *The Road to Wigan Pier*, his close observation of everyday life in the depressed areas of Northern England. Orwell's contact with the unemployed indicated that they adjusted themselves to their situation with stoic resilience. As unemployment dragged on for years, attitudes changed, from one that saw unemployment as a temporary difficulty for which individuals blamed themselves, to a fate affecting almost everyone and over which they had no control. Until war loomed on the horizon, Orwell (1937, p 162) opined, millions faced the prospect of going to their graves without ever working again: 'in streets where nobody has a job, getting a job seems as probable as owning an aeroplane and much less probable than winning fifty pounds in the Football Pools'. In this context, Orwell (1937, pp 164-5) further argued, lowered expectations and cheap consumer diversions militated against effective political action:

> When people live on the dole for years at a time they grow used to it, and drawing the dole, although it remains unpleasant, ceases to be shameful. Thus the old, independent, workhouse-fearing tradition is undermined.... The people are in effect living a reduced version of their former lives. Instead of raging against their destiny they have made things tolerable by lowering their standards.... They have neither turned revolutionary nor lost their self-respect; merely they have kept their tempers and settled down to make the best of things on a fish-and-chip standard. It is quite likely that fish-and-chips, art-silk stockings, tinned salmon, cut-price chocolate, the movies, the radio, strong tea and the Football Pools have between them averted a revolution.

Part of the difficulty with accounts like Orwell's and Jahoda et al's (and some recent social movement theory) is that the middle-class outsider takes up a position as an expert who examines the unemployed working class as an 'object' (Cole, 2007). Orwell is at least open about his own prejudices of being at once intellectually sympathetic but emotionally repelled by the relative deprivation of unemployed people so glaringly obvious to someone with his middle-class background.

A brief history of the NUMW

More directly significant for our concerns in this book is that such accounts tend to disregard the specific contribution that political activity can make to the experience and self-understanding of unemployment. So even in cases where there was a general equality of deprivation, contact with individuals and an active political culture could make a significant difference to the stoic fatalism predicted by Jahoda et al, Orwell and Runciman among others; at least for a minority of the total unemployed. As Emily Swankie (MacDougall, 1991, p 229, emphasis added) recounted her own experience of unemployed activism in the 1930s:

> It wasn't like nowadays where the differences are so obvious between the employed and the unemployed. Because *all around us then were unemployed*. And they were *more or less in the same position* as we were at that time ... we were on the outskirts of politics, just beginning to understand what was happening with the big unemployment that was in the country at that time. And I was interested in the marches that the National Unemployed Workers' Movement had ... I thought, 'That's great. Somebody's trying to do something or at least draw attention to how the people are living'.... So after one or two conversations with John Monghan [of the NUWM], whom I admired very much, as part of the ILP [Independent Labour Party] Guild of Youth activities – they were active in the protest movement against the Means Test at the time – and I was unemployed anyway, I decided that I would go on the Hunger March. But it was for no political reason other than my *strong resentment against the way that we had to live* and the lack of opportunity, the lack of jobs.

First-hand accounts like Emily Swankie's illustrate the contribution that social and political activism can make at different times and in different places. Testimonies like Emily's enable us to avoid reducing the unemployed to a static picture of relative deprivation imposed on a homogenous group, resulting in an identical psychological condition.

Inter-war cycles of protest

By far the most significant British social movement of the unemployed in the 20th century was the NUWM. Its importance rests on its successful efforts to mobilise the unemployed politically and its influence on local and national social policy. Protest reached its peak not simply when unemployment reached its peak but when severe cuts were threatened in the level of benefit. From a war economy that created full employment, unemployment rose to two million by 1921 and reached a peak of over three million in the years after the Stock Market collapse in 1929. The main phases in the cycle of unemployed protest were 1920-22 and 1931-36, although agitation went on in some form over these two decades and its repercussions were felt well beyond that. At some point in these years, around half of the British workforce personally experienced unemployment, which was concentrated in certain industrial areas of the country, especially mining communities, such as South Wales, Central Scotland and Northern England.

Unemployed protest was effective, in part, because it had a local focus around which people could be mobilised (Bagguley, 1991). In the 1920s, the main focus was on the locally elected Boards of Guardians. This gave rise to the phenomenon known as 'Polarism', after the election of socialists to the Poplar Board of Guardians in London raised the rate of relief beyond government scales (Branson, 1979). In 1929, Public Assistance Committees (PACs) were introduced to conduct elections on a county-wide basis and thereby (it was hoped) prevent the election of socialists intent on awarding generous rates of relief. But heightened unemployed mobilisation in the early 1930s continued to pressurise local PACs for a less stringent implementation of the Means Test and for higher relief. By 1934, the government aimed to undercut local autonomy of the PACs through a centralised bureaucratic system known as the Unemployment Assistance Board (UAB). This aimed to nationalise and depoliticise the rate of benefit by removing it from any direct local democratic control (Miller, 1979).

Unlike many other poor people's movements, the NUWM had a direct impact on national social policy. Its influence is clearly reflected in the Beveridge Report (1942) and the post-war policy of full employment. It also played a major role in preventing the unemployed from becoming recruiting material for British fascism, in contrast to the deteriorating situation in Germany where Nazis outfought the Communists to mobilise the resentments of the unemployed (Stachura, 1986). In Britain the NUWM mobilised the unemployed as part of wider anti-fascist confrontations such as the famous 'Battle of Cable Street'. It also made a significant contribution to the anti-fascist forces in Spain, not only volunteering to fight – one quarter of volunteers for the British International Brigades had been members of the NUWM – but even organising a workers' cooperative in a disused textile mill in Hawick in South East Scotland to send clothes to Spanish republicans. The temptation of fascism among the unemployed was also resisted day to day through the patient and practical advice and support that NUWM caseworkers gave to individual appeals for relief (Hannington, 1979).

1921-22: creating a national unemployed movement

The NUWM had its origins in the establishment in April 1921 of the National Unemployed Workers' Committee movement (NUWCM). Its formation and growth was a response to a rapid rise in unemployment and paltry poor relief. A violent police attack on an unemployed demonstration in London in October 1920 confirmed the need for a more coordinated national movement for local unemployed groups. Led by Wal Hannington, a young socialist toolmaker, and a network of engineering shop stewards, a London District Council of the Unemployed was formed under the slogan 'Work or full maintenance'. This placed the onus for unemployment not on individuals but on the authorities. It led to what Hannington (1979) called 'a new psychology' among the unemployed of collective action to demand rights, either work or benefits, rather than discretionary charity or insults about dole scroungers or 'malingerers'.

Local committees of the NUWCM were built according to a familiar pattern. First a mass meeting in the locality was called and a committee elected. Immediately, the committee organised a demonstration to demand – 'if possible peaceably' – 'adequate maintenance' from local Guardians of the Poor (Croucher, 1987, p 47). Delegates were sent to a national conference to thrash out the aims and methods of the organisation. With the involvement in the 1921 NUWCM conference of the Scottish unemployed movement, which had until then under the independent Marxist leader John MacLean jealously guarded its autonomy, a more fully British movement gradually emerged.

Unemployed agitation occurred in various parts of the country as the NUWCM took its campaign against overtime working, occupying factories and holding factory gate meetings. All this activity reached its apogee with the first national hunger march to London in the winter of 1922-23. This agitation seemed to prevent any further attacks on the unemployed of the kind that occurred in the year before the march. It also established unemployment as *the* major national issue of the day, something that the movement would do time and again until full employment in the war economy deprived it of its reason for existing.

1931: revival and repression

Membership of the NUWM broadly followed the fluctuating fortunes of the unemployed (see *Table 4.1*). As soon as a renewed prospect of employment appeared, the energies of activists would be consumed in pursuing jobs rather than agitation; after all, for many activists unemployment was the curse, not the system that created it. The NUWM emerged from a period of hiatus in 1931 to resist cuts to the dole and humiliating enforcement of the hated Means Test. Under threat of prosecution the income of each member of the extended family was calculated and deducted from relief awarded. A complicated system of means testing could result in the dole being stopped for an entire family by taking into account the earnings of an employed brother-in-law. Unemployed individuals were forced into depending on their relatives, with many young people driven out of the family home.

Table 4.1: NUWM landmarks and unemployment rates, 1921-39

Year	Organisational landmark	Unemployment rate (%)
1921	Founding conference of NUWCM	23.0
1922		14.6
1923	100,000 members	11.2
1924		9.4
1925		10.9
1926	10,000 members	14.5
1927		8.8
1928	Scottish conference; 10,000 members	9.8
1929	Sixth national conference; 20,000 members	9.7
1930	39,000 members	15.0
1931	20,000 members (August); 37,000 (December)	20.3
1932	50,000 members	22.0
1933	100,000 members; 349 branches	20.4
1934	Ninth national conference	16.2
1935	More than 100,000 members	15.5
1936		12.8
1937	Tenth (and last) national conference	10.7
1938		12.8
1939	Internal circular 'suspends' the NUWM	10.5

Source: Adapted from Kingsford (1982); Croucher (1987); Flanagan (1991); Perry (2000); Richards (2002)

In September 1931, as the cuts were announced, tens of thousands marched in Dundee, Birmingham, Manchester and Glasgow, where a pitched battle was fought with the police (Kingsford, 1982, p 134). Even more serious disturbances broke out in Birkenhead and Belfast. In Birkenhead, five days of rioting and fierce fighting were followed by police raids into working-class, predominantly Irish Catholic neighbourhoods (Croucher, 1987, pp 133-6). More than 100 men and women were hospitalised by indiscriminate police violence.

The ascending curve of revolt reached its height in Belfast, which had to contend with the institutionalised sectarianism of the state in Northern Ireland (Farrell, 1980, pp 125-32). Protestant domination meant that Catholics were more likely to be poor, unskilled and unemployed. Both Catholic *and* Protestant unemployed, however, were discriminated against by forcing them onto 'outdoor relief' where they had to work for relief payment. As far as organising goes, outdoor relief had the great advantage of collectivising the unemployed and made trade union forms of struggle possible. Hence, the small Unemployed Workers Committee, with no connections to the NUWM at the time, led by a redoubtable young Marxist, Betty Sinclair, was able to organise a strike of thousands of relief workers. In the fighting that followed, police shot dead two protesters and wounded 15 others, a curfew was imposed and British troops sent in. A fragile unity between Catholic and Protestant workers won major concessions that radically restructured the relief system in Northern Ireland, albeit at a terrible personal cost.

1935: a moment of madness

Unemployed struggles seemed to exist as a Sisyphean labour; just as the burden of reform was pushed up the hill a few steps it was no sooner rolled back down. Alternatively, as real material concessions were wrung from the authorities the original impetus for activity declined. Where the gains won by militant challenges always seemed to be temporary and precarious, protest took on a cyclical character. Hard-won reforms could be reversed in the form of cuts or harsher regulations as the scale and intensity of the movement receded. But with government counter-attacks, fresh struggles erupted, such as that over the UAB crisis of 1935 (Miller, 1979).

In attempting to depoliticise welfare, the UAB had the opposite effect. Areas where the NUWM was well organised had effectively forced better rates and procedures from local PACs, while weakly organised areas were at the mercy of the authorities. National rates and standardised bureaucratic procedures therefore improved the lot of the politically inactive areas while imposing cuts in areas with strong unemployed movements: 70% of claimants in the militant Glasgow area alone faced cuts. Threats to subsistence relief were therefore met by what social movement theorist Zolberg (1972) called a 'moment of madness' in the spontaneous, widespread explosion of militant street protest. In South Wales, 300,000 people demonstrated, calls were made for a one-day general strike and agitation spread like wildfire across Scotland and in Northern English towns and cities such as Blackburn, Bolton, Manchester, Oldham, Sheffield and Stoke.

> What happened in January and February 1935 was neither a political strike nor an organized demonstration like the Hunger Marches and the Jarrow Crusade. While various organizations arranged protest meetings and marches, the seriousness of the crisis was due to the wholly unexpected appearance at these events of tens of thousands of unemployed and employed workers outraged by the reductions in benefit taking place in their localities. (Miller, 1979, p 330)

This outburst of working-class rage wrecked government and the official labour movement assumptions about the essentially passive nature of the unemployed. Neither could its scale and militancy be attributed to the usual bogey-man of the numerically tiny 'communist agitators'. More important was the issue of shared experience of working-class communities as the threat of unemployment and the Means Test touched every family in some way or another. As one historian put it: 'A socially disorganized group of disparate poor law recipients simply could not have been mobilized with the strength, power and nationwide force shown by the unemployed in late January 1935' (Miller, 1979, pp 346-7).

The 1935 unemployment crisis conclusively demonstrated to wide sections of the working class just how out of touch politicians and government officials were with how they actually lived. It was the only time Runciman (1966, p 66) believed that a militant sense of relative deprivation – the 'extent and volume of protest was, by English standards, spectacular' – was aroused by modest expectations being raised by government statements only to be dashed by widespread cuts. Militancy was stimulated by rising expectations, forcing wholesale government concessions. The important point for Runciman was that the 1935 revolt was an isolated case, sparked by the government's mismanagement of an official reference group benchmark promising improved relief.

Forms of protest

The hunger march

Unemployed protest came to be strongly associated with the 'hunger march' or, in the case of Jarrow (a shipbuilding town in the North East of England), the 'crusade'. National hunger marches from various parts of Britain to London were organised in 1922, 1929, 1930, 1932 and 1936 (Kingsford, 1982). As well as national hunger marches, many regional marches were held, reaching a high point in 1933 (Croucher, 1987, p 157). This form of protest helped to frame the unemployed movement in terms of Christian imagery, despite the fact that the movement itself was avowedly non-religious or even atheistic. Walking hundreds of miles, poorly clad marchers publicly asserted their moral dignity and bodily suffering. Physical and moral discipline were highly valued attributes. A certain machismo was expressed in vigorous physical outdoor pursuits, epitomised by Communist leaders such as Wal Hannington, who was also a boxer, went swimming every day regardless of the weather and took long hikes (Croucher, 1987, p 35; Flanagan, 1991, p 193).

By symbolically shaming the authorities who denied the poor justice, the unemployed movement adopted a tactic of the weak that resonated with orthodox religious pieties associated with 'Bread and Work' (the title also of a recent outstanding account of unemployed struggles by Perry, 2000). The most famous image of this is the Jarrow crusade of 1936 (Wilkinson, 1939; Perry, 2005). Jarrow has achieved mythical status of a respectable and respectful, but ultimately futile march of 200 desperate but dignified local men requesting relief from hardship in the distressed shipbuilding town. Ellen Wilkinson (1939, pp 198-9), Jarrow's left-wing Labour Member of Parliament (MP), emphasised its deeply 'non-political' constitutional character and its cross-class support. She asserted that 'English men and women' differ from other nationalities in that 'they hate going on the streets' and only do with the greatest of reluctance as a last resort (Wilkinson, 1939, p 196).

Such symbolic framing of unemployed movements fits snugly into the gradual evolutionary model of British social policy discussed in Chapter One. Nevertheless, it is deeply flawed. Jarrow was exceptional as a localised movement generating official support (Perry, 2005). More typical of the 1930s was the NUWM – a national movement built and sustained by radical activists, some, but by no means all, influenced by the Communist Party, in the teeth of fierce hostility from the state, the press, the Labour Party and the trade union movement. Jarrow may have provided images redolent of stoic British traditions of deferential petitions, momentarily stirring the conscience of policy makers, in contrast to the militant street agitation of 'the Reds'. However, the NUWM not only made the Jarrow march itself possible but, more importantly, also posed a threat to political stability that was still being felt during the war.

If the NUWM made the Jarrow crusade possible, the NUWM's marches were themselves prefigured by the National League of the Blind (NLB) (Reiss, 2005). Indeed, the form of the hunger march as a coordinated descent into a central point in the capital city by separate contingents was first established by the NLB's 1920 march. Unlike the NUWM, the NLB was able to secure official backing of the labour movement leadership. The NLB was not a charity but a trade union for blind workers in their struggle against poverty wages and discriminatory practices, although its members were typically cast by officials as 'deserving cases' of the poor. Many newspapers reported the blind marchers who set out on Easter Monday 1920 in religious terms as 'pilgrims', calling for 'pity', and found the whole spectacle a 'revelation'. One Sheffield councillor claimed that it was an affront to 'civilisation and Christianity that these men should have to parade themselves in the public streets to call attention to their great needs' (quoted by Reiss, 2005, p 138). Yet these were members of the labour movement; the banners they carried demanded justice – not charity – including worker solidarity and citizenship rights.

By the time of the 1934 NLB march, the coordinated national march had become strongly identified with the NUWM, whose association with Communism led the NLB leadership to rebuff NUWM advances for a united march. Hunger marches allowed Communists to test their main rival, the Labour Party, for political leadership of the working class. Up to the mid-1930s, Communists tried to use the marches for propaganda purposes to expose in practice the Labour Party's failure to defend working-class living standards. In Grassic Gibbon's (1934, p 666; emphasis in original) great modernist novel of urban unemployed struggles, *Grey Granite*, the local Communist spits out the propaganda function of the hunger march:

> *And for God's sake take care on the line of march to keep the sods from straying or stealing or raising up trouble through lying with queans,*[2] they'd find the Labour locals en route were forced to give them shelter and help, never heed that, never heed that, rub it well in through all the speeches that the workers had no hope but the Communist Party.

An even more important contrast to the NUWM was that the Blind Marches 'were largely marches of the employed for the unemployed' (Reiss, 2005, p 150). Marchers had left jobs in the blind workshops and were paid from the funds of the NLB. No such fortune smiled on the NUWM activists, which was sustained only by the efforts of its own members. Orwell (1937, p 162) admired the unstinting commitment, tact and moral integrity of the NUWM activists he knew:

> This is a revolutionary organization intended to hold the unemployed together, stop them blacklegging during strikes and give them legal advice about the Means Test. It is a movement that has been built out of nothing, by the pennies and efforts of the unemployed themselves. I have seen a good deal of the NUWM, and I greatly admire the men, ragged and underfed like the others, who keep the organization going.

In so doing, individual activists faced police repression, employer blacklists, punitive cuts in the dole, and personal harassment. For instance, unemployed workers that went on the hunger marches to call attention to their plight found that their dole was cut on the basis that they were unavailable for work while they were marching across the country.

Moreover, NUWM activity was not restricted to spectacular, set-piece national hunger marches. Local branches – the 'basic unit' of the NUWM – provided a very direct form of participatory democracy (Bagguley, 1991, p 100). Different local branches emphasised agitation, casework or self-help; while Glasgow stressed the need for militant agitation, Edinburgh mainly devoted itself to casework. In practice, as Perry (2000, p 119) argues, agitation and casework were not seen as mutually incompatible since the NUWM would often combine protest and legal representation, for instance using demonstrations outside official buildings to back up deputations inside arguing for improved relief.

At moments of widespread mobilisation, such as the 1935 crisis, the hunger march seemed like an inadequate form of protest:

> The threat of violence was always present, and as frustration rose violence did break out in several places. From most accounts the protesters were sullen, angry and militant. They were quite different from the relative handful of tired men and women who trudged into an almost festive reception at the end of national Hunger Marches. (Miller, 1979, p 347)

Indeed, direct-action tactics could prove more militant than the Communist leadership were prepared to countenance.

A Communist front?

Branch life was shaped by the interrelationship between the working class, the labour movement, the Communist Party of Great Britain (CPGB) and the energies of the NUWM's most committed activists. Bound by parliamentary respectability, the official labour movement remained aloof from the unemployed struggles and played no significant part in the tumultuous events of the 1930s.[3] While the Labour Party and trade unions might cooperate with the NUWM at a local level, nationally the official labour movement was hostile, obstructive and unsympathetic to the independent militancy of the NUWM. Local relations between the NUWM and the labour movement could be uneven. For example, in a textile town like Paisley, the trades council and the Labour Party repeatedly spurned the advances of the NUWM, while across the River Clyde in the Vale of Leven (near the town of Dumbarton) in the early 1920s there was more cooperation (Rawlinson, 1992).

Part of the difficulty here for the NUWM's association with the CPGB was the twists and turns of the international Communist movement (Borkenau, 1962). On the back of the successful Russian Revolution in 1917, many socialists at that time were involved with the newly formed CPGB and so it seemed natural that Communists would play a leading role in the organisation of the unemployed and provide a political perspective on the need for the 'direct action' of protest as a militant form of working-class 'self-help'. In the 1920s, the newly formed Communist Party (CPGB) posed a revolutionary alternative to the gradual reformism of the Labour Party. In the 1930s, the Moscow-based international ommunist leadership claimed that 'unemployment revolutionises the working class' (Perry, 2007, p 121). Under such instruction, the CPGB took a dogmatic sectarian line of self-righteous ideological purity against the Labour Party and reformism, comparing it to 'social fascism' (Hallas, 1985). In this ultra-Left phase (1928-34), the CPGB alienated many socialists of all kinds. In the aftermath of Hitler's seizure of power in Germany, their next turn, called the 'Popular Front' (1935-39), adopted the need for a broad-based alliance of Communists with all non-fascist groups. In practice this meant that Communists had to acquire respectability and legitimacy from people they had been violently denouncing for years (Perry, 2000).[4]

However, the NUWM with its strong, responsive local roots could not be effectively controlled by the centralised CPGB leadership. Certainly, Communists like Wal Hannington and Harry McShane and scores of rank-and-file members lent to the CPGB the personal prestige that they earned through their unstinting activity among the unemployed. But, as Croucher (1987, p 104) notes, 'the dominance of Communists was not the dominance of CPGB headquarters'. Nor did they slavishly follow the zig-zags of the abrupt changes in Communist policy. Hannington and McShane were admonished by the international Communist leadership for refusing to subordinate the NUWM to the Trades Union Congress as part of the new Popular Front policy (Perry, 2000, pp 116-7).

Communists gave the NUWM a backbone of committed activists, inspired as they were by the (illusory) vision they had of the Soviet Union as an alternative world of peace, prosperity and human cooperation. Convinced in the righteousness of their cause, the certainty of their eventual triumph and the persecution that they must endure, Communists of this period are often dismissively compared to fundamentalist religious believers. But they were also self-educated 'worker-intellectuals', a self-styled modernist proletarian elite who earnestly studied and debated science, literature, history and philosophy (Macintyre, 1986).

Communism in Britain was not therefore an affair of middle-class dilettantes, as is often assumed. It was a proletarian creed that reached deep inside particular geographically concentrated working-class communities. Places like Mardy in South Wales, Cowdenbeath, Lumphinans and Lochgelly in West Fife, and Vale of Leven in Dunbartonshire were known as 'Little Moscows' (Macintyre, 1980). In the 'Little Moscows' a high calibre of local Communists appealed to and mobilised dense local loyalties as poverty and unemployment brought single-industry communities, often based on mining or textiles, into conflict with the local and national state.

Dilemmas of leadership

All social movements face dilemmas of leadership. Credibility has to be constantly demonstrated in response to the unexpected situations raised by mass mobilisation. Although they could often be stern, didactic and sectarian, their unflinching dedication, courage and intelligence gave Communists an elevated standing within many working-class communities. An anonymous worker's voice in Grassic Gibbon's (1934, p 533) *Grey Granite* mangles the language to convey how Communist militants acquired respect even among those who found their Marxist phraseology incomprehensible: 'Communionalists like Big Jim might blether damned stite[5] but they tried to win your rights for you'.

On the 1933 march to Edinburgh, Harry McShane, Communist leader of the Scottish NUWM, managed to keep hundreds of demonstrators active in fairly disciplined fashion for the three days and nights that they occupied the centre of Edinburgh, including parading through the Royal Palace of Holyrood with a band raucously playing socialist tunes, *The Internationale* and *The Rebel Song*. One night he was forced to make an instant decision when suitable accommodation was refused by the Edinburgh authorities. McShane instructed the marchers, male and female, to sleep that mild June night on the pavement of Princes Street, the city's prestigious shopping street. In the morning some women lay in the street to block the tramlines, while men shaved in the reflection of shop windows. Fifty years later marchers remembered the audacity shown by McShane's leadership:

> I think somebody offered us somewhere [to sleep] like Waverley Market or somethin'. And McShane and them wouldn't accept that, they says, 'No, no, we're not goin' there'. So they says, 'Oh, well, we cannae give you anything else'. And of course he says, 'Right, we'll sleep in Princes Street'.
> William McVicar
> (MacDougall, 1990, pp 177-8)

> So [McShane] said, 'Right, we'll sleep in the streets. And we'll pick the street we're gaun tae sleep in'. And they couldnae ha' picked a better spot than Princes Street! Under the Conservative Party headquarters, the Liberal Party headquarters, and the big luxury hotels, here was hundreds and hundreds o' angry unemployed. Obviously a sight like that is not seen every day, particularly in the capital city of Edinburgh! And here was these kind o' not too well dressed people whom they thought were foreigners in a sense, because they were coming to their town.
> Tom Ferns
> (MacDougall, 1990, p 143)

> We had overcoats and it was braw weather of course, it was nice. The first night we slept on Princes Street and in the mornin' a lot o' them were goin' across tae the shops and shavin' in the reflection o' the windaes. And the polis were goin' mad. But then McShane got his concessions anyway.
> James Allison
> (MacDougall, 1990, p 130)

> At dinner-time our field-kitchen came along and the police chief told Harry McShane, 'This is Princes Street. You can't feed here'. Harry told him, 'It was good enough for us to sleep here, it's good enough for us to feed here'.
> Hugh Sloan
> (MacDougall, 1991, p 282)

While this was not quite *Three Days That Shook Edinburgh*, as McShane (1933) was soon to dramatise the 1933 march in the pamphlet he wrote soon afterwards, these recollections illustrate vividly a capacity for decisive leadership among the experienced activists like McShane.

A male movement?

Feminist scholars have challenged the ideology of the male 'breadwinner' in the founding of the Beveridgean welfare state. The troublesome business of gender relations has also been obscured from some accounts of the unemployed struggles (Campbell, 1984). On the one hand, gender could internally divide and weaken the movement; on the other hand, the movement could also forge solidarity based on the shared class positions of men and women. Neither possibility – class unity or gender division – existed in a completely finished form; gender and class were always dynamically interrelated. Such stark alternatives are unable to adequately capture the stresses and strains of gender relations in the inter-war unemployed movement.

Working-class women often bore the brunt of unemployment, with many turning to prostitution simply to survive (Flanagan, 1991, p 192). From the start, women who worked in munitions factories were subject to a violently misogynist campaign and forced out of their jobs at the end of the First World War in their hundreds of thousands to make way for male soldiers returning from the front line (Flanagan, 1991, p 115). Unemployed ex-servicemen fought to intimidate women out of jobs that they felt rightly belonged to male 'breadwinners' temporarily displaced by the emergency demands of wartime mobilisation (Croucher, 1987, p 16). Hence, the earliest unemployed struggles of the inter-war years were waged by women; a women's Right to Work campaign was launched by the National Federation of Women Workers in 1919.

Against this domestic ideology, the NUWM struggled to overcome gender divisions among the unemployed. Women activists were always a minority within a minority (the NUWM) within a minority (the unemployed) of the entire working class. To begin with, however, women were expected to play a subordinate role in the movement to the physical endurance displayed by the typical male hunger marcher. When Mary Docherty, a young Fife communist, tried to join the 1929 march she was told by Wal Hannington, the male leader of the NUWM, that no women were allowed (MacDougall, 1990, p: 4). Instead, women organised dances, catering, fundraising and accommodation. Within local NUWM branches, women were usually in a small minority, although many branches were enlivened by the commitment of female activists.

By the late 1920s, this attitude began to change. Women marched in separate contingents on the national marches to London in the 1930s. They marched alongside men on the Scottish marches to Edinburgh in 1928, 1930, 1932, 1933 and 1938, and Glasgow in 1935. In 1929, the NUWM nationally set up a 'Women's Department' to organise unemployed women. By 1933, the number of local women's sections of the NUWM trebled from a mere dozen at the time of the 1932 march. Part of the reason for this was that women were subject to special discrimination by the government's Anomalies Register in 1932, which refused many married women unemployment benefit and tried to impose domestic service instead. In West Fife, the local NUWM paper, the aptly-named *Unemployed Demonstrator*, agitated against labour exchanges forcing women into domestic service:

> We have recently had cases in which girls were expected to sleep in old garages which 'the mistress' referred to as a 'bungalow'. Every girl should be on her guard as it is clear that rotten employers are using the [Labour] Exchange to force girls to accept rotten conditions. Report at once the NUWM. (cited in Croucher, 1987, p 131)

Despite the macho male culture among the marchers, working-class women's participation could prove a life-changing experience. On the 1932 march, working-class women took part in political discussions and public speaking, negotiated with authorities, and learned about birth control clinics. Some women formed delegations to make their case to government and its officials. A deputation was sent to meet the Prime Minster Ramsay McDonald in 1934. They were met by his daughter Ishbel, who once again tried to convince them over a cup of tea that unemployed women should enter domestic service. Under the self-assured leadership of the NUWM Women's Organiser, Maud Brown, the women angrily rejected her advice (Kingsford, 1982, p 196), although Mary Johnston (MacDougall, 1991, p 247) recalled the scene in somewhat more pleasant tones:

> We were shown up the stair into a big room and we just talked to her. Oh, very friendly, offered us tea. But funnily enough, on a point of honour, we refused it. Well, it wisnae discussed but we all seemed to say, 'No, we wouldnae have your tea'. I don't even know if it was that we felt it would be weakening our position if we accepted tea.

Women marchers, like male marchers, didn't always receive a friendly reception in the towns they passed through. On occasions where there was a lack of local sympathisers to offer accommodation, women had to force admittance to the local workhouse for somewhere to sleep for the night.

Women marchers also had to contend with the strict Puritanism of the labour movement, who were wary about offending the dominant mores of their time. Not only did this mean a prohibition on alcohol; it also meant that women not only marched separately but were required not to march in their bare legs. To quote Emily Swankie's (in MacDougall, 1991, p 232) experience again:

> I felt that the leaders of the march didn't want any criticism or anything untoward about the women who were walking to London. And we were asked to wear black stockings. There was a wee bit of Puritanism there too, but I think it was to avoid at all costs any bad publicity – women marching with bare legs.

Part of the reason for the 'iron discipline' on the 1934 march was the constant police surveillance and use of informers. Precautions against constant state harassment and monitoring helped to erode some of the organisation's internal democracy (Croucher, 1987, p 162).

Despite this, the NUWM challenged the dominant ideology of femininity by even daring to allow women to march, something that other progressive movements would not countenance. As Reiss (2005, p 150) has noted of the NLB's reluctance to allow women on their marches, 'only a revolutionary organization like the NUWM could risk sending women on a punishing trip to London in often adverse weather conditions without worrying too much about alienating contemporary notions of femininity'.

An example like the 1933 march to Edinburgh illustrates how the movement broke down some of its more rigid prohibitions when men and women not only marched together but slept together on the pavement in full public view (fully clothed of course). As Hugh Sloan (MacDougall, 1991, pp 281–2) recalled:

> That night a huge crowd of people turned out to watch us bedding down on Princes Street. I slept between old Maria Stewart from Methilhill and an old Miss Smith from Dundee on the pavement in front of the Gardens. Oh, there were plenty of women on the March. The women marched alongside the men. We all bedded down in our clothes on the pavement. We didnae have any pyjamas in these days!

Women were also at the forefront of some of the most dramatic cases of direct action, displaying a militancy often lacking in men-only protests. 'The methods of unemployed women were often more intimidating, and far less constitutional than those preferred by their menfolk' (Flanagan, 1991, p 194). In 1935, 2,000 women and 1,000 men formed an angry demonstration that stormed the UAB offices in Merthyr, destroying the records and wrecking the building, immediately winning improvements in relief payments from a panicked government.

1935 represented the high point for women's involvement, as well as for the movement more generally, with total membership standing in excess of 100,000. Women's conferences in Scotland, Nottinghamshire and Derby attracted large numbers of female delegates from the NUWM and women's organisations like Co-op Women's Guild (Croucher, 1987, p 174). Demands were raised for maternity benefits and birth control was debated. These issues were also taken up locally, as when the women's section in Arbroath demonstrated for a new maternity hospital. As Harry McShane later noted, the unemployed movement made a successful appeal to the specific conditions for working-class women that many other parts of the socialist movement never managed or even attempted (McShane and Smith, 1978: 131).

Unemployed movements as a myth?

The NUWM was officially dissolved in 1946. In reality it had ceased to function as a focus for unemployed activism by 1939 as mass unemployment declined through rearmament programmes. Since then its significance has been the subject of a raging dispute. For some, the unemployed struggles did not amount to very much, were sporadic, lacked revolutionary fervour and had little or no effect on social policy. For others, a radicalised, mass movement of the unemployed defined the inter-war years as a period of turbulent resistance and radicalisation, forcing the pace of reform. Each side of the debate accuse the other of peddling myths about ideological consensus or class polarisation.

For instance, the historian Bruce (1968, p 266) records how a 'debt' is owed to the leadership of the Labour Party who 'used all their influence against their less responsible followers to preserve the methods of parliamentary democracy'. That 'the situation remained under control' was thanks to the commitment of the Labour Party to parliamentary procedures and a government that 'took care not to drive opposition too hard'. All the distress visited on the unemployed 'was more or less patiently borne', protests were limited to rare local outbursts, without 'any substantial revolutionary activity among the unemployed' (Bruce, 1968, p 266).

This verdict has been repeated by 'revisionist' historians like Stevenson and Cook (1994). Among others, they minimise and obscure the efforts of the unemployed workers' movement. Instead, they emphasise the rising prosperity for large sections of British society in the 1930s. At no time was there any danger of radicalisation since shared national traditions made 'extremism' of the sort associated with the Communist Party and its influence over the unemployed movement 'alien' to ideas of British fair play and moderation in all things. For sociologists McKee and Bell (1986, p 149), the unemployed are too often perceived by radicals to have an almost automatic potential for collective mobilisation, a 'fantasy' employed by outsiders 'who know what's good for the unemployed'. Some sociologists also detect a rose-tinted, Marxist nostalgia for 1930s-style male collective action compared to the pitiful representations of a troubled masculine identity among the unemployed nowadays in films like *The Full Monty* (Cole, 2007).

On the other hand, the seismic shift represented by the Beveridge Report (1942) and the welfare state was not created in a vacuum. The interrelationship of crisis and protest in the 1930s should not be retrospectively stripped out of the founding politics of the British welfare state. Welfare reform did not come out of nowhere: the part played by unemployed struggles contributed directly to the set of conditions that made the welfare state possible. Considerable empirical evidence of its albeit uneven scale and intensity can be marshalled, although some historians and sociologists may choose to marginalise such sources, relying instead on official or police reports as authoritative accounts of the unemployed (Howkins and Saville, 1979). It is quite true that although it engulfed millions of workers in Britain, unemployment was not as catastrophic for political stability as it proved elsewhere such as in Austria and Germany. Nevertheless, the unemployed movement in 1930s Britain compares favourably to other countries in its scale, longevity and impact (Croucher, 1990; Flanagan, 1991; Perry, 2000, 2007; Richards, 2002).

Conclusion

Self-activity was considered essential by the NUWM to break the unemployed out of apathy and despair or, if you like, to heighten their sense of relative deprivation. Rank-and-file members of the NUWM may have had a transitory relationship to the organisation, especially for the vast majority who were not members of the CPGB. While at certain high points the NUWM could claim a membership of more than 100,000, at no time did it command the allegiance of more than a fraction of the unemployed, never more than 10% (at best). Hunger marchers were a minority within a minority, totalling no more than a couple of thousand. This appears to support claims that the NUWM was marginal to both the typical experience of the unemployed and the post-war shift in social policy.

Such a view seriously misunderstands the relationship between protest and reform. Certainly, Beveridge and Keynes were well aware of the potential for unemployment to provoke social unrest, political instability and class grievances. Only state-organised welfare reform managed from above, they thought, would prevent grievances from below being channelled in a militant direction, broadly confirming Saville's (1957-58) analysis introduced in Chapter One. One indication of this is that Beveridge's (1944) book *Full Employment* was subtitled *Misery Breeds Hate*[6] – a clear reference to the fear of unemployed militancy felt by some sections of the establishment. In contrast, his previous (1909) book *Unemployment* was subtitled *A Problem of Industry*, reflecting a completely different set of priorities – including 'idleness' arising from 'defects of character' rather than economic structure. Beveridge made this clear in the fevered atmosphere of the 1935 unemployment assistance crisis when, as Chair of the Unemployment Insurance Statutory Committee, he told a BBC audience that much more than a mere increase in benefit was necessary to deal with the problem of long-term unemployment (Miller, 1979).

In his famous report, Beveridge (1942) explicitly addressed the NUWM's demands. Social security reform abandoned the Means Test and gave claimants recognition rights to representation and advocacy within the procedures. In other words, the NUWM imposed on the state a new frame that had not existed before: the social right to work or benefit. Both Beveridge and Keynes influenced the welfare state because they responded to a political culture that was reshaped, at least in part, by the seemingly incessant struggles of the unemployed and the danger that unchecked grievances might result in even more far-reaching changes after the model of the Soviet Union. This sentiment was expressed clearly in Harold Macmillan's (1938, p 374) Conservative support for what he called 'paternal socialism' of the 'middle way':

> If, at this critical moment, we hesitate to be guided by the British tradition of peaceful change, then we shall move stage by stage towards the embitterment of class antagonism and the decay and destruction of our democratic institutions. The reply to the menace of political tyranny is to be made not when hatred has fanned the flames of popular discontent to revolutionary fervour, but in the period when it is still possible to achieve economic reconstruction and social amelioration by peaceful

means. Such a consummation would rob the revolutionary movements of their meaning, and apparent justification, by eliminating the social despair upon which alone they can be fostered.

Another indicator is that in 1945 the Labour Party adopted the electoral slogan of 'Never again!', opposing any return to the unemployment of the 1930s, and was swept to office in a landslide victory against Churchill, the famous wartime leader (Hennessey, 1992).

Apathy was not total even outside the ranks of the NUWM, as the huge unemployed demonstrations testified. Unemployment also had its consolations and diversions. Moreover, inactivity might be seen less as a 'rational choice' to 'free ride' than an irrational preference of psychological dissonance that joblessness can cause individuals. In any case, the courage, perseverance and spirit of self-sacrifice that the active minority of the unemployed demonstrated in the 1920s and 1930s cannot be accounted for as simply another 'rational choice' calculated between the costs and benefits of activism.

Account also needs to be given of how values and ideology mediate organisational forms. A fragile balance always had to be struck between the ideological and organisational goals of the committed political activists and the more immediate, practical exigencies of the unemployed (Valocchi, 1990, p 202). While the Communist Party itself became a dogmatic bureaucratic apparatus, it helped shape not only the organisational resources of the unemployed movement but also the sense of social justice and equality through its propaganda for a radical (if illusory) alternative to mass idleness and want.

Large-scale unemployment calls into question how the economy is organised around certain narrow social values, above all the priority to keep capitalism profitable. Collective action can lead to broad changes in public policy by helping to shift the grammar of politics. Keynesian economics did not become dominant simply because it was more intellectually coherent than the previous free-market brand of political economy. Nor did the Beveridge Report excite the hopes of millions because it deployed some memorable phrases. They responded to a new political grammar framed, in large part, by the inter-war struggles of the unemployed.

Notes

[1] In the event, the principle of subsistence was eroded as rises in the cost of living ate into the value of benefits.

[2] 'Lying with queans': sleeping with young women.

[3] Just as it stood aside half a century later from the anti–Poll Tax rebellion of 1990, which led to the defeat of the seemingly invincible Conservative leader Margaret Thatcher.

[4] Internationally the CPGB served as a Communist model for its work with the unemployed, although this seems to have been seriously misinterpreted abroad as a direct result of Communist forethought rather than an uneven response to immediate conditions. Perry (2007) shows how the French Communists tried to imitate what they saw as the success of the NUWM in radicalising the unemployed with direct lessons for building the French Communist Party through what was called 'the British turn'.

[5] Stite: nonsense, mumbo jumbo.

[6] Somewhat disconcertingly perhaps, the phrase 'the misery that generates hate' comes from Charlotte Bronte's novel *Shirley*, and was brought to Beveridge's attention by his wife Janet Mair (Deacon, 1981, p 88).

Further reading

The Road to Wigan Pier by George Orwell (Book Club Associates, 1937) conveys some sense of the condition of the unemployed in the 1930s.

Walter Greenwood's melodramatic novel *Love on the Dole* (1933) (Vintage, 2004 edition) gives a fictional account of the despair caused by unemployment. The novel was made into an even more melodramatic film in 1941, starring Deborah Kerr.

More convincing is *Grey Granite* by Lewis Grassic Gibbon (Polygon, 1934), part 3 of his epic trilogy *A Scots Quair*.

It is worth tracking down the autobiographies of the two leaders of the NUWM: *No Mean Fighter* by Harry McShane and Joan Smith (Pluto Press, 1978) and *Unemployed Struggles: 1919-1936* by Wal Hannington (Lawrence & Wishart, 1979). See McShane's (1933) account 'The March: The story of the historic Scottish hunger march', in the lively cultural politics magazine Variant, www.variant.randomstate.org/15texts/TheMarch.html

For more scholarly analysis, see especially the two fine studies by Matt Perry: *Bread and Work: Social Policy and the Experience of Unemployment, 1918-39* (Pluto Press, 2000) and *The Jarrow Crusade: Protest and Legend* (Business Education Publishers, 2005).

Ian MacDougall (Polygon, 1990, 1991) has collected oral histories from many Scottish participants in the unemployed struggles in the two volumes *Voices from the Hunger Marches: Personal Recollections by Scottish Hunger Marchers of the 1920s and 1930s*. Images of the hunger marchers can be seen at www.scran. ac.uk/database/results.php?field=event&searchterm=%22Hunger+march%22 &searchdb=scran

Some original documents on the NUWM can be viewed on the Working Class Movement Library website at http://wcml.ichameleon.com/contents/protests-politics-and-campaigning-for-change/unemployment/national-unemployed-workers-movement/

five

Fighting sickness: the women's health movement

Introduction: a National Health Service?

Sixty years after the foundation of the National Health Service (NHS) in 1948 that enshrined the principle of universal free healthcare at the point of delivery, the NHS continues to incite conflict between the government, medical professions, interested agencies and various social movements and social groups. Beveridge's welfare vision was premised on a nationalised health service (McCrae, 2003), however, it took Bevan's considerable political skill to overcome the opposition from the medical profession and other interested agencies to bring this vision to fruition (Webster, 2002). Although a limited free general practitioner (GP) service had been available since 1911, covering all manual workers in employment, this provision did not extend to workers' families nor did it provide free access to hospital treatment (Webster, 2002). While there also existed an extensive network of private and charitable hospitals throughout the UK, provision in areas of deprivation was poor as consultants gravitated to the wealthier areas and large urban centres. Bevan argued that the creation of the NHS would for the first time 'universalise the best' (Bevan, cited in Klein, R., 2001, p 20) and ensure that all people in the UK have access to high-quality health-care regardless of their means. These are admirable ideals. However, they have not been realised as class, gender, ethnicity, age, sexuality and geography continue to have a significant impact on health and life expectancy (Black et al, 1991; Whitehead, 1991; Doyal, 1998).

From the outset, the NHS has been plagued by controversy. Shortly after its foundation, the government recognised that Beveridge had significantly underestimated the cost of the new service since he had assumed that there would not be any increase in demand (Klein, R., 2001; McCrae, 2003). The cost of the NHS has continued to be an area of ongoing debate, especially the spiralling costs associated with new medical techniques and treatments, which has led the UK government to task the National Institute for Health and Clinical Excellence (NICE) to evaluate new treatments for efficacy and value for money in order to determine what will be made available on the NHS in England, Wales and Northern Ireland (see www.nice.org.uk). In Scotland, this role is carried out by the Scottish Medicines Consortium (SMC), which provides advice on new drugs to NHS Scotland and the regional NHS boards; however, this is purely an advisory role (see www.scottishmedicines.org.uk). The decisions taken by NICE, and the SMC in its advisory role, concerning the availability of treatments can be seen as another example of the erosion of medical power that has already been considerably undermined by the new managerialism and the imposition of market values arising from NHS reforms and from the growth of health consumer groups.

These debates have been accompanied by the growth of new political players in the form of a plethora of health social movements that have challenged government health policy, particularly the refusal to fund new treatments, hospital closures and the privatisation of NHS services, as well as providing a critique of medical authority and the power of the pharmaceutical companies. These new movements have been greatly influenced by the feminist challenge to medical authority and the failure of the welfare state to equally care for all people from the cradle to the grave. The women's health movement has been particularly important in highlighting the way in which the NHS has failed to 'universalise the best' and has demonstrated that who you are and where you live determine the healthcare you receive. In fighting against gender discrimination as patients, carers and health workers, the women's health movement has played a significant role in challenging medical authority and government health policy in order to ensure that the NHS is truly a national health service.

This chapter will briefly examine the origins of the NHS before proceeding to focus specifically on the women's health movement's critique of medical power and the NHS. The women's health movement was one of the first social movements to highlight differences in access, treatment and care on the NHS. Furthermore, the women's health movement illuminated the patriarchal nature of the NHS and how it acted to reinforce the dominant construction of gender, thereby serving to reproduce male power. The chapter will end with a consideration of the growing academic interest in social movements in health that have acted as a challenge to the organisation of healthcare in the UK including recent moves to privatise certain areas of the NHS and the continuing power of the medical profession to impose itself on our everyday lives.

In terms of social movement theory, the women's health movement acts as an exemplar of the way in which the embodied experiences of particular social groups can be used to legitimise a challenge to medical authority. This has been instructive for other groups of health users who following the lead of this feminist challenge have used their own experience of ill-health to challenge health service. Such movements can be characterised as a form of resistance to the encroachment expert systems into the lifeworld and in particular the way in which the foundation of the NHS has further extended the reach of the medical power into all of our everyday lives.

Origins of the NHS

The NHS was the outcome of a long struggle between the trade union and labour movements, local authorities, British Medical Association, Voluntary Hospital and various other interested groups. Ultimately, the NHS represented a compromise solution to the problem of improving the nation's health. Maintaining a healthy workforce and fighting force had been recognised by government since the end of the 19th century when the Boer War demonstrated the dreadfully poor health of the working classes in the UK. While it can be argued that the establishment of the National Health Insurance (NHI) scheme in 1911, which was the brainchild of Lloyd George, had been a significant step forward in offering limited protection to those in work, funded by deductions from their salary, this system did not provide for those not in work or dependents. Furthermore, McCrae (2003) argues that for some in Scotland the introduction of the 1911 NHI scheme actually led them to receive a poorer service. For example, many workers already paid for insurance for themselves and their family, through contributions to work or other schemes, but these were replaced by the more limited coverage of the NHI system. Nor did NHI solve the problem of the differential access to healthcare. For example, in 1883, the Napier Commission in Scotland found that the 300,000 people living scattered across the Scottish Highlands and Islands were served by a mere 103 GPs and still in 1912 a similar number (see McCrae, 2003). Provision elsewhere in the UK was also haphazard and irrational and tended to follow the ability of a particular population to pay for healthcare rather than need (Klein, R., 2001). Working-class women were particularly severely affected as they were largely excluded from the NHI scheme:

> Social investigations amply testified to the damaging consequences of poverty, ill-health, and inadequate sources of

social support. The worst affected were working class women. As dependents they were excluded from the meagre National Health Insurance (NHI) medical provision. They lacked the material resources adequately to support their families and were therefore forced to deny themselves medical assistance or even adequate diet. (Webster, 2002, p 4)

However, the NHI scheme only provided limited access to a GP and did not include hospital care. Access to hospital care was available, in the last resort, through the Poor Law, which instructed 'infirmary wards with a medical officer in charge' (Godber, 1988, p 38). These municipal hospitals could be distinguished from the larger voluntary hospitals that provided consultant-led specialist services and the smaller regional voluntary hospitals that often relied on GPs (Klein, R., 2001). Local authorities were key providers of healthcare such as offering some preventative services for children and mothers and midwifery services. The 1929 Local Government Act did attempt to make the provision of medical services more rational but was largely unsuccessful. For example Godber (1988, pp 37) argues that:

Hospital and specialist services in the late 1930s were unevenly distributed, inadequately funded, and lacked coordination. Most of the buildings were old, and the requirements of modern medicine were met by adaptations in inadequate space.

In the inter-war years, one of the most extensive reviews of health services was the 1937 Political and Economic Planning survey of healthcare, which concluded that the hospital system, in particular, was irrational and lacked unity, with voluntary and public hospitals competing with each other, 'only remotely regulated by the health departments' (Webster, 2002, p 5). Financially, the system was also unsustainable as voluntary hospitals were finding it increasingly difficult to support themselves through voluntary donations and charges levied on patients. Klein (2001, R., p 3) argues that 'bankruptcy of the voluntary sector was only staved off by the Second World War, when these hospitals drew large-scale benefits from the Government's scheme of paying for stand-by beds for war casualties'.

Between the First and Second World Wars, a number of reports offered various solutions to the problem of ensuring the health of the UK population. For example, the Dawson Report (Ministry of Health, 1920), which argued for a system of comprehensive and free healthcare for all (and was echoed by the 1926 *Report of the Royal Commission on National Health Insurance*), concluded that public health services needed to be funded from taxation rather than through a system of health insurance.

The most radical plan was proffered by the Socialist Medical Association in 1933, which proposed free healthcare for all and salaried doctors under the control of local authorities (see Klein, R., 2001). In Scotland, the 1936 Report of the Committee on Scottish Health Services (Cathcart Report) also recommended setting up a state medical service in Scotland and this was quickly accepted by the majority of Scottish MPs. However, the UK government was only willing to 'press ahead with those of the Cathcart reforms that could be carried out under existing legislation or extensions to existing legislation' (McCrae, 2003, p 203).

Despite the widespread consensus that something needed to be done to improve the nation's health and that the current system was not fit for purpose, there was little agreement on what a national health service would in the end look like and before it could become a reality, powerful interests would need to be placated. The Second World War was clearly an important influence on the foundations of both the welfare state and the NHS itself and the Beveridge Report (1942) linked the two. It was the Beveridge Report that really provided the impetus for the creation of the NHS since, as Webster (2002, p 8) argues, he 'both reflected and released a tide of expectations that could not be stemmed'. Following the Beveridge Report, the 1944 White Paper, written by Sir John Hawton, outlined plans for a national health service and its two key fundamental defining features of the philosophy of the NHS: that it should be free at the point of delivery and comprehensive (Klein, R., 2001). The White Paper had been very much a compromise and aimed at minimising opposition from the opposing factions, particularly from the GPs and voluntary hospitals who were both opposed to a unified service and against being brought under local authority control.

The process by which the White Paper became two Acts – the 1946 National Health Service Act, which founded the NHS in England and Wales; and the 1947 National Health Service (Scotland) Act, which created the NHS in Scotland – was far from straightforward. The Labour electoral victory in 1945 brought to an end the coalition government and provided an opportunity for a more coherent and radical social policy. Bevan was appointed as Minister of Health by Atlee and he reformulated the plan for the NHS that included the nationalisation and regionalisation of the hospitals and the setting up a tripartite system of control. Bevan also made many concessions in the process of translating the 1944 White Paper into reality, including allowing teaching hospitals to have special status under control of the Minister of Health and the participation of the medical profession in planning and running the service. Despite agitation from the Trades Union Congress, this right to participation was not extended to other health professionals (see Klein, R., 2001).

The setting up of the NHS was a triumph of the post-war Labour government and was an important step towards health for all. However, it quickly became apparent that the NHS was not going to be as successful in eliminating differential access to healthcare and inequalities in health as had been hoped.

The Feminist critique of medical power

Since the rise of second-wave feminism in the 1960s and the development of the women's health movement in the 1970s, the women's movement has been at the forefront of the critique of the NHS, particularly highlighting the way in which it has increased the medicalisation of women's bodies and extended the control exerted by predominantly male physicians. The critique of medical power has specifically focused on how the medical profession treated women and women's bodies as problematic, a problem stemming in many cases from their sexual and reproductive functions (Maines, 1999). From menstruation, through pregnancy and childbirth, to the menopause, women have been subject to the clinical gaze and medical interference to an extent that men have not been (Oakley, 1993). Women have been constructed not only as the weaker sex but also the sicker sex who require increasing levels of medical attention and surveillance. However, feminist academics have exposed these 'myths' used by medicine to legitimise their control over women's bodies by highlighting how medicalisation has led to the redefinition of healthy 'natural' processes, such as pregnancy and childbirth, as illnesses (see Oakley, 1993). They have also shown the way in which the medical profession has treated social problems experienced by women as illnesses (Doyal, 1994). For example, women are more likely to be diagnosed with a mental illness and were until very recently more likely to be 'compulsory admitted' to hospital than men. This has been, in part, explained by findings 'that the medical profession is more likely to view "feminine" characteristics as closer to mental illness' (Payne, 1998, p 86).

This feminist critique of medicine predates both the establishment of the NHS and second-wave feminism. For example, the extremely unpopular Contagious Diseases Acts (1864, 1866, 1869), which established a medical system for controlling prostitution and immoral behaviour by young women in the latter half of the 19th century, incited a mass movement fighting for their repeal. Suspended in 1883 and repealed in 1886 after two million people signed petitions opposing them, the campaign against the Contagious Diseases Acts politicised many women who went on to campaign on a variety of social issues including votes for women (Weeks, 1989).

The women's health movement can be seen as a response to the growing power that the medical profession exercised over women's lives, a power that was strengthened by the development of the NHS as it expanded the boundaries of medical authority, enabling it to colonise new areas. The NHS has certainly benefited women greatly, ensuring that women in the UK have access to high-quality medical services, particularly sexual and reproductive services (Doyal, 1994, 1998). The benefits of these services should not be underestimated; for example, the UK has one of the lowest maternal and infant mortality rates in the world and the average woman in the UK lives significantly longer than her male counterpart. However, Doyal (1998, p 4) argues even though the NHS has resulted in substantial health benefits for women, women's health advocates 'have amassed considerable evidence to show that women are treated differently to men in ways that objectively disadvantage them and they have campaigned for the removal of these discriminatory practices'. For example, although heart disease is the major cause of death of women under the age of 75 and is responsible for the deaths of more women than breast cancer, the belief that heart disease is predominantly a male disease means that women are less likely to respond to health promotion messages and evidence suggests that they are less likely to be referred for diagnostic tests (Sharp, 1998).

Following the establishment of the NHS, the medical profession have subjected women's bodies to greater levels of surveillance and social control, for example through medical dominance of maternity services and the extensive health screening programmes. Programmes such as breast and cervical screening extend medical surveillance to healthy populations and while this can be beneficial, it also has a darker dimension – disempowering women, subjecting them to both medical and moral control (for example, see Howson's, 1999, discussion of cervical screening). Feminism has led to a reassessment of women's position in society and produced a wide-ranging critique of the patriarchal structures through which women are oppressed, including medicine and the NHS. Challenging medical power has been a key feature of the feminist critique of women's structurally weak position (Doyal, 1994) that has manifested itself in a number of different ways, as a patient, as an unpaid carer and as a health worker. For example, women form the largest group of employees in the NHS and private medicine but they have predominantly been relegated to the less powerful roles of nursing and care assistants while their role as the major informal provider of healthcare is generally ignored by the medical profession (Graham, 1985; Doyal, 1994, 1998). This unpaid and unrecognised caring role performed by women as mothers, partners and wives has been fundamental to the development of the welfare state, with successive governments relying on women to act as informal health workers and carers for their family in order to artificially suppress the cost of the welfare state (Graham, 1985).

This has led feminist academics, such as Oakley (1993), to argue that medical power has been used to conceal and devalue the real contribution that women make to the nation's health by propagating myths about the actual providers of healthcare around the world as well as who is really the 'sicker sex':

> Women are the major social providers of health and health care, and they are also the principal users of health- and medical-care services. In these two ways, the truth of the matter negates the dominant cultural message … that doctors, not women, ensure health and that men, not women, are biologically the more vulnerable sex, with mortality and physical morbidity records exceeding that of women from the cradle to the grave. (Oakley, 1993, p 4)

Even though women are the real providers of medical care, medical paternalism and medicalisation has been accompanied by a process of infantilisation, disempowering women who are increasingly constructed as being incapable of making the correct choices for themselves about their own health and, in respect to maternity services, that of their babies.

> What we see involved here are issues of control and responsibility that come up again and again in looking at women's health. Who is in control of the process – of having a baby, of being ill, of determining the relative balance between housework and employment work? … At the present time, it is not often women who are in control of matters affecting their own health, and this situation arises not only through the overall medicalisation of life – a process which, after all, affects men too – but also through the infantilization of women as incapable of taking responsible decisions on behalf of themselves and their foetuses. (Oakley, 1993, p 13)

Therefore, to ensure the health of both mother and baby, a massive surveillance system has been constructed around the pregnant woman to ensure that she makes the right decisions. Once pregnant, women are expected to focus on the health of the foetus and to follow the ever-growing medical advice concerning what they can drink, smoke and eat while at the same time presenting themselves for numerous inspections and classes. If they do not, they are held personally and morally accountable for any foetal abnormality or miscarriage that subsequently occurs (Lupton, 1999).

Although this process of infantilisation may affect women more than men, because of the greater involvement of the medical professions in their lives, it has been a feature of the growth of medical power more generally. As Illich (1995) has argued, not only has medicalisation and the professionalisation of medical care resulted in a situation where we are increasingly unable or unwilling to care for ourselves as we strive for 'better health' but also medicine is unnecessary and dangerous.

The women's health movement

As we have highlighted above, the feminist critique of medical power and the NHS has illustrated the way in which the health service has, while purporting to be a universal system of healthcare, actually treated women in a qualitatively different way from men. It is the recognition of the way in which the health service has disadvantaged women that informed the growth of the women's health movement in the UK and has been significant in empowering women to challenge medical paternalism and misogyny both as service users and as formal and informal healthcare workers. Although the establishment of the NHS and the post-war welfare state has had many benefits for women, feminists recognise that these structures are 'markedly patriarchal' (Rose, 1990, p 210) reinforcing the dominant construction of gender and male power.

However, the origin of the modern women's health movement was not explicitly feminist but grew out of women's experience of maternity services. The National Childbirth Association (in 1961 renamed the National Childbirth Trust) was established in the mid-1950s to promote more natural childbirth after its founder, Prunella Briance, had lost her baby due, in her opinion, to excessive medical intervention. Although the National Childbirth Association could not be viewed as a feminist organisation, it did represent a movement of women coming together to effect change based on their own experience of maternity and as such represented a significant challenge to medical autonomy. In 1960, the National Childbirth Trust was joined by the more radical Association for Improvements in Maternity Services (AIMS), which was specifically concerned with empowering women to make their own decisions concerning the birth of their child (Allsop et al, 2005). AIMS was instrumental in the developing homebirth movement, which fought against the over-medicalisation of pregnancy and the medical profession's treatment of childbirth as an illness that required hospitalisation (see the AIMS website at www.aims.org.uk).

The medicalisation of pregnancy can be viewed as an exemplar for the way in which the development of the NHS, which was accompanied by the extension of medical authority, disempowered women. For example, not only did the development of obstetrics construct childbirth as a medical procedure that needed to be supervised by a suitably qualified medical expert, thereby devaluing women's own knowledge and experience, it also marginalised the traditional role of midwives, bringing them under the control of a predominantly male medical authority (Romalis, 1985; Barker, 1998). Medical power is based on having a monopoly over the delivery of medical services and on the prioritisation of Western medical science over other forms of medical knowledge.

> The representation of pregnancy as biomedical gave physicians a monopoly over the 'knowing' and therapeutics of pregnancy and concurrently undermining existing ways of knowing (experiential/folk wisdom). Additionally, a medical construction of pregnancy constituted bio-power through scientifically determined prescriptions for best ensuring a healthy pregnancy outcome. Such 'objective' advice created the basis for the legitimate control over the medically constituted human subject. (Barker, 1998, p 1074)

Initially, the medical profession opposed any interference of users in services. Many health professional during the 1950s and 1960s firmly believed in the 'doctor knows best' adage and even groups that were deferential to medical authority were viewed as potential threats to medical power. Hera Cook, (2004, p 313), for example, argues that it took relatively little for service user groups such as the National Association for the Welfare of Children in Hospital, an 'association, composed largely of middle class women ... seeking only to co-operate with nurses and doctors' to be viewed 'as extremely challenging'. It was universalism not democracy that provided the philosophical underpinning for the NHS and the medical profession have fiercely guarded their autonomy and power (Doyal, 1998).

The development of health consumer groups, such as the National Childbirth Trust, and the women's health movement were an important counterbalance to the extension of medical authority. These groups represented the organisation of a 'network of expertise and intelligence-gathering' (Baggott et al, 2005, p 124) that drew on the embodied knowledge of service users and sympathetic professionals from medicine and other relevant areas. Such expertise could be used to inform both medical practice and policy while simultaneously providing advice and support to those who required it.

The birth of an explicitly feminist women's health movement in the UK followed the first National Women's Liberation Conference held at Ruskin College in Oxford in February 1970. Four core demands arose from this first meeting: for equal pay, equal educational and employment opportunities, free and flexible childcare and free contraception and abortions on demand (Coote and Pattullo, 1990; Byrne, 1997). These demands reflected the women's movement challenge to the welfare state, particularly, the way in which 'the post-war welfare state had short-changed women, whether as users of services, as unpaid providers of welfare or as paid workers in the health and welfare services' (Williams, 2002, p 502). In challenging the structures of the patriarchal state, second-wave feminism sought to empower women to take control of their own lives and their own bodies. Concern about health was initially focused on women's sexual and reproductive health and on providing women with the freedom to choose when and if they wished to have children, influenced by the belief that women's liberation could only be achieved when women were released from the shackles of motherhood (Firestone, 1979). Although subsequently many feminists came to believe that motherhood gave women a special insight into the world not available to men and therefore should be lauded (Randall, 1987), the right of women to make their own choices about their bodies remains a core theme of the women's health movement.

However, this national agenda was not accompanied by the development of a national campaigning body unlike in the US. In the UK, the women's movement has always been largely an amorphous unorganised alliance of small groups and organisations, often based around local women's centres and refuges. This amorphous nature of the wider women's liberation movement was also reflected in the composition of the women's health movement, which was characterised by a 'loosely connected set of self-help groups' that:

> encouraged women to wrest control of their health and their bodies from (male) medical professionals, challenge the orthodoxy of the medical establishment and develop a way of understanding the body that was based upon the feminine qualities of self-awareness and body consciousness. (Moore, 2008, p 270)

An example of these feminist self-help groups is the string of well-women centres established during the 1970s and the 1980s that offered a limited alternative health service. These centres were more important in the American women's health movement where they acted as an alternative to the 'profit-driven male- and professional-dominated health institutions' (Morgen, 2002, p 74) whereas in the UK the focus was more on promoting change in the NHS (Kelleher et al, 1994; see also Stacey, 1985). Despite this, there were a number of these centres established in the UK, although they were more focused on self-help than on providing actual medical services. The first was established by the women at the Essex Road Women's Centre in Islington, London, in order to provide a variety of alternative health services and information for women such as abortion information, pregnancy testing, self-examination, health advice as well as providing 'information on doctors and their treatment of women' (Lovenduski and Randall, 1993, pp 233-4). Of greater importance than these centres was the much larger network of small, local self-help groups that formed the backbone of the women's health movement in the UK. By the early 1980s, there were some 20,000 active participants in the movement (Byrne, 1997).

For the women's liberation movement, such self-help networks were vitally important, not only for consciousness raising, but also for providing women with practical advice that would empower them to make their own decisions concerning their bodies and their lives. Empowering women to make their own informed choices was a core element to the feminist organising around the provision of contraceptive and abortion services. Throughout the 1970s and the early part of the 1980s, the fight for abortion on demand and the defence of the 1967 Abortion Act became the focal concern of the women's health movement. Although, in Britain (that is, excluding Northern Ireland), the 1967 Abortion Act meant that terminations, if agreed by two doctors, were permitted in cases of foetal abnormality or where continuing with the pregnancy was likely to result in physical or psychological maternal harm, this was not abortion on demand. However, the 1967 Act did not require the 'Ministry of Health to provide the necessary facilities, nor did it impose on individual consultants a duty to carry out the procedure', which resulted in the existence of wide variations in provision between health authorities (Klein, R., 2001, p 67). These variations underline the extent to which the belief that the NHS provides equal access to health services is a myth. Although the Society for the Protection of Unborn Children (SPUC), LIFE and pro-life sympathisers like to suggest that the 1967 Act opened the floodgates to abortion, this clearly was not the case. Ultimately, women's right to choose was dependent on medical approval. Shaver (1994, p 79) describes abortion in the UK as a woman's medical entitlement, not her right as in the US, and as such 'access is mediated by medical authority'. However, as terminations are only permitted within 24 weeks of conception (originally 28 weeks), the process of attending a GP for a referral to a consultant who would need to agree that an abortion was necessary can create problems of access. There is evidence that in certain parts of the country, access to terminations is limited and that, in these areas, GPs and health authority practice may force women to rely on the private or voluntary sector for their termination (Thomas, 1998), which may help to explain why despite the core NHS principle of universalism, half of all terminations in the UK are now conducted in the private sector (Shaver, 1994; Thomas, 1998).

As the 1967 Act was passed before the first Ruskin College meeting of the women's liberation movement, the focus of the women's health movement has been primarily on defending women's rights to choose from the predominantly Christian backlash against the Act. SPUC was established in January 1967 to rather belatedly oppose the passage of the Bill through Parliament and in 1970 the splinter organisation LIFE was formed by those critical of SPUC's willingness to compromise. The very real threat these organisations posed with the help of sympathetic MPs was brought home in 1975 when James White's Bill aimed at restricting the operation of the Abortion Act made it to the committee stage, having passed its second reading. In response, the National Abortion Campaign (NAC) was formed (Durham, 1991; Lovenduski and Randall, 1993) and mobilised tens of thousands of women in its defence of women's right to choose. The NAC was joined in 1976 by Co-ord (Co-ordinating committee in Defence of the 1967 Act), which was primarily concerned with acting as a bulwark against a well-funded and determined pro-life movement. Although James White's Bill failed, it was just the first of a number of parliamentary Bills introduced by pro-life MPs to undermine women's right to choose.

The next attack came following the election of the Thatcher government in 1979 when Conservative MP John Corrie introduced a Private Member's Bill to reduce the time limit for terminations from 28 to 20 weeks (Durham, 1991). The NAC's campaign against Corrie used the fear that the new Thatcher administration might mount a sustained attack against women's right to choose to encourage more than a 100,000 supporters to take to the street to demonstrate against the Bill (Lovenduski and Randall, 1993). This success represented the high-point of the pro-choice campaign in the UK as following the failure of the Corrie Bill, internal pressures in the NAC forced a split in 1983 between those who wanted the movement to remain focused on abortion and those who believed that a wider campaign on women's reproductive rights was essential. The split led to the establishment of the Women's Reproductive Rights Campaign in January 1984 and was also indicative of the wider tensions in the women's movement, with different groups beginning to challenge the movement's focus on the concerns of white, middle-class women (Lovenduski and Randall, 1993; Somerville, 1997).

Abortion has remained an important health issue for the women's movement. The campaign to Fight the Alton Bill in 1987-88, like the Corrie Bill, sought to reduce the time limit for abortions; however, it failed to achieve the mass mobilisation of the anti-Corrie campaign. Following anti-Alton campaign, a group of women concerned that abortion campaigns were always reacting to threats against the 1967 Act rather than pushing for better access to early abortions on the NHS, formed the Pro-Choice Alliance (Lovenduski and Randall, 1993). Despite this revitalisation of organising around abortions, the movement was unable to stop the time limit for abortions being reduced from 28 to 24 weeks through the government-sponsored 1990 Human Fertilisation and Embryology Act. However, the extent to which this was actually a victory for pro-life campaigners is questionable since they have consistently failed to significantly undermine either the 1967 Act or the belief that women should have the right (within limits) to abortions. Pro-life campaigners, in the end, were bitterly disappointed with the Conservative administrations under Margaret Thatcher and John Major, who were, despite their belated support, far less concerned with imposing a 'traditional' morality than introducing sweeping monetarist economic changes and challenging the unions (see Durham, 1991). In terms of the NHS, this translated into the Conservative governments challenging medical autonomy through managerial reforms and introducing mechanisms to promote 'good housekeeping', including increased private sector involvement in the NHS in order to ensure value for money (see Klein, R., 2001).

Defending women's rights to abortion continues to be a key issue for the women's movement. However, during the 1980s, focus shifted to other concerns (anti-nuclear, pornography, male violence, reproductive rights). In part this reflected the fragmentation of the women's movement and a decline in the active women's health movement towards the end of the 1980s (Laughlin, 1998). However, this has been accompanied by a growing recognition of the specific needs of women by policy makers and by health authorities. As Williams (2002, p 503) argues:

> Feminist politics of the 1970s and 1980s can be seen to have had some enduring influences upon the subsequent provision of welfare services... This was not only in creating new services to meet women's specific needs, but also in the development of equal opportunities policies, anti-oppressive strategies and empowerment strategies for users within public and voluntary sector services.

An example of this is the way in which the women's health movement influenced the establishment of well-women clinics and created a climate in which many alternative women's health projects were able to successfully obtain statutory funding, thereby becoming 'partially or wholly integrated into the mainstream' (Benato et al, 1998, p 201). There has also been growing cooperation between the voluntary sector and statutory sector service providers to meet the needs of women service users (for example, see Benato et al, 1998; Griffiths and Bradlow, 1998; Laughlin, 1998). While there is always a danger that co-option and professionalisation can lead to the loss of autonomy, it is also a reflection that the concern of women is being taken more seriously by the NHS and both national and local governments.

Social movements in health

In challenging medical authority, the NHS and government health policy, the women's health movement has been an important influence on the growing numbers of health-oriented social movements. These movements can be divided into three main groups:

- *health access movements*, which aim to increase access to health services for specific groups;
- *constituency-based movements*, which challenge inequalities in health and access to services for a particular constituency, for example those movements that organise around gender, ethnicity, class and sexuality;
- *embodied health movements*, which coalesce around a particular illness such as breast cancer, AIDS, gulf war syndrome or ME (Brown and Zavestoki, 2005).

There is a considerable overlap between these different types of health movements; for example, many AIDS activists define themselves as gay activists and AIDS predominantly as a gay issue (King, 1993). Similarly, the women's movement has informed the practice of a range of different health access movements and embodied health movements. Neither do all health social movements fit easily into these three categories. For example, it is difficult to categorise the complementary and alternative medicine movement, which fights for medical recognition (or very least acceptance of the value of this alternative medical model by governments and funders) of these alternative therapies and treatments (Goldner, 2005). This is further complicated by the situation that many health movements may also fight for access to these complementary and alternative therapies and treatments. Access to such services was, for example, a major part of the local activism of Body Positive and Buddy groups, which acted as advocates for people living with HIV/AIDS particularly before the development of combination therapies substantially increased the life chances for the majority of these people. At the same time, these groups can also be fighting for access to new experimental treatments or to drugs that are not yet available in the UK. In so doing they highlight the way in which the universalism of the NHS is restricted to those treatments and drugs that the government and the health authorities are willing to fund.

The extent to which these movements challenge medical power and health policy also vary considerably, with some movements primarily aimed at helping medical science, forming alliances with practitioners to fight for increased funding and increasing public awareness while others seek to challenge accepted medical knowledge. The campaign to improve public awareness of breast cancer and public support for breast cancer research is a good example of a movement that does not seek to challenge medical science but is primarily aimed at helping it. Kolker (2004) argues that one of the major changes that have occurred over the past 20 years in health social movements has been the shift from their focus on the 'problem of patient care' to a focus on securing research funding and greater public awareness of a particular condition. The breast cancer movement has been particularly successful in transforming an individual trouble into a public problem and inciting public discourse around this once-stigmatised issue (Kolker, 2004). Some health social movements involve an alliance of activists and members of the medical profession, for instance pro-choice activists have worked with sympathetic doctors and nurses to ensure adequate provision for terminations and act as a bulwark against the pro-life movement (Joffe et al, 2004). Other movements, however, have sought to overturn the accepted medical dogmas and counter the stigma of medical labels. The anti-psychiatric movement that challenged the right of the medical profession to label people as mentally ill (Crossley, 2006) and the gay liberation's campaign to have homosexuality removed from the American Psychiatric Association's (1968) list of mental illnesses (*DSM-II*) are good examples (Marshall, 1983).

Similarly, self-help groups that offer sufferers of chronic illnesses an alternative support mechanism can also act as a challenge to the medical profession. Kelleher (1994, p 113) characterises the self-help movement as a new social movement since they are 'resisting the domination of the life-world by expert systems, in this case the expert system of medicine' (see also Habermas, 1981). This is particularly apparent in the growth of embodied health movements of which a core feature is the production of a 'politicized collective illness identity' that challenges 'normal scientific practice', blurring 'the boundaries between lay and expert forms of knowledge, and between activists and the state' (Brown et al, 2004, p 54). The women's health movement has been extremely influential in encouraging the growth of the embodied health movements, particularly, through the legitimation of the embodied knowledge of health service users. For example, Potts (2004, p 141) argues that that the environmental breast cancer movement has drawn on a feminist epistemology to legitimatise the alternative expertise of activists on the basis 'that the personal, subjective and the partial count'. In doing so, the women's health movement has facilitated the prioritisation of patient's rights in the NHS and in challenging the widespread medical view that the patient's opinion is of little consequence in the clinical decision-making process.

The problem of defining a health social movement has also become increasingly complicated as it is more difficult to distinguish between social movements and voluntary sector providers, between activists and service providers. The women's refuge movement, for example, grew out of the women's liberation movement while at the same time providing a network of safe houses for women and children subject to domestic abuse. This network receives statutory funding to provide refuges and has relied on its charitable status to raise funds for its work (Pahl, 1979) while simultaneously being engaged in a political struggle against male violence and the wider patriarchal nature of society. Similar issues arose with the professionalisation of AIDS activism during the 1980s: for example, although the Terrence Higgins Trust (THT) developed as a response of the lesbian, gay, bisexual and transgender (LGBT) community to HIV/AIDS, it had by the late 1980s become almost totally reliant on statutory funding and professional workers, which resulted in the trust becoming less focused on gay men and AIDS (King, 1993).

However, while health social movements are diverse, they all act to some extent as health advocates for certain social groups or seek to support and defend the NHS. In recent years, the defence of the NHS has become more important as successive governments have eroded public provision by an increasing reliance on the private sector.

The NHS has always been a compromise settlement that sought to placate powerful opposition to universal provision of healthcare. These compromises have meant that the NHS continues to fail to live up to its promise of eliminating differential access to healthcare, yet, despite its inadequacies, the existence of the NHS as a form of socialised healthcare free to all at the point of delivery is as necessary today as it was in 1948. Therefore, although many social movements have been critical of the organisation and operation of the NHS, few movements would advocate the dismantling the NHS. Quite the opposite: 'the critique from the margins … were very critical of existing state provision, but the context of this criticism was not to the undermining of welfare as such, but making it more accountable to the people who use it' (Cowden and Singh, 2007, p 9). Unfortunately, this critique has at times been used by the government to justify attacks on universal provision and the ability of the public sector to deliver a high-quality health service. Cowden and Singh (2007) also argue that the ideology of the user involvement has also been used by New Labour to strengthen the managerialism of the NHS, enabling managers and ministers to use the notion of user choice and what users want to defend their actions against the wishes of frontline staff.

The process of privatisation within the NHS followed the 1979 election victory of the Thatcher administration and had begun as a cost-cutting exercise that aimed to challenge the power of the health service unions and the authority of consultants, as well as to privatise, in the first instance, auxiliary services such as laundry and cleaning. Despite claims to the contrary, this agenda has been continued by New Labour following its election in 1997 and supported across the political spectrum – often against the wishes of the rank-and-file members of all mainstream parties (Pollock, 2004; Ruane, 2004, 2007). Hence, there has been considerable continuity between New Labour and the previous Conservative administration, even if the language of market efficiency has been replaced with the language of modernisation:

> Under the Conservatives the reduction of the Welfare State in the interest of economic efficiency was emphasized, New Labour emphasized 'modernization', though the difference in rhetoric conceals important continuities between New Labour and Thatcherism. The dominant theme of social policy in health and welfare provision continues to be defined in terms of a public policy agenda designed to reduce the role of the state through a strategy of commodification and privatization. (Cowden and Singh, 2007, p 10)

While a number of trade unions have been active in their opposition to privatisation, professional associations have been more muted and many of the larger service user organisations, having been co-opted into the polity, have taken a more pragmatic approach to the privatisation policy (Ruane, 2004, 2007; see also Allsop et al, 2005). While there is considerable public unease to the idea of privatising the health service, and there have been a number of high-profile campaigns against hospital closures in particular areas, there has yet to be a public awakening to the dangers posed by current health policy (see Ruane, 2004).

Conclusion

Although the extent to which the women's health movement has informed the development of the NHS and health policy has been questioned by academics (see Doyal, 1998), and that in recent years the movement has seemingly gone into terminal decline, it would be wrong to underestimate the influence that the movement has had on social movements in health. A defining characteristic of both the women's liberation movement and the women's health movement has been the tactic of drawing on women's personal experience and embodied knowledge and using it as a political weapon. The development of a large network of women sharing their own personal experience underpinned the feminist challenge to medical authority and health policy and has been an important inspiration to a growing number of embodied health social movements and health consumer groups. These groups along with the women's health movement have defended the NHS and fought for the rights of patients to have equal access to health services. The women's health movement has succeeded in drawing attention to the discrimination experienced by women in the NHS and the failure of the NHS to provide for the specific health needs of women. In doing this,

> The women's health movement sets and resets health objectives from below, while making space for individual women to make their choices, and constantly presses governments to ensure that health services are available either free or affordable, so that choice is affordable. (Rose, 1990, p 214)

This fight has become all the more important as both Conservative and Labour administrations have sought to increase private sector involvement in the delivery of health and personal care, which has undermined the universalism of Beveridge's vision. Health social movements straddle the boundaries of 'old' and 'new' social movements, in that they are concerned with ensuring access to high-quality health services and the latest drug therapies and continue to fight against the privatisation and closure of these services while simultaneously making space for their adherents to discuss the legitimacy of their own embodied experience. In this way, such movements can be characterised as a form of resistance to the encroachment of expert systems into the lifeworld (Habermas, 1981, 1987b) and in particular the way in which the foundation of the NHS has further extended the reach of the medical power into all of our everyday lives.

Further reading

There is a growing body of research on social movements in health that has led social movement theorists to identify different types of health social movements. The collection *Social Movements in Health* edited by Phil Brown and Stephen Zavestoski (Blackwell, 2005) provides a good overview of the topic, while *Speaking for Patients and Carers: Health Consumer Groups and the Policy Process* by Rob Baggott, Judith Allsop and Kathryn Jones (Palgrave Macmillan, 2005) offers important insights into the impact of the growth of consumer groups on the policy process.

A history of the women's health movement in the UK has not been published. However, *Into Our Own Hands: The Women's Health Movement in the United States, 1969-1990* by Sandra Morgen (Rutgers University Press, 2002) provides an American history.

On women, health and the NHS, *Essays on Women, Medicine and Health* by Ann Oakley (Edinburgh University Press, 1993) is a good discussion of various ways in which women are medicalised, while *Women and Health Services* by Lesley Doyal (Open University Press, 1998) provides a wider discussion of women's experience of the health service.

For a discussion of privatisation of the health service, see *NHS plc: The Privatisation of Our Health Care* by Allyson M. Pollock (Verso, 2005).

Useful websites

NICE ~ responsible for approving all medicine available on the NHS in England, Wales and Northern Ireland: www.nice.org.uk

Scottish Medicine Consortium ~ provides advice to the Scottish Health Boards concerning all new drugs and therapies: www.scottishmedicines.org.uk

The Association for Improvements in Maternity Services (AIMS) ~ has been an advocate for pregnant women for nearly 50 years: www.aims.org.uk

Abortion Rights ~ was formed by the merger of the National Abortion Campaign (NAC) and the Abortion Law Reform Association (ALRA) in 2003: *www.abortionrights.org.uk*

six

Fighting squalor: urban social movements

Introduction

As historic sites of power, cities have also long been central to forms of protest and rebellion (see Allen, 1999). From the Paris Commune of 1871, through upper-class fears of 'the mob' in London in the second half of the 19th century, rent strikes and industrial agitation in Glasgow during and immediately after the First World War, the 'race riots' that engulfed US cities in the 1960s, Paris 1968 (where student protests and a general strike toppled the de Gaulle government), riots against racism and police oppression in major English cities in the 1980s and early 1990s, the Poll Tax riot in London in 1990, to Seattle, Genoa and Florence, sites of some of the most notable anti-neoliberal globalisation protests, the entanglements of cities and uprisings and insurgence have a long and proud history. Across the cities of the global North and South, protest and rebellion are everyday features of the urban landscape – and indeed shape that landscape. In the context of late 20th- and early 21st-century 'globalisation' where, in a small number of 'global cities', power appears to have become even more concentrated, the city occupies centre stage. However, as Portaliou (2007, p 165) reminds us, 'the city is not only the place of power, but also of grassroots resistance'.

For Sassen (2004, p 651), one of the key theorists of the global city, the strategic networks and relations that connect global cities offer up new opportunities for protest:

> Among the actors in this political landscape are a variety of organizations focused on transboundary issues concerning immigration, asylum, international women's agendas, alter-globalisation struggles and many others. While these are not necessarily urban in their orientation or genesis, they tend to converge in cities. The new network technologies, especially the Internet, ironically have strengthened the urban map of these transboundary networks....
>
> Global cities are, then, thick enabling environments for these types of activities, even though the networks themselves are not urban per se.

While new opportunities for mobilisation and resistance have opened up in recent times to vastly differing degrees across different cities, long-standing protests such as, for example, squatters' movements and anti-road-building protests, have become more radicalised and organisationally adept, and new protests have erupted around the environmental issues in the city, defending green spaces and public spaces. In passing, we must also acknowledge the growth in more reactionary and regressive movements in the city and beyond, including right-wing protests around housing provision and allocations, 'NIMBYism' (not in my back yard; see McClymont and O'Hare, 2008, for a critical discussion of this), and in the US and UK in particular, urban vigilantes, and diverse forms of suburban conservatism and protectionism.

As we will encounter as we progress though this chapter, recognising that cities are important factors in popular protest and insurrection is one thing, disentangling 'the urban' dimension from the main other issues and targets of protest and rebellion is another matter altogether. As Sassen (2004) highlights, protests that frequently take place and erupt in urban locations around, to borrow the term she deploys, 'trans-boundary' issues (environmental issues, migration, gender, anti-globalisation and so on), may not originate in the city nor be an 'urban' issue per se – reminding us also that protests are a feature of rural and non-urban areas. The relationship between cities and protest movements is therefore a complex and dynamic one.

The focus of this chapter is on the question and nature of 'urban social movements', the term itself denoting such almost as a sub-branch of social movement analysis and studies. Echoing our point above that cities and protest go hand in hand, the discussion here considers some of the ways in which the city has been important for our understanding of struggles around welfare issues in the UK – notably around housing and, to use the term employed by Beveridge (1942), 'squalor'. Housing has been a central point of contention in welfare protest and struggles in the UK from the late 19th century, arguably an ever-present source of social movement mobilisation – albeit in differing guises and forms. Given the centrality of housing, one of the key case studies that we discuss in this chapter is concerned with housing struggles.

Housing is, of course, not a specifically city or urban issue. Housing provision, or more correctly the supply of affordable quality housing to rent – or the lack thereof – has frequently been an issue that has also concerned rural communities. It also interrelates with other issues such as the Poll Tax, with protestors involved in the Poll Tax rebellions of the late 1980s and early 1990s (see Lavalette and Mooney, 2000) drawing links between the undermining of public housing provision and local government finance and taxation – and as we will see with regard to protests over housing stock transfer in the early 2000s, it also relates to wider protests against privatisation.

Taking housing as a case study immediately throws up questions about 'old' and 'new' forms of social movement, echoing our explorations in the chapters in Part One and elsewhere in this book. 'Housing struggles' are generally seen as representative of 'older' forms of social movement – around material needs and social justice. As we will see, however, such distinctions are much more problematic when we add the urban dimension too.

There are, then, as we proceed to move to the substance of our discussion, complex issues around old and new forms of social movement. That urban movements based on collective services are place based means that they may not have transboundary and/or transnational links and connections. What indeed makes a social movement an *urban* social movement?

Urban social movements

In Chapter Three, we briefly introduced the concept or notion of an urban social movement (USM), and its location within the theoretical frameworks developed by urban theorist and sociologist Castells. It is Castells' work, notably his 1983 book *The City and the Grassroots,* that has largely shaped the arguments that have ensued since in the USM literature – and in the wider urban studies field – providing a set of conceptual and analytic tools, the usefulness and applicability of which has been much contested. Castells' starting point is with what he calls 'the urban question' (1977a). In advanced capitalist societies, he argues, the state at local and national levels becomes ever-more involved in the provision of social goods and services, in part through pressure from above from business but also as a consequence of protest from below. Such 'collective consumption' – while apart from the antagonistic relationship between capital and labour at the point of production – reflects both a new phase and a new form of conflict between capital and labour. However, reflecting Castells' Marxist pedigree, as the state becomes more and more involved in the provision of collective consumption, he sees new contradictions emerging around the failure of the state to provide the services being demanded and the protests this in turn generates. The social reproduction of labour power, therefore, becomes central to class conflict in the city.

Starting from the central premise that 'urban social movements have been among the sources of urban forms and structures throughout history ... the historical conditions peculiar to our societies make their impact much more evident than ever before' (Castells, 1983, p xix), *The City and the Grassroots* provides a wide range of detailed empirical accounts of USMs that stretch from a study of the Comunidades of Castilla, 1520-22, taking in an exploration of the tenants' movement in Glasgow during the First World War, the urban uprisings in the US in the 1960s through to union activism in Paris, demands for rights for sexual orientation and minority ethnic groups in San Francisco and to squatters' movements in Chile, Mexico and Peru among other case studies. From this he developed his central theory of USMs:

> [U]rban protest movements, in our societies and in our epoch, ... develop around three major themes: 1) demands focused on *collective consumption*.... 2) defence of cultural identity associated with and organised around a specific *territory*. 3) *political mobilization* in relationship to the state, particularly emphasizing the role of *local government*. (Castells, 1983, p xviii, emphasis in original)

Thus, for Castells, USMs are characterised by their diversity and different forms of mobilisation: those that mobilise to demand state provision of goods and services, in other words decommodified 'collective consumption'; 'community movements', which are involved in 'the search for cultural identity, for the maintenance of autonomous local cultures, ethnically-based or historically originated' (Castells, 1983, pp 319-20); and 'citizen movements', which struggle for territorially or neighbourhood-based self-management. There is another aspect of Castells' theorisation here that merits attention and is, we would argue, significant for our understanding of social movements in general – but here for USMs specifically today.

While Castells sees USMs as primarily defensive or reactive, he is also clear that they can be transformative. They crucially involve struggles over and around urban meanings. USMs are a 'collective conscious action aimed at the transformation of the institutionalised urban meaning against the logic, interest and values of the dominant class' (Castells, 1983, p 305). While Castells sees USMs as unable to transform society, urban mobilisations and struggles can, in the words of Susser (2006, p 212), make 'ideals seem "realizable"'. For instance, the tenants of Glasgow who organised the Glasgow rent strike in 1915 were successful in transforming the dominant understanding of housing from a commodity to a social right and entitlement. We will return to this particular theme later in the chapter in relation to the issue of 'right to the city' but here we wish to emphasise that in the process of struggling, new forms of protest are thrown up, existing forms of power challenged and new imaginings of city life developed.

With such an ambitious project it will come as no surprise that Castells' arguments provoked a good deal of debate and controversy. Here we focus on a particularly significant aspect of this, the question of social class. As we have seen in other chapters, the relationship between class and social movements represents one of the key points of contestation that runs through social movement theorising – and this is also true of USMs. Indeed, arguably it is in relation to USMs that some of the most notable skirmishes have taken place between those who remain committed to social class analysis, particularly classical Marxist class theory, and those who tend to see social movements (including USMs) as generally independent and autonomous from class action. Let us explore this by briefly considering the Glasgow rent strike of 1915, around which some of the most heated arguments have been voiced.

Glasgow 1915 was 'One of the most important rent strikes in history', claims Castells (1983, p 27). While he recognises that this struggle was rooted in working-class communities on the Clyde, often led by working-class women (see Damer, 1980; Melling, 1983), that it was a struggle located 'in the sphere of consumption' (1983, p 31), the resulting outcome – the 1915 Rents and Mortgage Restrictions (War Restrictions) Act (generally regarded as the key legislation that was to lead to council housing itself in 1919) – was supported by sections of local industrial capital (although opposed by the private landlords) who wished to avoid housing conflicts becoming also industrial conflicts, as well as having a vested interest in ensuring the satisfactory housing of workers. Waged by a largely artisan community with a 'strong cultural identity' and who were not directly in a struggle with the industrial capital class meant that, for Castells, victorious though the Clyde rent strikers were, it was not a class struggle in the classic sense. He argues (1983, pp 36-7):

> [B]oth from the point of view of the movement and from the point of view of its political effects, the Rent Strike appears as an episode of the class struggle. Yet the absence of any direct confrontation with the dominant fractions of capital, the deviation of the demands towards the request for state intervention, and the actual support of the capitalists for the new housing policies, clearly challenge any interpretation of the Glasgow Rent Strike as an anti-capitalist movement.

Before considering some of the critical responses to these claims, we should pause to reflect briefly on some of the key aspects of the 1915 rent strike on Clydeside as a form of mobilisation and protest. Renowned Clydeside Revolutionary and latterly Communist MP Willie Gallagher (1978, pp 52-3, emphasis in original) commented:

> In Govan, Mrs Barbour, a typical working class housewife, became the leader of a movement such as had never been seen before, or since for that matter. Street meetings, back-court meetings, drums, bells, trumpets – every method was used to bring the women out and organise them for the struggle. Notices were printed by the thousand and put up in the windows: wherever you went you could see them. In street after street, scarcely a window without one: WE ARE NOT PAYING INCREASED RENT.

Such forms of resistance were radically innovative at the time, supplementing street defence committees, protest meetings and demonstrations. But the centrality of women to the protest, now recognised as pivotal in most accounts of the rent strike, also stands out as significant. Many of the forms of protests developed in the communities of Glasgow and other West of Scotland towns such as Clydebank represented direct action at it best – forgoing the rules of conduct that often characterised the likes of trade union-organised protest at the time. In this one case study we are encouraged, then, to think about the diversity of forms of protest and resistance that have emerged in the city over time.

To return to the critical responses to Castells' arguments, critics writing from a Marxist perspective, such as Damer (1980, 2000), have sought to foreground the class nature of the Clyde rent war of 1915 (and of the early 1920s) by focusing on the class nature of the local state and by arguing that the rent strikers were able to transcend sectional and sectarian divisions and attain a higher level of class consciousness. In so doing, they clearly understood, he argues, that Glasgow's landlords were a capitalist class and that together with the shop stewards movement in the Clyde's shipyards and engineering plants, leaders of the rent strike mobilised and led 'on the basis of a struggle against capitalism as a system' (Damer, 1980, p 106). Further, Damer argues that although the Clyde rent strike might be labelled as an urban or consumption struggle, they remain a facet of the overall class struggle:

> While they may not be directly related to struggles over the immediate process of production – or at least, not at first sight – this does not mean that they are not class struggles. The way to theorise these struggles is to locate them in the process of social reproduction, and the class struggle over reproduction and social welfare issues – rent, housing, health, education – is as bitter, if not more bitter, than struggles at the point of production. (Damer, 2000, p 94)

This is a debate that ran for some considerable time (see Lowe, 1986). It is important for us in that it flags important controversies around the analysis and understanding of USMs, but it also highlights how Castells de-emphasises class relations and class mobilisations, offering a 'vision of community movements and urban struggles that goes beyond class conflict' (Susser, 2006, p 214). Thus, for many of the contributors to recent commentary on *The City and the Grassroots* (see *IJURR*, 2003, 2006; *City*, 2006), Castells' willingness to embrace different understandings of class, particularly from the Weberian tradition (confirming his departure from Marxism, see also Castells, 2006), and in his recognition of identity and citizenship as important factors that generate urban protest, makes him relevant to social movement theorisations today.

Castells' work has been important in developing a conceptual framework for our understanding of the context of the struggles around collective consumption in the city, both historically as well as those taking place now. His particular focus on the role of the local state is especially important (see also Cockburn, 1977, Lowe, 1986). The local state functions almost as a local manager for the national state, regulating forms of collective consumption and thereby enabling the successful reproduction of labour power. The intervention of the local state arises as a consequence of the failures of the market to meet such aims. The failure of the private sector to provide suitable housing for the working class, for instance, has consequences for the reproduction of the next generation of workers – thereby threatening the process of capital accumulation itself.

However, as the local state becomes ever-more enmeshed in collective consumption activities, the political fallout from such involvement also intensifies. Financing such consumption can result in a fiscal crisis from which the state cannot easily disengage and attempts to do so generate new forms of protest and resistance against cuts in service provision. In turn, this serves to give rise to different social movements in the city – to urban social movements where the local state becomes the focus protest. This is a theme that will be highlighted again later in this chapter.

Social movement and urban social movement analysis: parallel worlds?

In a world where global protest and social movements have become so pronounced over the past decade or so (see Chapter Eleven), USMs can appear almost as a 'left-over' from previous eras of struggle, seemingly a parochial form of resistance in a world now characterised by transnational spatialities, networks and connections. The interest in the development, organisation and dynamics of new social movements since the late 1980s means also that USM concerns and mobilisations around the provision of collective goods (housing, education, health and so on) have generally been superseded, with the material concerns of USMs replaced by the growing concern with issues of identity and recognition of new social movements. This throws up important questions about the relationship between USMs and social movements in general – whether old or new. While largely overtaken by an interest with new social movements and, more significantly, with the global justice movements, nonetheless, USMs have continued to exercise researchers, theorists and, of course, activists. After what seems to have been years of general neglect, there has been some rekindling of interest in USMs evidenced, as we noted earlier, by special issues of journals devoted to reflections on the nature of urban movements today (see *IJURR*, 2003, 2006; *City*, 2006). In no small part, such reflections emerge as a consequence of the role of the city in global protest movements, but also that the city continues to be a locale of continuing protest around collective issues such as housing and health and, an issue that has generated significant protest movements and insurgence in cities the world over, the supply of clean and safe water.

Pickvance (2003, p 104), a key commentator writing in this field, argues that the analysis and exploration of USMs tended to develop in isolation from social movement theorising in general (see also Miller, 2006, p 208). In part this is because an interest in USMs tended to evolve from some of the dominant concerns of urban studies, urban geography and politics and while urban sociology was an important factor in provoking such an interest, it was arguably not as influential as it was in other areas of social movement theorising. Pickvance further argues, a point we have already made above, that those who were interested in new social movements tended to avoid USMs as a form of older social movement, which, like the labour movement, was concerned with material struggles.

This isolation, for Pickvance, had several lasting consequences: USM writers were generally concerned with the effects of USM struggles, with outcomes, for example improved housing provision or better healthcare, rather than with type of organisation. A second positive effect was that USM theorists were particularly concerned with questions of political power, of the nature of the state both at local as well as national levels. A further related emphasis in USM literature was a focus on the political environment and context within which urban protests and movements developed: the particular economic, social and political conditions under which USMs emerged were often related to issues of urban poverty and related material deprivations but also to the increasing role of the state in delivering collective goods and services. However, Pickvance also notes that the relative detachment of USM theorising from social movement theory in general meant that there was less concern with processes of mobilisation and further, that USM analysis tended to shy away from an interest in voluntary associations, pressure groups and service user groups. In no small part, this once again highlights the key question that has featured in the USM literature for over three decades, 'whether urban social movements are distinctive because they are urban and how distinctively urban social movements contribute to constructing the urban' (Lake, 2006, p 194).

The contemporary relevance of USMs

What is the relevance of this for our understanding of social movements, particularly USMs in the early years of the 21st century? The first point we wish to stress, following Pickvance (2003, p 106), is that USMs make demands that span a range of issues: from material concerns to demands for greater participation, entitlements and 'non-material' issues such as recognition and voice. And as Mayer (2006, p 204) argues,

> [U]rban movements continue to emerge and thrive, the structural conditions for conflicts over the meaning of the city have hardly disappeared, and studies of urban politics and social movements indicate that such conflicts and mobilisations around them are frequent. If anything there is an intensified connection between social community and socio-spatial environment.

At the outset we highlighted that there has been a renewed interest in USMs given the centrality of the city as the locale for global social movement protests, although aspects of what might have been termed USMs in the past have today often been subsumed under the umbrella of protest that is the global justice movement. But USMs – as with social movements in general – were always diverse, fragmented and dynamic. As we have seen, many of the concerns of the USMs overlapped and interrelated with those of other movements that did not have a city or urban focus and a number of USMs have been subsumed under gender, race, identity and cultural movements. However, new USMs have either emerged, or long-standing ones revitalised, as a consequence of state action and erosion of many of the gains and victories that were hard won during the 1960s and 1970s – and which have been thrown into reverse by the neoliberal onslaught of the 1980s, 1990s and early 2000s.

Neoliberalism has, we would suggest, also contributed to the revitalisation of USMs in other contexts. We will consider some aspects of this in the case studies that follow, but here we would highlight resistance to welfare state dismantling, in particular the attack on state housing provision, the privatisation of public utilities and the closures of publicly provided amenities such as leisure centres, community facilities and the like, with swimming pool closures often a particular source of community mobilisation (see Mooney and Fyfe, 2006). Importantly, such protests have allowed campaigners to develop links that may have been either neglected or not possible in the past. Service user groups and trade unions have come together in many towns and cities to resist either the privatisation, or closures, of hospitals, schools and other public services and amenities (Mooney and Law, 2007). In turn, this has also enabled wider links to be made to protests and campaigns organised nationally, transnationally and globally in ways that often transcend what were frequently held up as some of the key limitations of 'traditional' forms of USM campaigning. 'Privatisation' and commercialisation of the public sector are key targets of global movement protestors, enabling direct links to be made between campaigners across different spaces.

While such an erosion of public services, that is, of collective consumption, undermines the basis of many USM protests, at least theoretically, in the context of neoliberalisation in recent times it has worked, albeit unevenly, to re-ignite protests around collective consumption and the provision of public goods and services. However, and this has been widely argued, in the context of privatisation, public sector and welfare state dismantling and rampant marketisation and commercialisation, the relationship between protestors and the local state/urban authorities is now often less clear cut. As Mayer (2006) argues, the activation and integration of 'civil society' 'stakeholders' into the fabric and institutional architecture of urban policy making has fundamentally altered political structures in the city. She continues:

> Local governments, whose political leverage and competence has diminished and who therefore have vanished as direct antagonists for the urban movements, now play the role of steering partnerships and furthering civic engagement: they are contracting with 'third sector' and community-based or faith-based organisations thus embedding parts of the local movement scene within 'activating' structures and spatially oriented programs....While the demands for participation that were on the agenda of the earlier movements are now realized in public-private partnerships, community boards and round tables.... (Mayer, 2006, p 205)

While Mayer perhaps over-stresses the erosion of the local state and of local government here, nonetheless she does point to a clear and pervasive development that has affected a number of social movement organisations in the recent past. However, as Mayer (2006, p 205) again recognises:

> New mobilizing impulses and new coalition building impetus have, however, been derived from the (re)localization of issues which anti-globalization movements have identified on other scales, putting 'old' social justice topics (unemployment, poverty, workfare, security, or surveillance) back on the agenda.

We would dispute that such social in/justice topics have ever been off the agenda. Indeed, to go further, the suggestion that 'old' issues had in some sense been addressed through state-sponsored collective consumption, that material needs had been met, neglects that for many who were involved in USMs in the UK and elsewhere, important that the gains of the past were, they never fully met the material needs or aspirations of working-class communities. However, many of those who have been involved in more recent campaigns against the privatisation and marketisation of key areas of public provision now find themselves defending the kinds of state-provided services that were once the target of protest (see LEWRG, 1980; Ferguson et al, 2002). As we will see, this results in new tensions and dilemmas.

Fighting for and defending state housing: from Glasgow 1915 to housing stock transfer, 1990s and 2000s

> There is evidence that the country is moving towards a wide acceptance of the principle that services provided by the people for themselves through the medium of central and local government, shall compare in standard with those provided by private enterprise. As it is with hospitals and clinics, so it should be with schools and houses. The council house should in the future provide the amenities, space and surroundings which hitherto have often been the monopoly of private building. (Grundy and Titmuss, *Report on Luton*, 1945, quoted in Kynaston, 2007, p 154)

Council housing did not always have the image and status of housing of last resort that for many it has now (see Hanley, 2007). We can see in the above report, co-authored by Richard Titmuss, that in the aftermath of the Second World War, there was a desire that council housing should at least match the quality of provision enjoyed in much of the private sector. In 1945, it was estimated that some five million new homes were required 'in quick time' (Timmins, 1995, p 141). Tackling 'squalor', the phrase used by Beveridge in his 1942 Report, referred primarily to rent levels and subsidies – and also to issues of town planning (see Timmins, 2001). However, addressing housing shortages, tackling the squalor of slum housing and severe overcrowding and improving the overall quality of housing stock were to become key goals of the post-1945 welfare state.

While state housing was to represent much less of a policy departure than other areas of the Beveridgean welfare state, such as healthcare (see Chapter Five), nonetheless, housing was for many the most acute need that had to be addressed by the 1945 Labour government. However, by 1945, state housing provision had already been accepted as a key principle and across the UK council estates were part of the landscape of most towns and cities – and in many rural areas too. From the Glasgow rent strike of 1915, leading to the 1919 Housing and Town Planning Act and further pieces of legislation introduced by minority Labour governments in 1924 and in 1929/30, subsidised housing for rent had become central to the development of state welfare provision.

Glasgow 1915 was but one episode, albeit perhaps one of the most important episodes of protest and agitation around housing provision in the UK. Throughout the 1920s and 1930s and into the post-Second World War era, housing remained a major political issue and source of urban protest movements of various kinds. Of course, the term 'housing struggles' encapsulates a rather broad range of campaigns, from single-issue protests, locally based and grassroots campaigns to nationally organised movements and protests. Throughout the history of state housing in the UK there have been numerous rent strikes, campaigns around housing shortages, squatters' and tenants' movements and campaigns against proposals to sell council homes to the private sector (see Bradley, nd, 1997; Burn, 1972; Piratin, 1978; Lowe, 1986; Johnson, 2000; Johnstone, 2000). In returning to the point we made above, that struggles around 'old' issues such as state housing continue to be a feature of the housing and political landscape today, we turn to a brief consideration of the campaigns against housing stock transfer under New Labour in the late 1990s and 2000s. These serve to highlight some of the contradictions that Castells outlined as local states attempt to reduce service provision in the context of financial crisis or of tax cuts for the wealthy.

On coming to power in 1997, the New Labour government inherited from the previous Conservative administration an approach to council housing that was essentially about transferring council housing out of the local authority sector and allowing rents to increase significantly. Houses were transferred either through the Right to Buy legislation introduced in 1979, which gave sitting tenants the right to purchase their council house at greatly reduced cost, or, increasingly during the 1980s and into the 1990s, through other transfer programmes, which saw complete estates removed from the local authority sector. This was to reach unprecedented levels with New Labour (see Robbins, 2002; DCH, 2003; Ginsburg, 2005; Mooney and Poole, 2005; Watt, 2008).

Housing stock transfer (HST), as it has become known, involves the removal of council housing from council control and its transfer to a diverse range of alternative 'social landlords', from local housing associations to quasi-private landlords and quangos. In some cities, one of the most notable being Glasgow, this involved the transfer of the entire stock to a new landlord, Glasgow Housing Agency (see Daly et al, 2005). The programme of housing stock transfer has renewed tenants' struggles across the UK. While recognising that this is uneven geographically, and the campaigns are arguably more fragmented than in the past, nonetheless, that there has been, *is*, such a campaign to prevent HST reminds us that the kinds of issues that have been associated with old USMs, continue to be part of urban struggles today. For opponents of HST, transfer amounts to little more than the wholesale privatisation of an important public asset – and to an erosion of a public service that meets the housing needs of millions of people across the UK. It is important to acknowledge that while the campaign to prevent transfer has seen some notable successes (Birmingham and Edinburgh being two of the most significant), elsewhere (in Glasgow and Liverpool for instance) it has not prevented transfer.

The Defend Council Housing (DCH) campaign is a UK-wide campaign to resist council house transfers but which also argues for direct investment in council housing as a way of renewing the stock (after decades of neglect). DCH has the characteristics of a single-issue campaign – to prevent transfer. Drawing on existing tenants' organisations and UK-wide tenants' movements, it has also gathered support from left-wing groups and parties, community activists, public sector trade unions, as well MPs and councillors opposed to transfer proposals. DCH is both a resource and also a national campaign, which has been able to generate some considerable support from tenants not previously involved in campaigning. Estate-based campaigns and meetings are supplemented by national rallies and through the use of the internet campaigners are able to learn from successes and defeats, and share experiences and tactics. Other tenants' organisations have remained independent and while many have opposed transfer, in a number of cases, repeating developments from the 1970s and 1980s, attempts have been made to incorporate some leading tenant and community activists into the new forms of housing governance that have developed on the back of transfer.

It is important not to make claims for the campaigns to defend council housing that do not survive close attention. That there has been a campaign is significant. And while this campaign has been primarily defensive, that is, fighting to maintain a publicly provided and democratically accountable service, campaigners have also sought to resist the demonisation and stigmatisation of council tenants (as 'welfare dependents') as well as the ongoing residualisation of the council housing sector (see Johnstone and Mooney, 2007; Watt, 2008). However, and to return to an earlier point, many campaigners have found themselves in a position of having to defend the very state housing that they had protested and struggled over in past decades. There is a tension here between defending state provision yet at the same time seeking to look beyond such provision (at least in the way that has existed in the past) to imagine a new form of publicly provided housing that meets the aspirations of successive generations of tenants' movements attaining the kind of quality provision highlighted by Grundy and Titmuss above. That the DCH campaign has been successful in resisting some transfers there is no doubt. However, arguably it has been much less successful in generating a vision of a new kind of state housing that does not appear simply as a return to the past.

There have been other significant developments with the DCH and related campaigns to protect public housing provision – campaigners have been able to draw immediate and direct links with the privatisation of council housing and other types of privatisation, highlighting the role of banks and other private financiers in privatisation in general, raising issues about local democracy and 'real' community participation from below – as opposed to top-down imposed community involvement as advocated by new housing landlords and agencies – and also through this relate to the kinds of global campaigns against commercialisation and privatisation.

Fighting for the city: a right to the city

Let us return to an issue that we considered above in relation to Castells – that USMs are transformative, that is, they enable the generation and mobilisation of new ways of thinking and acting, producing new imaginaries in the process. Arguably, such imaginings are vital to the protests of many of the USMs involved in campaigns today. In particular, the meaning of the city and the question of right to the city have become central to the diverse resistances to the neoliberal-driven restructuring and reimagining of urban space. In this respect, we can talk of the privatisation of the city: reflected in gentrified neighbourhoods and elite enclaves, 'safe' and heavily policed retail and leisure areas for the affluent consumer, which confine particular spaces to the 'desirable', while regulating city spaces in ways that seek to exclude the 'undesirable'.

This brings us back to the central issue raised by Castells of the meaning of the city and of making claims to the city. In the context of urban entrepreneurialism, urban politics has been transformed in many respects. Place-marketing and urban re-imaging is accompanied by inter-urban competition, the pursuit of 'flagship' events and attracting inward investment and the entrepreneurial classes (see *Local Economy*, 2004; Law and Mooney, 2005). The city of the new is contrasted with the old city, the city of decline, dependency and disorganisation. Creative classes versus dependent classes! In this regard, urban 'boosterism', urban entrepreneurialism and city re-imaging can be understood as regressive movements, seeking to marginalise welfare and collectivised consumption as key aspects of urban life (in many Western countries at least). In important respects, they aim to order the city in ways that are conducive to capital accumulation and which support and help to reproduce the activities and lifestyles of the already privileged. They seek to combat alternative perspectives around the city, which are dismissed as outmoded and/or redundant. They advocate visions of the modern city as a knowledge centre and information hub, which is connected with similar cities elsewhere. The overarching objective of such movements, which bring together city elites, business, transnational corporations and not a few academics and 'advisors' (see Allan, 2008), is a city in which control is wrenched from democratically accountable bodies, where urban 'regeneration' and 'renewal' come to be regeneration from above in the interests of capital. Thus, in ways that are different from the social movements we have discussed in this chapter, they also make demands on the state to act in particular ways, securing the city as a site of privatised forms of production and consumption.

In Glasgow, European Capital of Culture in 1990, and Liverpool, European Capital of Culture in 2008, where particular city stories and images are valorised and others marginalised, and in numerous other towns and cities across the UK and elsewhere, the question of whose city it is has been repeatedly raised by protestors. Against the marginalisations, exclusions and disenfranchisements that we have flagged here, the issue of what French philosopher Henri Lefebvre in 1968 called 'the right to the city', for all city dwellers, is immediately brought into sharp focus (Lefebvre, 1968/1996; see also Harvey, 2003a). The re-division of urban spaces, the privatisation of urban space and the marginalisation of 'problem places' and 'problem populations' is not uncontested (see Leontidou, 2006; Mooney, 2008). The importance of 'discursive resistance' in the face of exclusions, stereotyping and stigmatising should not be underestimated – it is part of the struggle for the city. Cities today, as in the past, represent contested terrains in which some of the most significant protests and resistances are taking place today. Urban activism continues to be a key element of global struggles against neoliberalism – in ways that draw on the protests of the past but which also seek to develop new forms of resistance.

Once more on the importance of the city today: 'race', migration and asylum

We have argued throughout this chapter that cities remain vitally important for our understanding not just of USMs but also of social movements in general today. We have highlighted that protests in the city are entangled and interrelated in many diverse and complex ways with 'wider' social movement struggles and protests. Struggles to defend green spaces in the city and the diminution of urban communities in the face of urban motorway construction and large retail and commercial developments have been revitalised in recent years. Urban movements continue to emerge and they continue to protest and this has also led to new fusions between 'local' urban and transnational protests against the privatisations, marketisations and commercialisations associated with neoliberal political agendas.

One of the clearest examples of such fusions is in the protests that have emerged in many towns and cities in the UK to defend asylum seekers and refugees over the past decade. Government policies have seen asylum seekers dispersed to some of the more run-down areas of urban Britain;

sometimes this has resulted in tensions with existing residents, racist attacks and murders. It has also and more frequently given rise to new alliances and organisations and to new forms of solidarity. These have developed in response to the brutally harsh conditions that many asylum seekers and refugees find themselves in, and in response to the frequent raids and detention of asylum-seeker families by Home Office officials and the police on the way to forced deportation (see Mynott, 2002; Sales, 2002; National Coalition of Anti-Deportation Campaigns at www.ncadc.org. uk; see also Chapter Nine).

These protest movements are important in drawing our attention to more of the different ways in which 'globalisation', wars and global and transnational policy developments are giving rise to new patterns of migration and in turn which are encouraging the development of new protest organisations. While in the context of the UK there is a long tradition of protest around deportations, recent government policy and practice has served to push this to new levels. There are numerous campaign groups across the UK today who are mobilising around the defence of refugees.

There are, for us, two particularly significant aspects of this that we wish to flag here. First, campaigns to defend refugees once again bridge 'old' and 'new' movements in that they integrate concerns with material needs, housing, health, education and so on with issues of recognition, voice and identity in ways that render the distinction between old and new highly ambiguous and problematic. Mobilisations around the failures of collective consumption come to be universalised to issues of racism, neoliberal globalisation, war and oppression but also to questions of social justice and solidarity. This draws our immediate attention to the global and transnational dimensions of social movements.

The second important aspect of this for us is that it draws attention to one of the most neglected aspects of social movement study – including the analysis of USMs – the role of 'race' and ethnicity in urban protest movements. Social movements around 'race' have often been overlooked (see Gilroy, 1987) yet some of the most notable forms of urban protest have mobilised around issues of racism and oppression. Throughout the 1970s and 1980s, demonstrations against police harassment were a regular feature of urban protests (Widgery, 1986) while in the 1980s and 1990s, 'rebellions' or 'insurrections' against harsh and racist policing and racism in general broke out in Birmingham, Bristol, Leeds, Liverpool, London and Manchester (see Kettle and Hodges, 1982; Benyon and Solomos, 1987) and which have continued into the early 2000s in other towns and cities in England. The continuing protests around the forced deportations of refugees and asylum seekers and other mobilisations around racism will hopefully lead to more study and analysis of the role of 'race' in social movements and in particular to the ways in which such protests interconnect with other ongoing resistances of the kinds we have charted in this chapter and elsewhere in this book.

Conclusion

Against claims that in the context of the rise of global social movements, USMs will decline and become less significant, in many respects the opposite has occurred. There has been a revitalisation and re-energising of protest in the city – and while there are many diverse targets, as we have seen these come together in some cases as protesters seeks to universalise their campaigns, drawing links with other mobilisations. And protests and campaigns continue to emerge around 'traditional' collective consumption issues. However, it would be mistaken to assume or to imply that USMs have not changed. The welfare state has undergone significant transformation in the UK and elsewhere. USMs in the pre- and post-1945 epoch were instrumental in demanding more and better-quality collectivised state provision, while criticising the paternalism, invasiveness, exclusions, marginalisations and failures to meet needs that accompanied this. But such material issues, issues of social justice, have hardly disappeared in the context of state withdrawal and the increasing role of the private and profit-making sectors in 'heartland' social welfare provision. Collective consumption and the social reproduction of labour continue to be central issues around which protests are generated and reproduced in the contemporary city.

New forms of organisation and new protests have emerged – there is a growing awareness of the interconnectedness of protests – locally, nationally and transnationally – even if this is not always and everywhere reflected in formal organisation. Against the view that today USMs might appear somewhat parochial, USMs are drawing from the experiences of protestors in the global justice movement and from campaigns across many global cities to develop their own campaigns. As Leontidou (2006, p 265) among others points out, 'transnational and local movements merge, overlap and coincide in the city. The new urban social movements are simultaneously global and local movements'. These movements have, as we have highlighted in this chapter, sought to challenge the dominant meanings of the city that are being advanced by neoliberalising movements. In this regard they are not 'solely' reactive but seek to construct alternative visions of the city and of social solidarity and organisation. In this transformative role, USMs encompass demands for material needs to be met, for social justice rights, greater participation and democratisation and – against misrecognition and othering – demand voice and social recognition.

This brings us back to the debates around social movement theorising that were introduced in Chapter Three, especially the different approaches offered by American and European perspectives. As we noted in this chapter, USMs can and have been interpreted as older forms of social movement, in the terminology deployed by European new social movements theory. However, we have sought to highlight the dynamic nature of USM protest, the changing organisational approaches and forms of struggle that have been adopted. Many of the issues around which USMs mobilise have been 'around' for some considerable time – and they promise to remain so for the foreseeable future. But such mobilisations invoke a wide assortment of responses, which means that labelling USMs as an 'old' form of social movement is less than helpful, especially given the struggles that characterise many contemporary global cities. As for American resource mobilisation theory, while its focus on single-use campaigns may make it seem more pertinent for our understanding of USMs, its focus on 'mainstream' forms of protest and politics leave it unable to capture the radical and transformative aspects of many USMs both today and historically. In this respect, there are close parallels between the demands of USMs and the goals of social movements organising around many of the other key issues that are discussed throughout this book.

Further reading

The city and USMs were important elements of the discussions that took place at the 2006 World Social Forum in Bamako, Caracas and Karachi. From this a *World Charter on the Right to the City* was developed, which builds on the writings of Lefebvre discussed in this chapter (see www.forumsocialmundial.org).

The activities of many USMs and the day-to-day protests that characterise contemporary cities are frequently given voice in the alternative media and protest publishing, which has developed a new momentum of its own in recent years. Among the many publications that have emerged, we highlight three as indicative of this development:

Mute   www.metamute.org
Nerve   www.catalystmedia.org.uk
Variant   www.variant.randomstate.org

Useful websites

City Strolls: *www.citystrolls.com*

Defend Council Housing campaign: *www.defendcouncilhousing.org.uk*

IndyMedia: *www.indymedia.org.uk*

National Coalition of Anti-Deportation Campaigns: *www.ncadc.org.uk/*

seven

Fighting ignorance: social movements and the making of modern education

Introduction

Conflicts around education policy have a long history that dates back to the 19th century when the struggle for free universal educational provision became synonymous with social movement struggles for civil rights in the form of freedom of association, assembly and speech, and for political rights in the form of extensions to the franchise. In the early 20th century, these struggles were enjoined by the newly visible labour movement's mobilisation for social rights and social welfare (Marshall and Bottomore, 1992). When taken together and considered from the perspective of education, these social movement demands for rights can be conceptualised as mobilisations for 'the conditions of education' – something that finally achieved qualified success in the creation of the Beveridgean welfare state during the years 1944-48. The pivotal 1944 Education Act (often referred to as the Butler Act after the Conservative Education Minister R.A. Butler who sponsored it through Parliament) tackled 'ignorance' and was the first of Beveridge's 'five giants' to be reformed (Timmins, 1995).

The Butler Act set out the framework for the modern British education system and subsequent years are marked by further social movement campaigns and struggles concerning its development and reform. These conflicts were initially taken forward largely by the labour movement (and in particular teaching trade unions), which in the 1950s and 1960s sought the introduction of comprehensive schooling as a way of tackling the reproduction of social hierarchy – and then from the late 1960s onwards by the 'new' social movements – the students' movement, which focused on issues pertaining to higher education provision; and in particular the women's movement and other identity rights mobilisations, which have sought an end to educational discrimination and campaigned for equality of provision. More recently again, during the era of neoliberal hegemony (in the period stretching from the Thatcher to Brown governments), there have been numerous local community campaigns to defend schools from closure, and wide-ranging national campaigns and protests against the educational reforms of successive governments, which have introduced competition and marketisation and removed democratic control and accountability under the guise of 'freedom' and 'diversity'.

This chapter will trace the interlinked impact of social movements and educational protest movements on the historical development of the British education system. The focus here is for the most part limited to schooling – a consideration of conflicts around higher education is more than the space for this chapter would allow (see, for example, Crick and Robson, 1970; Harman, 1998). The chapter will begin with a discussion of the pre-Beveridge and Butler era when the struggle for the conditions of education was most acute; it will then move on to consider the making and impact of the modernising Butler Act, before concluding with a brief survey of the key contests of the post-Butler era when movement mobilisations around what might constitute an 'educative society' moved centre stage. A short case study of the first- and second-wave women's movement will illustrate how social movement theory can be used to illuminate the historical dynamics of conflicts around educational reform. It will be argued throughout that education policy outcomes are determined by the shifting contours of the strengths and weaknesses of the class interests, organisational forces and activist networks that are involved in the social movement/state interface.

Before Beveridge and Butler: the struggle for the conditions of education

Throughout the 19th century, radical social reformers campaigned for state provision of universal compulsory schooling. These campaigns were often bound up in a wider coalition of interests with progressive demands regarding extensions of the franchise, the emancipation of women, religious equality and the improvements in working-class living, working and housing conditions. Viewed through the educational lens, these wider demands can be understood as social movement demands for 'the conditions of education' (Simon, 1974). Organisations like the Society for Useful

Knowledge, the British and Foreign Schools Society and the National Society were established in the early years of the 19th century to advance a progressive 'middle-class' educational agenda, which aimed at 'enlightened' social and economic modernisation. Prominent utilitarian liberals like Jeremy Bentham, James Mill and John Stuart Mill argued inside and outside of Parliament that the extension of education to all classes should be central to the development of a modern meritocratic social order and a democratic political system. This could not happen while the ruling class was reproduced through a handful of exclusive fee-paying public schools and elite universities and the other classes at best had access to fragmented, voluntary (usually Church-run) and underfunded alternatives.

Ambitious experiments in the provision of free schooling for the working class were conducted at the Guest family's Dowlais iron works in Wales and by Robert Owen at New Lanark in the lower Clyde valley in Scotland during the 1820s and 1830s. Working-class activists such as Richard Carlile, Thomas Hodgskin, William Lovett and William Thompson argued for working-class education for both children and adults as a means of challenging exploitation and oppression – unlike their middle-class counterparts they were often put in prison for public expressions of their views (McCoy, 1998). Unofficial forms of self-education were (by necessity) widespread among the working class for both adults and children through the use of private teachers, reading groups, libraries and the more political corresponding societies. Socialist followers of Owen in the 1830s and 1840s provided an extensive education programme where women could participate as equals, and were among the pioneers for feminism before the mobilisation of the organised women's movement from the 1860s onwards (Purvis, 2005). After the setback of the 1832 Reform Act (which failed to extend the franchise beyond the propertied classes), working-class power matured through the rise of Chartism in the 1840s and the growth of trade unionism. Arguments for the extension of voting rights and the extension of state educational provision to the working class became synonymous. When the Reform Act of 1867 finally extended the franchise (after a period of bitter working-class agitation led by The Reform League that culminated in a government ban defying mass demonstrations and riots involving upwards of 80,000 people in Hyde Park), it 'brought approximately a million artisans on to the voting registers, and in terms of the Benthamite creed, made universal education a political necessity' (Simon, 1974, p 12).

The process of 'parliamentarisation' or 'democratisation' changes the form and content of social movement mobilisations. As political process models indicate (see Chapter Three), repertoires often become circumscribed to operate within a legal-rational framework, claims made often become narrowed to focus on what can realistically be attained by reform, while social movements themselves usually proliferate because a new more favourable vehicle for the realisation of claims made on the state has been created. Within social movements there may also be splits and schisms as factions and coalitions form to take different positions on how to operate within (or indeed outside) the new constitutional framework. Tilly (2004, p 53) summaries the political effects as:

- Reducing the political importance of long-established chains of patronage for the conduct of national politics.
- Creating significant new opportunities for political entrepreneurs who could produce temporary links between state officials and multiple groups of aggrieved, connected citizens.
- Accentuating government ability to speak on behalf of a unified, connected people.
- Setting out an institutional framework for regular semi-public sittings of representative bodies that in turn become geographic and temporal sites for claim making.

In Britain, democratisation created the conditions for the emergence of key labour movement organisations such as the Trades Union Congress (TUC) (formed in 1868), and mass reformist political parties to represent the interests of organised labour (the Independent Labour Party in 1893, the Labour Party in 1906). This enabled further claims to be made on the state for extensions of civil and political rights and a new impetus for claims associated with welfare issues and social rights (Marshall, 1950). The National Union of Teachers (NUT) was formed early in this history in 1870, and it played a key role in using the new political framework to advance the broad agenda of progressive educational interests. This involved strategic engagement with the ever-shifting coalition of interests between the labour movement, radical liberals and religious dissenters against the established churches and conservative political establishment.

The 1870 Education Act for the first time set out the framework for the development of a system of compulsory elementary schooling for all children between the ages of five and 12. Where existing provision (usually church-run 'voluntary' schools) was unable to fulfil demand, School Boards would be elected by local ratepayers to set up Elementary Schools to make up the shortfall. School Boards were able to apply for capital funding in the form of a government loan and would receive small annual grants based on the results of an inspection regime and parental fees (Boards would pay for the fees of the poorest pupils). The Act was contentious from a number of different perspectives: the churches (and in particular the Church of

England) opposed it because it removed their near monopoly over the control of education; many conservatives opposed it because aside from the danger of educationally empowering the 'dangerous classes', 'education was viewed as a private matter rather than a public issue in which the state had a right to intervene' – compulsion in particular was viewed as an infringement of individual liberty and parental choice, while even the Liberal MP William Foster who drafted the Act, emphasised that parental responsibility should be encouraged by retaining school fees (McCoy, 1998, p 114). The Act was passed because a new political opportunity structure (Tarrow, 1994) had been opened up by the conjunction of the new political rights granted by the 1867 Reform Act and the recognition among important sections of the ruling class that educational reform was necessary in terms of economic modernisation – a labour workforce educated in basic numeracy and literacy was required if Britain was to remain competitive with its imperial rivals (Salter and Tapper, 1981). From the perspective of the working-class movement, the Act should be viewed as at least a partial victory because 'while the full demands of the most advanced working class bodies were not won in 1870, elected School Boards were established on which it became possible to gain representation and these gave scope for further advances' (Simon, 1974, p 12).

Reaction and retrenchment: the 1902 Education Act

During the next three decades, working-class aims vis-à-vis education increasingly came to be formulated in a more or less explicitly socialist form, articulated by the trade unions, political parties of labour and campaigning pressure groups such as the Fabian Society – in other words, socialism came to operate as the master frame through which educational demands were formulated (see Snow et al, 1986; Chapter Three). The socialist movement provided a powerful vehicle for different strands of the struggle for 'the conditions of education' to coalesce around and to ferment dialogue and debate on what might constitute a future 'educative society' (Simon, 1974). The widespread election of radical liberals and socialists to School Boards, the success of the Elementary Schools in recruiting numbers (75% of working-class children aged 12-13 were on their registers in 1893-94) and their increasing tendency to provide places beyond the age of 12 (almost 200,000 children aged 13-14 in 1894-95) (Simon, 1974, p 177), meant that a conservative backlash was almost inevitable.

In 1902, an Education Act (sometimes referred to as the Balfour Education Act after A.J. Balfour who sponsored it through Parliament) was passed by the Conservative government against the implacable opposition of the NUT, the wider labour movement, liberals and religious non-conformists. The 1902 Education Act replaced the School Boards with local education authorities (LEAs) through which the Catholic and Anglican establishments could reassert control over both school infrastructure and curriculum. The new LEAs would also control the expansion of fee-paying secondary education whereby pupils could transfer at the age of 11 if they were successful in a competitive examination. For religious dissenters this was deemed 'Rome on the rates' and a campaign of non-payment led by the radical Baptist preacher Dr John Clifford and the national passive resistance movement followed in the wake of the Act. Resistance in the North of England was so strong that Clifford stood and actually won as a parliamentary candidate for the Liberal Party in a Leeds by-election for a safe Tory seat in July 1902. In the autumn of 1902, mass demonstrations in Leeds of between 70,000 and 100,000 people were addressed by sixteen MPs speaking from six different platforms. Campaigns of organised opposition to the 1902 Act led by religious non-conformists and labour movement activists continued sporadically for the next decade and are widely credited with facilitating the election of the reforming Liberal government of 1906 (see Simon, 1974).

British education in the early 20th century: class division, differentiation and government stasis

Hobsbawm (1990, p 169), writing from the perspective of the labour movement, is scathing about the reactionary nature of the 1902 Act and the general backwardness of British education in the early years of the 20th century:

> Unfortunately, the public school formed the model of the new system of secondary education, which the less privileged sectors of the new middle class were allowed to construct for themselves after the Education Act of 1902, and whose main object was to exclude from higher education the children of the working class.... Knowledge, especially scientific knowledge, therefore took second place in the new British Education system, to the maintenance of a rigid division between the classes.... The British therefore entered the twentieth century ... as a spectacularly ill-educated people.

Aside from the Liberal government, which introduced limited free secondary schooling (a requirement for 25% free places) in 1907 based on the 1902 Act, the only other significant pieces of legislation regarding education in the decades before the Second World War were the 1918

Education Act, which made schooling across the UK compulsory up to the age of 14 and abolished Elementary School fees, the 1918 Education Act (Scotland), which facilitated the development of separate state-funded Catholic schools and the 1936 Education Act, which raised the school-leaving age to 15 but with major exceptions (for example in rural areas where young farm labourers where required). The years prior to the First World War and the inter-war years thereafter were a period of relative government stasis regarding education policy making because although dissatisfaction with educational provision remained widespread, little was actually done to address the issues of class division, sex discrimination, religion, infrastructure and curriculum, which exercised continuous debate and campaigning among labour movement activists and progressive teachers (Barber, 1994).

Education for the majority of working-class school pupils and students was of the three R's variety (reading, writing and arithmetic) taught by rote in highly structured disciplined environments that strongly resembled the type of work environments that they would enter on leaving education. Middle-class parents of course had more choice as to where to educate their children – the expensive fee-paying public schools continued to attract the most wealthy; grammar schools catered for the professional new middle classes; and for a minority there were the benefits of the experimental schools associated with progressive educationalists like J.H. Badley, A.S. Neil and Cecil Reddie. These pioneers of humanist experiential education were part of a wider international 'new education movement' (which built on the work of the 19th-century German educational philosopher Freidrich Froebel and included, for example, John Dewey and Maria Montessori), which aimed to put the child at the centre, and unusually for the period aimed to provide equal educational opportunity for the fulfilment of aspirations regardless of sex (see Hilton and Hirsch, 2000).

The educational issue that perhaps aroused the greatest controversy in the inter-war years was that of school differentiation – that is, different schools for different 'types' of pupil. Before the Second World War, eugenics was a popular form of explanation for class, 'race' and sex differences – in the 1920s and 1930s it was given a fresh coat of pseudo-scientific paint with the development of psychometric testing and new schools of educational psychology, which claimed to be able to categorise different 'types of mind', which had different potentials for development. This dovetailed neatly with the form of conservative ideology that was prevalent among the ruling elites and even influenced thinking among some socialists who supported the notion of 'separate but equal schooling'. The government commissioned Spens (Consultative Committee on Secondary Education, 1938) and Norwood (Committee of the Secondary School Examinations

Council, 1943) to write reports into the future of education, both of which advocated the creation of a three-tiered educational system (the eventual structure adopted by Butler), and can be seen as a high point in the influence of psychology on state educational policy (Lowe, 1988, p 6).

In 1923, the Assistant Masters Association (male grammar school teachers) became the first teacher organisation to oppose differentiation and to make a clear policy of supporting the comprehensive idea of free secondary education for all in one type of school (multilateralism). As the motion mover at their annual conference argued:

> [I]f secondary schools of different types were set up it would mean that there would be in secondary schools of the present type (ie, grammar schools) a class which was bound to be looked upon as something socially superior to the children who would attend the new schools of the distinct types. (Simon, 1997, p 14)

Thereafter, support for a comprehensive framework came from the TUC, other teacher organisations such as the NUT and the wider labour movement. The Labour Party remained split on the issue so that although it had adopted multilateralism 'in principle' in 1939, its education committee fell into line with the 'scientific' argument for differentiation that had prevailed in the formulation of the National Government's Board of Education's reconstruction policy during the war years (Lowe, 1988).

Beveridge and Butler: the conditions for education achieved?

During the years of the Second World War, a 'major public movement' emerged to make claims on government for progressive educational reform (Barber, 1994). At its heart was the Campaign for Educational Advance, which was formed in 1942 and consisted of the TUC, the NUT, the Workers Educational Association and the Co-operative Union. Chaired by the leading socialist educationalist R.H. Tawney, this organisation held over 200 well-attended meetings across the UK in its first year and published numerous articles and pamphlets in support of a left-wing reformist agenda that included free comprehensive schooling, raising the school leaving age to 16, removal of all church control and even the abolishment of the fee-paying public schools. The broad sweep of demands made by this protest movement were far too radical for the political establishment and the Education Minister Butler to accept – however, had it not mobilised, it is unlikely that the Butler Act would have made even the modest concessions to a progressive educational agenda, which it eventually did give. As Barber (1994, p 11) argues, the educational protest movement

> helped him [Butler] to convince his colleagues of the need to act, and it provided ammunition ... in making the case for Treasury support. Above all, it gave him the strength to knock the heads together of those in the churches who tended to put self-interest before national interest in educational advance.

The churches, of course, mobilised to defend their interests. As Timmins (1995, p 66) notes, just two days after his appointment as Education Minister in 1941, Butler met the Archbishop of Canterbury and then just three weeks later met deputations from the Free Church and the Church of England. The public schools mounted a similar rearguard action through the Conservative Party, the House of Lords, the churches again and eventually through the Fleming Committee Report (Board of Education, 1944), which Butler had commissioned to investigate the issue – published in 1944, this report advocated a limited 'assisted places scheme' whereby public schools could offer up to 25% of places funded by LEAs. Adopted by Butler as a compromise, the scheme soon foundered as public schools chose not to open up these opportunities in the post-war period (Timmins, 1995, p 86). Claims from very different political directions were being made on the state and the 1944 Education Act, which proceeds from those claims, represents a compromise that in the end satisfied neither side. Despite its compromise nature the Act is nevertheless pivotal in the establishment of the modern British education system and in the formation of the wider welfare state.

The White Paper that preceded the 1944 Butler Act framed its aims in meritocratic terms: 'the nature of a child's education should be determined by his capacity and promise and not by the financial circumstances of his parent' (*Educational Reconstruction*, 1943, cited in Halsey et al, 1980, p 27). The 1944 Act established for the first time a unified framework of free universal compulsory schooling for children and young people from the age of five to 15. Unlike the centralised education systems of other European nations (Moore, 2004), in England the central state would continue to devolve responsibility for delivery to the LEAs (although unlike the pre-war years the churches would only remain in control of schools to which they contributed 50% of building costs), while in Scotland, Wales and Northern Ireland the Act was interpreted to apply to different regional contexts (Phillips, 2003). Local authorities were charged with providing pupils with

> such a variety of instruction and training as may be desirable in view of their ages, their abilities and aptitudes, and of different periods which they may be expected to remain at school including practical instruction and training appropriate to their respective needs. (1944 Education Act, cited in McKenzie, 2001, p 176)

This strong emphasis on 'variety', 'ability', 'aptitude' and 'appropriateness' meant that selection was built into the fabric of the schooling system where different types of school would cater for 'different types' of pupil. The tripartite schooling system as it came to be known was made up of grammar schools, which aimed to cater for pupils who were deemed academically able; secondary moderns, which aimed to cater for pupils of a more general level of ability; and technical schools, which aimed to cater for pupils with practical abilities. Selection was to take place at the age of 11+ through the use of intelligence tests, school records and parental aspirations. Although allocated to different schools with different purposes, an ideal of 'parity of esteem' was supposed to hold the notion of educational hierarchy in check. In practice, however, the demand for grammar school entry far outstripped supply (something that varied significantly between LEAs and was determined largely by historical accident), and a competitive 11+ examination had to be introduced to ration places – those who 'failed' this test usually had to attend a secondary modern (very few technical schools were ever opened), which was widely perceived as providing an inferior form of education for pupils of inferior ability whose aspirations should be confined to low-status manual occupations (Halsey et al, 1980).

In essence, the Act provided pupils 'an equal opportunity to compete for the best education for which they could be selected' (Warnock, 1997; McKenzie, 2001, p 177), but even then this 'equal opportunity' was limited because it left the fee-paying public schools, church schools and the independent sector largely unreformed, thus contradicting the meritocratic theory that was supposed to underpin its practice (Halsey et al, 1980). While these were key shortcomings, the Act did deliver a range of educational support services that extended the boundaries of educational welfare, including school transport, free milk, medical and dental treatment and the provision of free school meals for all who needed them. It also extended the notion of education to incorporate the wider community's needs for cultural and recreational amenities – hence, local authorities were enabled to provide nursery schools, adult classes, play schemes, swimming baths, community centres and other education-related activities (McKenzie, 2001).

The Second World War provided an opening in the political opportunity structure for a network of interlinked progressive social movements around education, health, employment and housing to make radical claims on the state for new social welfare rights. Socialist ideas of equity and social justice provided the ideological master frame that bound these movements together in a community of interests so that although there were often internal differences regarding strategy and tactics, a more or less coherent reform programme could be framed and then advocated. Although the Butler Act was full of shortcomings and compromises, when taken together with Beveridge's welfare reform package and its wider service provision, it did represent a fundamental shift towards 'the conditions for education'. Hence, although the educational reform protest movement did not achieve its most radical aims, it did achieve key demands for universal free secondary schooling, the reinstatement of local authority control and the raising of the school leaving age to 15. Like the Education Act of 1870, it created an enabling framework for further advance. On the other hand, the ruling establishment managed to protect the reproductive core of the class structure with fee-paying public schools left largely unscathed by Butler – this was as Timmins (1995, p 86) notes 'a great lost opportunity' because the early 1940s was perhaps the only period during the 20th century when 'the political will and the political votes to integrate them to the national education system just might have been assembled'. Moreover, the tripartite education system that now formed the basis of education for the majority would also serve to reinforce competition and reproduce social distinction. The Butler Act represented a compromise between opposing class interests organised into movements during the Second World War from above and below to make competing claims on the state. Compromises rarely please anyone for a long period of time and the social rights achieved in relation to education merely served to fuel the desire for further reform – in the post-war period the labour movement would seek to extend, and the new movements to redefine, these rights far beyond the boundaries of Butler.

Post-Butler: the social movements and the struggle for an 'educative society'

> Education is the most political of subjects, for it is firmly about the future. It defines the sort of society people want to see. At one extreme, for those who believe that the next generation should be more equal than the present one, the demand is for equal access to equally good education for all.... At the other is a belief that there will always be inequalities and that it is

> better to organise for that reality, selecting out the high fliers
> to ensure that they do fly high and are thus able to support the
> mass for whom it might be safer all round if expectations were
> not too greatly raised. (Timmins, 1995, p 65)

The conservative philosophy pointed to in the latter half of Timmins'
summary had been the overarching frame for the British establishment in
the 19th and early 20th centuries, and the Butler Act with its emphasis on
the 'scientific' differentiation of schooling was simply a modern twist on an
old elitist idea. However, in the post-war period, a combination of a shift
in public social aspirations (itself stimulated by the meritocratic promises
of the post-war settlement), the recognition that access to educational
credentials was required for the fulfilment of social mobility and the need
to facilitate technological modernisation of the economy, meant that
pressure for a shift towards the last of these perspectives as embodied in
comprehensive education was building. As Dale (1989, pp 99-100) says,
'the post-war settlement created an enormous burden of legitimation; by
pledging itself to achieve so much, by accepting responsibility for so much,
the State gave itself the problem of delivering what it had promised'. This
legitimation crisis became systemic by the 1960s and was to lead to the
breakdown of the post-war settlement in subsequent decades. The 'new'
social movements, as Habermas (1981) and Offe (1984) argue, embody
a reaction to this structural crisis that occurred in different ways across
the advanced liberal democracies and which remains as yet ongoing and
unresolved (Habermas, 1976; see also Chapter Three).

In Britain, the tripartite education system contributed strongly to
the crisis of political legitimation because it clearly could not deliver
the equal opportunities for attainment that Butler had promised and
that were increasingly being demanded by the public. In particular, the
11+ examination, which lay at its heart, was increasingly questioned by
parents, teachers and social scientists as a reliable indicator of ability – for
example, the Robbins Report (Committee on Higher Education, 1963)
attacked the deterministic notions of intelligence that underpinned it. The
Labour Party officially adopted comprehensive schooling as a key strand
of its education policy in 1953 and during the 1950s and early 1960s it
worked in a loose coalition of progressive interests with the wider labour
movement, liberals, teachers organisations and local authorities to forge
a new educational consensus around equal opportunities and education
for the new technologically driven economy that was coming into being
(Tomlinson, 2005). When Labour was finally returned to power in 1964,
the 'new consensus' was finally able to be put into practice and, in 1965, the
Education Minister Tony Crosland issued Circular 10/65 (*The Organisation*

of Secondary Education), which required local authorities to introduce a system of comprehensive schools.

Although the Conservative government of 1970-74 (with Margaret Thatcher as Education Minister) removed the mandatory requirement for LEAs to go comprehensive, during the next two decades comprehensive expansion was rapid, with Wales and Scotland reaching almost 100% comprehensive schooling by the mid-1980s and England reaching 94% (Simon, 1997). The remaining 6% in England was made up largely of grammar schools, which, as Phillips (2003, p 5) argues, 'was particularly significant for creating a symbolic and visible alternative to comprehensive schools in the 1980s and 1990s'. The Labour government of the 1960s also oversaw a major economically driven expansion of the university sector (a process continued under Thatcher and Major in the late 1980s and early 1990s), and the establishment of the Open University, which opened up educational opportunities for adults that they otherwise would not have had.

Comprehensivisation meant that although class, ethnicity and gender differences continued to mediate attainment levels, young people were being educated in a largely egalitarian framework that would have been unthinkable to previous generations (Sked and Cook, 1988). Large sections of the Conservative Party and the British ruling class have never fully accepted that this type of education should prevail and remain wedded to the selective philosophy described earlier. In the 1950s and 1960s, vociferous anti-comprehensive sentiments were constantly articulated in the right-wing press and through Conservative-sponsored campaigns to 'save our grammar schools' – these campaigns intensified through the economic and political crisis years of the 1970s and 1980s when 'progressive education' became bound up with 1960s 'radicalism' and 1970s moral 'permissiveness' to be blamed for the assortment of ills in wider society. Attacks on notions of levelling down, a progressive curriculum, 'political correctness' and 'trendy lefty' teachers became part and parcel of the process of the 'demonisation of education' (Tomlinson, 2005, p 22).

This negative framing process prepared the cultural ground for the neoliberal education reforms of the Thatcher, Major and Blair governments, which have done much to undermine and reverse the egalitarian gains brought about by comprehensivisation. Since the 1988 Education Act, which set the elites' educational backlash in motion, a national curriculum for England has been introduced; LEAs' powers have been significantly reduced; parental choice over where to send children has been significantly enhanced (a change largely favouring the middle classes); comprehensive schools have been given the opportunity to 'opt out' of local authority control; league tables comparing school examination results have been introduced; new forms of differentiated schooling (city technology colleges, city academies, faith schools and so on) have been encouraged; and business interests have made significant inroads into education through Private Finance Initiatives in relation to school building and maintenance and through school sponsorship. This elite backlash has of course been contested by coalitions of trade unions, progressive educationalists and parents groups, but with neoliberalism in the ascendancy it has been, and continues to be, a difficult rearguard action.

Case study: closing the gender gap – the educational impact of the first- and second-wave women's movement

Despite the widespread reversals of the neoliberal years, one of the major achievements of a social movement in Britain in the 20th century that continues to go from strength to strength is the rise in female educational attainment. As Moore (2004, p 19) argues, 'the outstanding feature of educational change in the second half of the twentieth century was the gender revolution. Girls first caught up with boys in terms of educational credential attainment in the 1970s, and then by the 1980s a gender gap opened up in favour of girls, which has remained constant ever since. Research shows that the cluster of issues affecting school performance is complex and interactive, and in relation to girls' attainment levels cannot simply be put down to educational actions (changes in subjects, assessments, classroom behaviour or wider educational programmes, policies and procedures); rather, 'what is clear is that successive generations of girls have been challenged by economic and social change and by feminism' (Arnot et al, 1999, p 150).

Before the Second World War, education for the majority of female children was designed to deliberately lower aspirations and provide training for a traditional domesticated family role:

> [T]he ideal end state for all women, irrespective of their social class background, was marriage and full time wife-hood and motherhood. In particular the bourgeois family form of a wage earning husband and a financially dependent wife and children was considered the essential building block of civilised society. (Purvis, 2005, p 191)

This 'ideal' was of course rarely realised in practice, with working-class mothers being forced to undertake poorly paid home-based jobs (such as sewing) to supplement the household income, single working-class women usually working in domestic service or factories, and lower-middle-class single women working under conditions of discrimination in male-dominated professions (for instance teaching) to earn a living. When the movement for women's suffrage became a serious force for progressive change in the years leading up to the First World War, the issue of female education became synonymous with the issue of female political emancipation (in many ways mirroring the movement for working-class male suffrage in the mid-19th century) (Purvis, 2005). This was a broad cross-class movement involving working-class trade unionists (especially textile workers who were predominantly women) as well as teachers and 'independent' women from the upper echelons of British society (as well as male activists from across the classes as well) – it also contained currents of feminism (socialist, liberal, radical and so on) that would surface again and take new forms in the second-wave women's movement from the 1960s onwards (Walby, 1994).

Both of the key first-phase feminist social movement organisations of the period – the National Union of Women's Suffrage Societies (NUWSS) and the more militant Women's Social and Political Union (WSPU) – engaged in educational activities to raise the aspirations and confidence of supporters and women generally. At its height, in the years leading up to the First World War, the WPSU attracted hundreds of thousands to its rallies, had 11 regional offices, 30 paid organisers, 45 paid office staff, its own publishing house (Women's Press) and a newspaper called *Votes for Women* with a circulation in excess of 50,000 (Purvis, 2005). The very fact that this level of organisation existed and was able to draw large numbers of women (and men) into its orbit was significant in terms of political education as well as education in the traditional sense. In her commentary, Purvis (2005) points to the sense of empowered self, enhanced political consciousness and group solidarity that WPSU activists gained through the very process of organising, campaigning and taking collective action (often for the WPSU through direct action). From the American resource mobilisation perspective, these are selective benefits gained by participants who were active in the women's movement. Barker (1999, p 27), writing about the positive psychosocial effects of engagement in social movement activities, argues in a more general sense that:

> Such processes have effects on those who participate in them. Not uncommonly they entail considerable affective aspects. All action has both cognitive and affective sides, but 'extraordinary action' is liable to have 'extraordinary' affective qualities. Collective action, 'successful' or not, alters the balance of confidence in society.

The WPSU and the wider women's suffrage movement clearly operated to successfully educate activists in both an intellectual and an emotional sense. Its 'extraordinary' lawbreaking and socially transgressive activities (such as heckling and spitting at politicians; breaking windows at fashionable shops; vandalising art treasures; pouring acid onto golf courses; 'locking-on' to railings outside Parliament; hunger strikes; and of course the death of Emily Davison after she ran onto the Epsom racecourse) created a strong collective identity among the activists concerned, got significant press coverage and generated widespread debate around suffrage for women in the public sphere – from the perspective of European theories of social movements this type of public communicative dialogue is a prerequisite for progressive social change (see, for example, Habermas, 1981). It is also notable that despite its high level of organisation, the WPSU consistently maintained its radical tactics and uncompromising political stance – something for which resource mobilisation perspectives cannot properly account.

The first-wave women's movement provoked a reactionary social movement to emerge and engage in opposition concerning the direction of the 'balance of confidence' for women in British society. The movement for women's suffrage was challenged from 1908 by the Women's National Anti-Suffrage League, an organisation of approximately 42,000 female members. True to its ideological basis, it merged in 1910 with the male-dominated National League for Opposing Woman Suffrage. Anti-democratic and anti-labour, this movement aimed to preserve male control of the political sphere and to reassert patriarchal structures in wider society (Bush, 2007). The First World War was the turning point in this struggle – it opened up a new political opportunity structure in the state because female labour was required to undertake jobs traditionally done by men. In 1918, the suffragettes attained a major victory when women over the age of 30 were granted the vote, and then finally in 1928 won the war over the franchise when the voting age was equalised at 21. In many ways, this was a pyrrhic victory because women remained largely excluded from political office by the male-dominated political parties and widespread patriarchal attitudes among the voting public.

The inter-war years saw a regression in terms of female employment opportunities, with women being forced out of jobs to make space for the demobilisation of some four million men who needed employment. This process was coupled with a reinforcement of the patriarchal ideology of male as 'breadwinner' and female as 'homemaker' across key social institutions including education (where numbers of female teachers declined) and through the circulation of new mass circulation magazines such as *Good Housekeeping* and *Women and Home*. As mass unemployment was created through the depression years of the 1930s, male employment was prioritised, with marriage bars on female employment being strongly enforced and women's influence in the male-dominated trade unions waning (Pugh, 2000).

Like the First World War, the Second World War drew women into traditionally male-dominated employment spheres and, although demobilisation again negatively affected many sources of employment, this was balanced by extensive new opportunities in education, health and administrative bureaucracies offered by the Beveridgean welfare state and the post-war reconstruction. Like the 1920s and 1930s, the 1940s and 1950s were marked by an ideological attempt to reinforce the ideal of female domesticity through media representations and gender socialisation within the education system. However, this time the gap between ideal and reality, as well as aspirations and possibilities for fulfilment, came to be increasingly critically questioned by women (including large numbers of married women) whose life orientations had moved from the private to the public sphere through their experience of sustained employment. These stirrings of a new feminist consciousness finally began to coalesce in the 1960s as the second-wave women's movement began to take shape through a complex network of interlinked micro-mobilisation contexts (McCarthy et al, 1988): 'begun in kitchens, in classrooms, in lecture theatres and in workplaces, this movement started campaigning for social change, particularly by making demands *for* and *by* women' (Arnot et al, 1999, p 63). The state would play a key role as target and mediator of feminist demands, which the British women's liberation movement formulated in 1969 as 'equal pay for equal work; equality of educational opportunity; abortion and contraception on demands; and twenty-four hour nurseries' (Arnot et al, 1999, p 63).

After a period of intense campaigning by trade unions and a myriad of different women's groups and organisations using both conventional and unconventional tactics, the government did finally address these demands with legislation including the landmark 1970 Equal Pay Act 1970 and the 1975 Sex Discrimination Act (which included important clauses on education) but it did not move on the limited abortion provision of the 1967 Abortion Act and has acted since only in a piecemeal manner on the issue of nurseries. By the early 1980s, a combination of the impacts of academic post-modernism (which fetishises difference) and political change meant that feminism had ceased to be a visible coherent women's movement that made claims on the state. Instead, it had fragmented into a number of different protest campaigns (for example, against rape, violence against women or pornography) and into different competing factions and currents. Its lack of visibility as a campaigning movement does not, however, mean that feminism has disappeared (indeed, many movements oscillate between visibility and latency); rather, it continues to operate through submerged networks (Melucci, 1989) at the level of culture – for example in law, academia and the media.

The impact of feminism in terms of the interrelated spheres of legislation, employment, education and cultural norms and values has significantly and positively altered the status of and opportunities for women in British society. In terms of education, first-wave feminism operated to prepare the ground for the conditions for female education – it raised public consciousness of female political inequality, raised women's political confidence and won important civil and political rights. After the Second World War, Butler's tripartite education system clearly could not deliver for raised public expectations regarding social mobility and improved life chances (see Chapter Seven). A key component of this legitimation crisis was a failure to address women's aspirations (and those of their daughters), which had been raised by the experience of working in health, education and administration in the new public welfare sector. This dissatisfaction fed into a new feminist consciousness that mobilised the second-wave women's movement during a period in the late 1960s when the political opportunity structure was particularly open due to a combination of the first Labour government in 13 years, the breakdown of the post-war political settlement and the imperative to modernise the economy. The open political opportunity structure was complimented by an open educational opportunity structure in the sense that Labour was committed to the introduction of comprehensive schooling, and with that an ethos of equal opportunity. This ethos meant that the government was relatively receptive to feminist arguments regarding the need for legislation to tackle gender inequalities in the form and content of education (including pedagogy, the curriculum, careers advice and teacher training).

Aside from the equal opportunities legislation of the 1970s, feminist pressure eventually led to the setting up of the Equal Opportunities Commission in 1970 as a new regulatory body regarding gender issues (this was followed by the Commission for Racial Equality, which followed the Race Relations Act in 1976). What was key though to raising female educational attainment levels was, as Arnot et al (1999, p 151) argue, the 'space offered by a decentralised system of education and the associated notions of teacher professionalism and autonomy. In the "secret garden of the curriculum" teachers were able to challenge traditional female roles and offer girls the chance to experiment and reflect on their personal ambitions' (1999, p 151). Feminism operating vis-à-vis education as both a visible political movement making claims on the state, and as a less visible cultural movement (where the personal is political) to challenge codes in terms of aspirations, norms and values has meant that the education system has been changed to work for women rather than against them. Even the educational reforms of the neoliberal era have not been able to reverse the educational gains made by women as women's attainment levels continue to outstrip men's. It is arguable though that the ongoing conservative 'backlash' (Faludi, 1992), against the progressive gains of the 1960s and 1970s, has meant that 'in respect of education the effects have been to convert girls' educational successes into a moral panic about boys' failure' (Arnot et al, 1999, p 151). Educational attainment continues to be mediated by gender alongside 'race' and class, a process that teaching professionals and teaching unions argue will not be tackled by current policies that merely serve to reinforce social differentiation and enable the reproduction of social hierarchies.

Conclusion: social movements and education policy

'England rouse thy legions
Ere it be too late,
Foes of right and foes of light
Would storm the schoolhouse gate.'
(Hirst Hollowell, 1902, *Battle Song of the Schools*, in Simon, 1974, p 222)

All social movements make some claim or another on education whether it be for equal opportunities and an end to discrimination, or for proactive education programmes in favour of one issue or another. The brief history of the making of the British education system recounted in this chapter illustrates that there is no singular continuous historical social movement for educational rights or educational reform. Rather, education (as a key source of social reproduction and development) has been incorporated in different ways into the ideological framing (see the discussion of 'framing' in Chapter Three) and policy demands of the key social movements that have been active in shaping the welfare state in the modern era. Educational protest movements that are concerned specifically with government education policy (see the discussion surrounding Byrne's [1997] distinctions of types of movement in Chapter Three) are, however, significant in a historical sense – these movements have periodically challenged the state or demanded reform. Hollowell's song quoted above was bought by approximately 33,000 people at the Leeds demonstrations in 1902 and sung at subsequent public events organised to oppose the reactionary 1902 Education Act (Simon, 1974). This educational protest movement like those of later years was made up of loose networks of activists from across the classes, and coalitions of social movement organisations from wider oppositional social movements.

Educational protest movements have waxed and waned through cycles of protest depending on state policy, available resources and the relative openness of the political opportunity structure (Tarrow, 1994; see the discussion of political process theory in Chapter Three).

The labour movement and the women's movement in its first phase fought for the conditions of education (basic civil, political and social rights) – democracy and then socialism providing the master frames, which climaxed in the making of the Beveridge welfare state and the Butler Education Act. In the post-war period, conceptions of an educative society that provided meritocratic equality of opportunity regardless of class, gender or 'race' moved centre stage and the education aspects of the post-war settlement represented by tripartism in schooling came under attack as part of the wider crisis of legitimation. Again the labour movement took the lead, campaigning for comprehensive schooling, and when this was achieved from the mid-1960s onwards the second-phase women's movement and other contemporary movements emerged (around 'race', disability and sexuality) to make further claims on the state for equal opportunities and an end to discriminatory practices.

The state responded to these claims with equal opportunities legislation and new regulatory organisations in the 1970s and there has been some limited progress in addressing new movement demands vis-à-vis education in the intervening years. Of all the achievements of social movements in the 20th century, the 'gender revolution' in educational attainment for women wrought by the women's movement has been among the most notable. The era of neoliberalism has, however, seen the retrenchment of differentiation in education, with class divisions solidifying, social mobility going into reverse and the elites taking back social and political ground that they had lost in the 1960s and 1970s. The current campaigns in the first decade of the 21st century led by teachers' unions against public-private partnerships in relation to school infrastructure, and against the creation of self-governing academies (see, for instance, the Anti-Academies Alliance) and faith schools are the latest in a long history of social movement mobilisations and conflicts around the contested terrain of education.

Further reading

There are a number of excellent histories of the relationship between the labour movement and the struggle for educational reform – two of the best are the classic *Education and the Labour Movement 1870-1920* by Brian Simon (Lawrence & Wishart, 1974) and *Education in the Post-War Years* by Roy Lowe (Routledge, 1988).

A lively account of the Butler reforms is provided in *The Five Giants: A Biography of the Welfare State* by Nicholas Timmins (HarperCollins, 1995) in the education chapter of his book, while *The Making of the 1944 Education Act* by Michael Barber (Cassell, 1994) looks at the Butler reforms in more detail.

Two collections – *A Feminist Critique of Education* edited by Christine Skelton and Becky Francis (Routledge, 2005) and *Practical Visionaries: Women, Education, Progress* edited by Mary Hilton and Pam Hirsch (Pearson Education, 2000) – provide a good source material on the educational impact of the women's movement and the early feminist pioneers respectively.

Education in a Post-Welfare Society by Sally Tomlinson (Open University Press, 2005) brings the debate concerning the contestation of educational reform up to date.

Useful websites

See contemporary educational campaigns and related social movement organisations at the following websites:

Anti-Academies Alliance: *www.antiacademies.org.uk/*

National Union of Teachers: *www.teachers.org.uk/topichome.php?id=54*

Campaign Against National Curriculum Tests, Targets and School League Tables: *www.teachers.org.uk/story.php?id=2264*

British Humanist Association Campaign Against Faith Schools: *www.humanism. org.uk/home*

Part Three

Contemporary social movements and social welfare

eight

Contesting the family: LGBT and conservative counter-movements

Introduction

'The family' plays a pivotal role in society: not only can the family offer a 'safe' refuge from the stresses and strains of modern life but it also potentially provides our identity and place in society. In the Beveridge Report (1942), the welfare state was predicated upon the traditional nuclear family with its male breadwinner and wife/mother engaged in the unpaid work of raising the family and looking after the home (Wasoff and Dey, 2000). Successive governments have relied on the traditional nuclear family as the foundation for their welfare policies, and families that deviate from this model have been frequently constructed by the state as 'problem' families and as legitimate targets for state intervention (McKie et al, 2005). For example, during the 1980s and 1990s, there was widespread demonisation and targeting of single mothers by the media and the UK government.

Although the family has been attacked, particularly by feminists as patriarchy's chief institution, the majority of people believe that the family is both a necessary and a positive force in society. During the second half of the 20th century, the family underwent a massive transformation, such that not only has the age of first marriage significantly increased, traditional gender roles within the family have been challenged, families are smaller and more liable to breakdown, but also what we consider to be a family has changed. This transformation reflects not only the changing way we live our lives but also the critique of the traditional nuclear family by feminists and lesbian, gay, bisexual and transgendered (LGBT) activists among others. However, not everyone is happy with the changing nature of the family;

Christian activism on both sides of the Atlantic has prioritised the defence of the nuclear family and 'traditional' family values in their fight against the permissive society.

In recent years, aspects of family policy and the official definition of 'the family' have been heavily influenced by ongoing conflict between conservative religious groups (such as the Christian Institute, CARE and the Evangelical Alliance) and LGBT organisations (such as Stonewall, OutRage! and the Equality Network). Section 28 of the 1988 Local Government Act and its subsequent repeal, the equalising of the age of consent, gay adoption and civil partnerships all reflect a wider debate concerning the legitimacy and origins of homosexuality. For example, Section 28 (Section 2a of the 1988 Scotland Act 1988 in Scotland) enshrined in law the view that heterosexuality was superior to homosexuality and that lesbian and gay relationships were no more than 'pretend family relationships'. Since coming to power, however, New Labour's family policy has led to a more inclusive definition of the family that has included lesbian and gay male partnerships, which has eroded the ascendancy of the traditional nuclear family despite considerable opposition from Christian and conservative groups. This more inclusive family policy represents the success of LGBT campaigners to influence public policy and wider public opinion. One of the primary obstacles that LGBT rights campaigners have had to overcome is the 'protection of children' frame widely used by Christian activists and others who oppose the redefinition of the family and related issues such as the extension of adoption rights to gay and lesbian couples. The use of such a frame constructs homosexuality as a contagion that can be transmitted to young people by proselytising lesbians and gay men. Furthermore, gay men, in particular, are often constructed as a sexual threat to young people; sexual predators able to seduce young 'heterosexual' males into the carefree gay lifestyle.

This chapter will detail the 'war over the family' during the latter part of the 20th century when the family emerged as one of the primary battlegrounds in the ongoing conflict between reactionary Christians and conservative movements and the more progressive social movements, particularly the LGBT and women's movements. The chapter will consider how the recognition of lesbian and gay couples as more than 'pretend family relationships' has been indicative of a waning in the dominance of traditional Christian values in society. This has been reflected in major legislative changes that have included the repeal of Section 28, changes in adoption laws and the enactment of civil partnership legislation that have given lesbian and gay couples the right to marry in all but name.

In terms of social movement theory, this chapter demonstrates how Christian crusaders have used a 'protection of children' frame to undermine the permissive changes of the late 20th century and to challenge the campaigns for LGBT rights (for a good discussion of faming strategies in the conflict between the Christian crusaders and LGBT rights campaigners in the US, see Miceli, 2005). While Christian crusaders had limited success using the 'protection of children' frame during the 1980s (see Thompson, 1994), during the 1990s and the 2000s the political opportunities (for a discussion of political opportunities and LGBT activism in the UK, the US and Canada, see Rayside, 2001) associated with New Labour's electoral victory in 1997 and devolution in Scotland, Wales and Northern Ireland in 1999 has enabled a resurgent LGBT movement to successfully challenge Christian power in the UK. The chapter also draws parallels with the symbolic nature of the temperance crusade at the turn of the 19th and 20th centuries (see Gusfield, 1986) and the Christian defence of the family in late 20th century. For example, it can be argued that the importance of Section 28 was related to the fact that it enshrined in law that lesbian and gay partnerships were not equivalent to heterosexual marriage and were no more than 'pretend family relationships'. In this way, as with the temperance movement in the US in the early 20th century, the passing of Section 28 was a symbolic victory that was used to demonstrate the dominance of Christian values and the crusader's definition of the family in the UK even though in reality the significance and power of Christian values were waning.

The family and Christian rearmament

The changing family patterns in the UK such as the rising divorce rate, growing numbers of lone-parent families and cohabiting couples and the official recognition of lesbian and gay relationships, have for many conservative groups amounted to a 'crisis' in the family. In the UK, conservative religious organisations, such as Christian Action Research and Education (CARE), the Christian Institute and the Evangelical Alliance, have despaired at what they perceive to be the erosion of traditional family values and government recognition of a diversity of family forms. For such groups, the promotion of traditional nuclear family values is central to their fight against the permissive society and is a necessary part of their wider moral rearmament of society.

For Christians, the centrality of the family stems not only from their belief that marriage is ordained by God (Evangelical Alliance factsheet for Election) but also because the family is the primary conduit through which the Christian faith is transmitted to successive generations:

> Marriage creates new relationships uniting the families of husband and wife. Stable married families are a primary carrier of values. It is in married families that values are most effectively passed down through the generations. It is where children learn right from wrong and where they learn to get along with others and control their own selfish impulses. (Christian Institute, 2002, p 7)

Therefore, the family is the cornerstone upon which a Christian life is built and any attack on the family is an attack on Christianity and God. The defence of the family has taken many forms, from the fight against abortion rights to the current controversies over sex education, gay adoption, gender recognition, civil partnerships and the legal recognition of cohabiting heterosexual couples. Although Christian activism has a very long history dating back to the 18th century with organisations such as the Society for the Suppression of Vice (see Thompson, 1994), the current 'war over the family' has been closely related to the legalisation of abortion in 1967 in the UK and the *Roe v Wade* (1973) judgment of the American Supreme Court, which legalised abortion on demand in the US in the first trimester of pregnancy. Berger and Berger (1983) argue that the legalisation of abortion was a step too far for Christian activists and they have worked tirelessly since then to undermine women's right to choose.

In the UK, the undermining of the family was perceived by Christians to arise from the government's increasing unwillingness to promote Christian values through legislation and the growing power of secular humanism. The permissive reforms of the 1960s – the 1959 Obscene Publication Act, 1967 Sexual Offences Act, 1967 Abortion Act and 1969 Divorce Reform Act – represented what they believed to be a disastrous transition from a Christian to a secular society:

> In 1967 came the Sexual Offences Act, which legalized homosexual practices in certain circumstances; and worst of all, legislation to 'amend' the Infant Life Preservation Act of 1929, which opened the door to the Abortion Act of 1967 and subsequent Abortion Law Reform Legislation which has resulted in the slaughter – how can we describe it otherwise? – of over two million unborn babies.

> In 1969, too, came the Divorce Reform Act which has undermined the sanctity of marriage and the stability of home life and has caused untold misery to hundreds of thousands of young children.... And so has come the transformation of

society from one based on the morality of the bible and the Christian faith to the ethics of a secular society. (Whitehouse, 1985, pp 25-6)

In response to this growing permissiveness, Christians began organising. The National Viewers' and Listeners' Association (NVALA), originally launched as the Clean Up TV Campaign in 1964, and the Society for the Protection of the Unborn Child (SPUC) formed in 1967, arose to challenge this permissive legislation and through the use of often secular language and arguments sought to uphold traditional Christian values (Durham, 1991). Framing their crusades in such a way was vital to widen the appeal of their campaigns to a largely secular audience. The most successful frame has been the 'protection of children frame' used as a justification, for example, by Mary Whitehouse to argue for greater censorship of violent and sexual television programmes, pornography and video 'nasties' (see Durham, 1991; Thompson, 1994; for a classic discussion of framing, see Snow et al, 1986; on framing by Christian and LGBT activists, see Micelini, 2005; see also Chapter Three). This frame underpinned the campaign for Section 28 and against the extension of adoption rights to lesbian and gay couples. The crusade against the permissive society was strengthened by being joined by the more explicitly Christian Evangelical Nationwide Festival of Light launched in Trafalgar Square in September 1971, which was renamed Christian Action Research and Education (CARE) in 1983 (see www. care.org.uk) and the establishment of the Christian Institute in 1990 (see www.christian.org.uk).

'Pretend family relationships'

Throughout the 1980s, Christian crusaders such as Mary Whitehouse and conservative Christian organisations aimed to use the sympathetic Thatcher administration to turn back the growing tide of permissiveness. Successful attacks against adult cinemas, sex shops and 'video nasties' acted as important symbolic victories (Thompson, 1994), however, despite high hopes that the Thatcher administration would aid them in their moral reinvigoration of society, the primary focus of the Thatcher revolution was economic (see Durham, 1991). Although the Thatcher and Major administrations often deployed the rhetoric of traditional family values and used the family support mechanisms as a means of reducing the costs of the welfare state, religious groups were disappointed with what they perceived to be the Conservatives' anti-family economic policies as well as their failure to support a range of Bills including the limitation of abortion rights for women (although the Major government did eventually support the reduction of the legal time limit for abortions from 28 to 24 weeks) and the ban on topless page three models in the tabloid press.

One of the major Christian successes was the Thatcher administration's eventual support for Section 28, which aimed to restrict the promotion of homosexuality as a 'pretend family relationship' by local authorities or any organisation funded by local authorities. Section 28 had been the outcome of the controversy surrounding the stocking of the book *Jenny Lives with Martin and Eric*, a story of a young girl living with her father and his boyfriend, as a teaching resource by several London boroughs. However, the real issue behind Section 28 was not that primary school children had access to this book (which they did not) but Christian concern that sex education in school was being used to promote lesbian and gay relationships as an equally valid alternative to heterosexual marriage. Initially introduced as a Private Members Bill in 1986 by the Earl of Halsbury and promoted by the Conservative Family Campaign, Section 28 fitted into a wider Christian crusade against both sex education materials and homosexuality, a crusade that had occupied Christian fundamentalist groups for over a decade (Durham, 1991; Annetts and Thompson, 1992).

The passage of the Section was interrupted by the 1987 General Election; however, when it was reintroduced by David Wilshire in December 1987 it was then formally adopted by the government on the basis that there was 'growing concern' about the use of ratepayers' money for the promotion of homosexuality. However, there were two more important underlying reasons for the government's support of the clause: first, it provided the government with the opportunity to further attack and curb the activities of Labour-run councils (Smith, 1994); and second, it acted to deflect growing Christian criticism of the Conservatives' 'anti-family' economic policy (Thompson, 1994). Supporting Section 28 provided the government an opportunity to reward Christian support of the Conservative Party without compromising their free-market ethics (Annetts and Thompson, 1992).

Legally, Section 28 had relatively little impact, however, it had a significant symbolic value enshrining in law that gay relationships were not, and could not be taught as, equal to heterosexual relationships and marriage. Parallels can be drawn between Section 28 and the American temperance movement's victory in achieving prohibition in 1920, which acted as a symbolic affirmation of the dominance of the crusaders' values even though more and more Americans were rejecting these values. Although the 18th amendment to the American Constitution provided a legal affirmation of the dominance of the temperance ethic, it did not guarantee them popular support and, within 13 years, prohibition was struck down; a blow from which the temperance movement never recovered (Gusfield, 1986). Similarly, Christian activists in the UK could not have envisaged that their success in getting Section 28 on the statute book would reinvigorate and repoliticise LGBT communities, encouraging them onto the offensive. Just as prohibition acted as a swan song for the American temperance movement, Section 28 represented a high point in the Christian defence of the family and its campaign against the extension of LGBT rights.

The lasting legacy of Section 28 was the recognition by the LGBT communities of the need to work together to set an agenda for change rather than continue to engage in what Peter Tatchell (1992, p 238) has referred to as 'fire brigade activism':

> The end result of this 'fire brigade activism' is not merely a defensive politics, but an absence of any thought-out, coherent political strategy for lesbian and gay equality.... Faced with homophobic attacks, of course we have to respond. However, we also need to find a way to set our agenda and make our demands.

After Section 28, lesbian and gay activism became much more proactive and more visible. Stonewall (established in 1989) and OutRage! (established in 1990) were very much conduits of this new proactive LGBT activism. Stonewall, in particular, was primarily set up to lobby legislators on a range of issues, including the equalisation of the age of consent, LGBT employment rights, women's reproductive rights and the recognition of lesbian and gay partnerships. Stonewall emulated the lobbying activism of the earlier Homosexual Law Reform Society, which was established in 1958 to facilitate the transition into law of the 1957 Wolfenden Report's recommendation that consensual homosexual acts be decriminalised for adults over the age of 21 (Report of the Committee on Homosexual Offences and Prostitution, 1957). This was achieved in 1967 in England and Wales, 1980 in Scotland and finally in 1982 in Northern Ireland. This type of professional lobby organisation is more prevalent in the US where the more decentralised political system offers far greater political opportunities for lobbyists (Engel, 2001; Rayside, 2001). The political lobbying of Stonewall can be contrasted with OutRage!, which reflected the more informal and democratic structures of the Gay Liberation Front (GLF) in the early 1970s and ACT UP in the 1980s, using direct action and civil disobedience to challenge discriminatory practices and injustices against the LGBT communities throughout the 1990s. For example, one of OutRage!'s first major protests was a 'Kiss-in' in Trafalgar Square, London in September 1990 to highlight the use by police of the 1986 Public Order Act to arrest gay men for kissing in public (Lucas, 1998). This theatrical protest was used to publicly embarrass the police and ensure maximum media coverage. Therefore, rather ironically, despite the failure of the

LGBT communities to 'Stop the Clause', Section 28 became a watershed for lesbian and gay politics in the UK (Plummer, 1999; Engel, 2001). The battle over Section 28 led to the creation of a more confident community and created networks through which a newly politicised generation of activists could challenge discrimination against LGBT people.

> Clause 28 became Section 28 of the Local Government Act on 24 May 1988. Rather than shutting up the gay community, the effect of the legislation was to give them a voice, and to make it angry. The gloves were now off.... More positively, for many people the experience had shown that there was political strength in numbers. Section 28 sparked off local and national networks which became the basis for continuing action. (Lucas, 1998, p 6)

Repealing the Clause

While the Conservatives remained in power there were relatively few opportunities for the LGBT communities to effect change. Although there were some victories for LGBT activists, for example the decriminalising of homosexuality in Scotland in 1980 and Northern Ireland in 1981 and the reduction of the age of consent for consensual male homosexual acts to 18 in 1994, the Thatcher and Major administrations had largely remained hostile to the extension of LGBT rights and the increased visibility of the LGBT communities (Smith, 1994; Engel, 2001). However, the election of New Labour in 1997 and Scottish and Welsh devolution in 1999 substantially enhanced the LGBT movement's political opportunities (see McAdam, 1996). These opportunities were limited under the Conservatives, far more so than the American LGBT movement faced under the Reagan and Bush (Senior) administrations, because the centralisation of the British political system and party discipline results in the UK having a relatively closed political system (Engel, 2001; Rayside, 2001). Hence, political opportunities are often determined by the ability of movements to cultivate close links with elite allies such as political parties in the hope that they will honour their promises to the movement when they eventually become elected. While it might be true that organisations such as CARE and Stonewall purport to be non-party-political organisations, the Conservatives tend to be more sympathetic to the traditional family value arguments of Christian organisations while New Labour has generally been more sympathetic to the gay rights agenda. For example, New Labour had pledged that it would repeal Section 28 and lower the age of consent for male homosexual acts from 18 to 16, bringing it in line with the age of consent for both heterosexual and lesbian sexual acts. However, the New Labour government encountered considerable opposition from reactionary voices in the House of Lords, which thwarted the equalising of the age of consent at 16 in 1999, forcing New Labour to eventually rely on the Parliament Act to force the 2000 Sexual Offences (Amendment) Act through the Lords.

New Labour was even slower in bringing forward legislation to repeal Section 28 and, with the delays to the lowering of the age of consent, this was causing considerable frustration among LGBT activists. David Northmore (news editor for *Pink Paper*), for example, writing in *The Guardian* argued in 1999 that despite New Labour's gay-friendly posture, three key demands remained unresolved: the age of consent was still 18, Section 28 had not been repealed and homosexuals were still banned from serving in the armed forces (*The Guardian*, 13 January 1999).

When the government finally announced its intention to repeal Section 28 in the 1999 Queen's Speech, there was real concern that the vehicle chosen for the repeal – the Local Government Bill – would inevitably lead to the jettisoning of the repeal in order that the government could meet the deadline for the London mayoral contest. In the press it was even suggested that ministers were well aware that the repeal of Section 28 'would be blocked in the Lords' and that 'it could be jettisoned if the Lords throw it out' (*The Independent*, 25 October 1999). Inevitably, the government was forced to drop the repeal to ensure that there was no delay in the London mayoral election and on 25 July 2000, Ms Armstrong, speaking on behalf of the government, stated that the repeal would be dropped because of opposition in the Lords. However, Ms Armstrong indicated that the government would look for an appropriate vehicle 'to ensure that we repeal the legislation and make it clear that we want both a tolerant and supportive society for all our citizens, and proper respect and protection for children at school' (Hansard, 25 June, 2000: col 1036).

In Scotland, the Liberal–Labour administration in control of the newly devolved Scottish government was in the enviable position of not having a second chamber, and therefore no obstacle to reform. However, this was not to be the case. Following the Scottish Executive's announcement on 28 October 1999 that it was its intention 'to secure repeal at the earliest opportunity, and [that] appropriate provision will be made within the Ethical Standards in Public Life Bill' (*The Guardian*, 29 October 1999), an alliance of Christian groups tried to stop the repeal of Section 2a of the 1988 Scotland Act (as Section 28 was known in Scotland). This powerful coalition of both Catholic and Evangelical Christian voices was bankrolled by Brian Souter, the multimillionaire chairman of Stagecoach, the international transport company. Souter, a devout Christian and member of the Trinity Church of the Nazarene in Perth, pledged one million pounds to fight the repeal of Section 28. The money would be used to help fund the campaign that was being led by the Scottish School Boards Association (SSBA). A spokesperson for Souter explained that his actions were not about homophobia but democracy:

> Mr. Souter believes that this is an important issue of democracy. It is not homophobic. It is essential that all Scottish parents realised what the implications are of scrapping Clause 28 and the kind of explicit material which could then be forced on their children in the classroom. (BBC News Online, 14 January 2000)

There were two main concerns voiced by proponents of the clause: first, the need to protect children from sexually explicit gay material; and second, to ensure that homosexual relationships were not seen as the moral equivalent of heterosexual relationships and marriage.

In Scotland and in England and Wales even relatively moderate religious voices were concerned that the scrapping of the clause may lead to the acceptance of gay relationships as equivalent to heterosexual marriage. For example, Archbishop Carey argued that the government must 'resist placing homosexual relationships on an equal footing with marriage as the proper context for sexual intimacy. With or without Section 28, we need to be sure that there are adequate safeguards in place for schools and pupils' (*The Guardian*, 24 January 2000). Section 28 provided legislative backing for the Christian definition of the family and that gay relationships could be no more than 'pretend family relationships'.

The scrapping of Section 28 initially in Scotland and then in the rest of the UK was indicative of a change of mood in the country concerning LGBT rights and a decline in influence of the Christian movement. Although the Christian Institute, the Catholic Church and Brian Souter's campaign in Scotland sought to raise fears that young children were at risk from homosexual proselytising in the classroom and may be forced to view sexually explicit gay material that could threaten their 'normal' sexual development, there was no groundswell of public opinion against the repeal. This is, in part, related to a growing acceptance among the general public that you cannot teach someone to be homosexual. For example, Matthew Waites (2005, p 551) argues that:

> The debates over Section 28 and adoption have both side stepped arguments about the fixity of sexual identities in important ways. Mainstream (heterosexual) support for 'equality'

in these contexts has been won via arguments that encounters with lesbian and gay people in the context of education and parenting do not influence sexual-identity formation.

However, these debates also took place against the background of strong support for the family and marriage both in Westminster and in the Scottish Parliament at Holyrood (Dunphy, 2000, p 189). The Scottish Executive, although it more quickly repealed Section 28, sought to placate opposition from the Church and Brian Souter's campaign by offering guidance to the Directors of Education that 'Pupils should be encouraged to appreciate the value of stable family life, parental responsibility and family relationships in bringing up children and offering them security, stability and happiness' (Scottish Executive Circular 2/2001). A similar offer was made in Westminster; however, this still failed to placate the opponents to the repeal in the Lords. In the end, it took another three years before Section 28 was repealed in England and Wales through an amendment to the 2003 Local Government Act (Waites, 2005).

The failure of the Christian lobby to stop the repeal of Section 28 in England and Wales and Section 2a in Scotland can be seen as indicative of both the success of the new proactive LGBT movement and the growing acceptance of LGBT communities in the UK. Although the New Labour government in Westminster and the devolved administrations in Scotland and Wales continue to strongly support the family and emphasise its importance, there has been a growing recognition of and support for a diversity of family forms/non-traditional households (CRFR, 2002; Wasoff and Hill, 2002). The repeal of Section 28 and Section 2a offered LGBT activists the opportunity to fight for a more inclusive family, one which recognised same-sex partners.

Civil partnerships and the redefinition of the family

Until relatively recently, successive governments' family policies have been aimed at bolstering the traditional nuclear family against rising rates of lone-parent families, divorce and cohabitation, believing that the nuclear family and traditional family values are a panacea for the majority of society's ills. Both the Thatcher and Major administrations considered that the family, through an expansion of its welfare activities, could be used to roll back the boundaries of the welfare state (Clarke and Langan, 1993). The Conservative governments also reinforced the exclusion of lesbians and gay men from the family, not only through Section 28, but also through other various pieces of legislation such as the 1990 Human Fertilisation and Embryology Act. This Act, for example, demands that before artificial insemination is given to any woman, careful consideration is taken of the welfare of any child born of the procedure and this includes the need for a father. Such a stipulation, while effectively prohibiting lesbians and single heterosexual women from receiving treatment, reinforces the dominant construction of heterosexual marriage and the patriarchal family (see Smith, 1994). This failure to legally recognise lesbian and gay relationships has had serious consequences, for example the loss of one's home following the death of a partner (see Auchmuty, 2004). However, the election of New Labour in 1997 gave LGBT activists high hopes that they would be able to push forward the equality agenda in a way that had not been possible under the Conservatives.

In terms of family policies, New Labour has accelerated the shift to more explicit and more punitive family policies that have been reflected in a growing willingness of the government to intervene directly in family life. In the past, intervention had largely been restricted to dealing with 'problem' families but now has extended to greater state involvement in supporting, for example, childcare. Such policies have acted to blur the boundary between the private sphere of the family and the public sphere in which governments usually operate (Wasoff and Cunningham-Burley, 2005). The Labour government's often punitive family policies have been aimed at supporting two-parent families and reducing child poverty through, for example, the Child Support Agency and its heavily criticised welfare-to-work programme (Wasoff and Cunningham-Burley, 2005). The Blair administration has continually stressed that two-parent families provide the best environment to raise children and believes that in supporting the family it will ultimately strengthen society and reduce poverty and crime. In this way, New Labour's family policies continue to reflect those of its predecessors, further evidenced by its emphasis on selective benefits and individual responsibility and the continuation of market-oriented reforms, even if these are now dressed up in the language of social justice (Wasoff and Dey, 2000).

However, while continuing to support the family and emphasising that healthy children need healthy families, the Labour administration has promoted a more inclusive definition of the family (CRFR, 2002; Wasoff and Hill, 2002). Although this was not immediately apparent, signs of a greater willingness to recognise lesbian and gay partnerships could be glimpsed in Stonewall's successful campaign in 2000 to force the government to change the immigration rules 'to permit same-sex partners to enter the country under the same test as that applied to unmarried heterosexual couples' (Auchmuty, 2004, p 107). This was accompanied by the 2002 Adoption and Children Act, which not only recognises lesbian and gay partnerships but also accepts that they provide stable and loving environments for raising adoptive children.

The most important evidence of this more inclusive approach to the family has been the 2004 Civil Partnership Act, which is indicative of the growing political acceptance of the LGBT communities and their rights agenda since 1997. It also represents the most significant evidence of the greater acceptance of 'non-conventional households' by the UK government and the devolved administrations. The Act gave lesbian and gay couples the opportunity to formally register their partnership in a civil ceremony, providing the same rights and responsibilities as marriage does for heterosexual couples (Land and Kitzinger, 2007). This legislation was initiated following a decade of campaigning by Stonewall and also followed the setting up of registration schemes in London in 2001 and Manchester in 2002. It would appear that LGBT activists in securing the civil partnership legislation have won a major victory for equality, thwarting the attempt of Christian crusaders and supporters of 'traditional' family values to characterise gay relationships as 'pretend family relationships' that should have no legal validity. However, while civil partnerships do offer lesbian and gay couples 'marriage in all but name', names are, as Auchmuty (2004, p 102) argues, important:

> Even though the expressed aim of the British government's proposals was to offer lesbian and gay couples a form of legal protection equivalent to marriage, it is clear to me that marriage is more than simply a set of rules. It has a symbolic significance that exists beyond, and sometimes in spite of, legal and material reality. Marriage confers upon individuals the highest social status and approval. That is what makes the concept of registered partnerships or civil unions qualitatively different from marriage, even if, legally speaking, they guarantee the same rights.

Although the UK government has ensured that lesbian and gay couples who register their partnership have similar rights as heterosexual married couples, they are still excluded from the institution of marriage. This was underlined by a legal ruling in 2004 that upheld that the Canadian marriage of Susan Wilkinson and Celia Kitzinger was not a valid marriage in the UK. This ruling was appealed on the basis that the failure to recognise their Canadian marriage was an abrogation of the 1998 Human Rights Act. The 2006 appeal judgment of Sir Mark Potter, which followed the passing of the 2004 Civil Partnership Act, upheld the original judgment and ruled that their Canadian marriage is now treated as a civil partnership and that doing so does not constitute a violation of their civil rights (see Harding,

2007). However, some LGBT activists and feminist commentators are critical of the failure of the New Labour government to offer real equality. Harding (2007, pp 224-5), for example, argues that 'denying same sex couples access to marriage is a reinscription of (hetero) patriarchal ideals of the "traditional family"', which she suggests is 'a method of bolstering and re-inscribing gender roles within the family'.

Therefore, while civil partnerships have been widely supported within the LGBT communities and social movement organisations such as Stonewall and the Equality Network in Scotland have been advocates for the legislation, some activists and academics have been critical of the way in which the Civil Partnership Act reinforces the exclusion of lesbians and gay men from the institution of marriage, even if civil partnerships represent an important step forward in the fight for lesbian and gay rights. Arguably, the Act has not offered equality but rather has enshrined discrimination in law. Peter Tatchell, for example, writing in *The Guardian*, has argued that 'By legislating a two-tier system of relationship recognition Labour has, in effect, created a form of legal apartheid based on sexual orientation. In a democracy everyone is supposed to be equal in law. Separate is not equal' (*The Guardian*, 19 December 2005).

However, it should still be recognised that the civil partnership legislation and other legislation such as the extension of adoption rights to couples including gay and lesbian partners have significantly altered the legal definition of the family and have undermined the ascendancy of the orthodox Christian definition of the family. However, Christian activists and groups have refused to accept these changes and are actively working to undermine LGBT rights. For example, despite the passing of the 2007 Sexual Orientation Act, which bans discrimination on the basis of a person's sexual orientation by any public body, commercial organisation or individual, the Christian Institute successfully financed the case of Miss Lillian Ladele, a registrar in Islington, who was threatened with dismissal for her refusal to officiate at civil partnership ceremonies because of her strong Christian conviction that homosexuality was a sin. The employment tribunal upheld Ms Ladele's claim that she was treated less favourably on the grounds of her orthodox Christian beliefs and that she was subject to 'direct discrimination on the grounds of religion and belief' (*Ladele v Islington Borough Council*, 2008). However, this tactic has not always been successful. The government, for instance, rejected Christian adoption agencies' argument that as a matter of conscience their religious faith should allow them to discriminate against lesbian and gay couples who wish to adopt, although they were given extra time to comply with the law.

Conclusion

The family continues to be an important site of social movement conflict between conservative religious and the LGBT and women's movements. One of the key contemporary debates has been constructed around the question of what actually constitutes a family. In the war over the family, Christian crusaders, conservative supporters of traditional family values and LGBT activists have all sought to influence government family policy with varying degrees of success. For example, successive governments have subscribed to the Christian crusaders' belief that the traditional nuclear family is essential for the stability of society. This has led to the demonising of 'problem' families who do not conform to this idealised family pattern, particularly single mothers who have been accused of being a drain on the nation's resources and responsible for much juvenile delinquency.

However, the traditional nuclear family has been promoted by both Conservative and Labour administrations as a panacea to a plethora of social problems and has been used to reduce the cost of the welfare state. However, since the New Labour victory in 1997, LGBT activists have been successful in forcing the government to accept a more inclusive definition of the family, one that accepts that lesbian and gay couples may also constitute 'real' families. The repeal of Section 28 that had labelled lesbian and gay partnerships as 'pretend family relationships', the extension of adoption rights to lesbian and gay couples and the enactment of the civil partnership and sexual orientation legislation represent a significant step forward for LGBT rights while at the same time undermining the gains made by Christian crusaders particularly during the Thatcher administration. Yet this success is soured by the continual refusal of the government to offer true equality. While the 2004 Civil Partnership Act has ensured that lesbian and gay couples have substantially the same rights as heterosexuals, they are still denied the right to marry, just as heterosexuals are denied the choice of a civil partnership.

In terms of social movement theory, this chapter illustrates the importance of framing to successful social movement campaigns. Christian crusaders have very successfully used a 'protection of children' frame to undermine the permissive changes of the late 20th century and LGBT rights. In fighting back, the LGBT movement has framed its demands in the language of equality, discrimination and justice. However, the success of the LGBT movement in the last 10 years in achieving the equalisation of the age of consent, the repeal of Section 28, adoption rights for lesbian and gay couples and recognition of lesbian and gay partnerships is also the result of the substantial political opportunities created by the New Labour election victory in 1997. The chapter also draws parallels with the symbolic nature of the temperance crusade at the turn of the 19th and 20th centuries (see Gusfield, 1986) and the Christian defence of the family in late 20th century. For example, it can be argued that the importance of Section 28 was related to the fact that it enshrined in law that lesbian and gay male partnerships were not equivalent to heterosexual marriage and were no more than pretend family relationships. In this way, as with temperance movement in the US in the early 20th century, the passing of Section 28 was a symbolic victory that was used to demonstrate the dominance of Christian values and the crusader's definition of the family in the UK even though in reality the significance and power of Christian values are waning.

Although the LGBT movement is often characterised as a 'new' social movement and as engaging in a cultural politics, that politics is also concerned with challenging and influencing the state. Since the decriminalisation of homosexuality, Christian and LGBT activists have sought to influence public thinking on sexuality yet each has also needed to engage with the more mainstream institutional politics to ensure that their values are backed up by legislative change.

Further reading

For a good discussion of the family and family policy, see *Families in Society: Boundaries and Relationships* by Linda McKie and Sarah Cunningham-Burley (The Policy Press, 2005) and *Family Policy* by Fran Wasoff and Ian Dey (Gildredge Press, 2000).

Sex and Politics: The Family and Morality in the Thatcher Years by Martin Durham (Macmillan, 1991) provides a good discussion of the moral politics of the family during the 1980s.

If you would like further information on LGBT history in the UK, see *A Gay History of Britain: Love and Sex between Men since the Middle Ages* by Matt Cook et al (Greenwood World Publishing, 2007) and *Coming Out: Homosexual Politics in Britain from the 19th Century to the Present* by Jeffery Weeks (Quartet, 1990, revised edition).

On the lesbian and gay movement, *The Unfinished Revolution: Social Movement Theory and the Gay and Lesbian Movement* by Stephen Engel (Cambridge University Press, 2001) is a good recent discussion of the gay and lesbian movement in terms of social movement theory, while *OutRage!* by Ian Lucas (Cassell, 1998) is an extremely enjoyable history of that organisation.

MatthewWaites has written a number of very good articles on the contemporary debates on the age of consent, and the repeal of Section 28. In particular, see 'The fixity of sexual identities in the public sphere: biomedical knowledge, liberalism and the heterosexual/homosexual binary in late modernity', *Sexualities*, 2005, 8 (5): 539-69.

Useful websites

Centre for Relationship and Family Research: *www.crfr.ac.uk*

Equality Network ~ a Scottish LGBT rights organisation: *www.equality-network.org*

Stonewall ~ the main LGBT lobby organisation in the UK: www.stonewall.org.uk

For those interested in Christian anti-gay activism, see:

Christian Institute: *www.christian.org.uk*

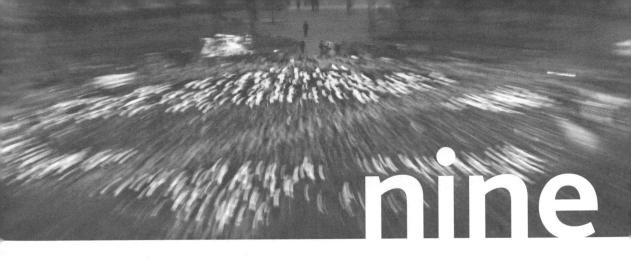

Contesting discrimination: anti-racist movements

Introduction: discrimination and civil rights

The latter half of the 20th century saw a growing number of contemporary social movements framing their demands in the language of 'civil rights', influenced by the success and tactics of the American black civil rights movement of the 1960s. The civil rights 'master frame' (see Snow and Benford, 1992) at once legitimatised the movement's activities and transformed their grievances into an injustice, which has been identified as a key micro-mobilisation process (see Gamson, 1995; Klandermans, 1992). In the UK, the demand for equal rights and an end to discrimination were core elements of the women's, lesbian, gay, bisexual and transgendered (LGBT), black and disability social movements' agenda and the success of the movements can be seen in the raft of anti-discrimination legislation passed by the British government. For example, the 1970 Equal Pay Act, 1975 Sex Discrimination Act, 1976 Race Relations Act and 1995 Disability Discrimination Act are all the outcome of the pressure these movements exerted on the government (see Lawrence and Turner, 1999). However, it is also possible to argue that such legislation, while representing an important victory in the fight for the rights of all people to be treated equally, has not ended discrimination. Hence, women are still paid less than men, racism is still endemic in our institutions, lesbian and gay couples are denied the right to marry (although civil partnerships legally recognise their relationships, separate is not equal) and disabled people, older people and young people are all prevented from fully participating in the social and economic life of the country.

This is not to underestimate the positive impact that these hard-won changes have had on society. However, these successes have often been accompanied by a process of incorporation as movements have been brought into the polity through the creation of equal opportunity posts and government funding (see also Chapter Eight). Such changes have led to the emergence of a more professionalised movement that is more akin to American interest groups and this invariably has the effect of weakening the radicalism of the original movement. This process by which social movements begin as 'challengers' but as they become more established and concerned with issues such as maintaining funding they become increasingly incorporated into the polity has been widely documented by social movement theorists (see Lo, 1992).

One of the major recent legislative changes has been the 1998 Human Rights Act, which incorporated the European Convention on Human Rights into UK and Scottish law and came into force on 2 October 2000. This Act has provided even greater opportunities for social movements to demand full rights for their constituents and legally challenge discrimination and discriminatory practices. However, it remains unclear to what extent the Act will actually undermine a culture of discrimination, nor will it end discrimination by all sections of the government, for example in certain areas discriminatory practices will remain in force, such as immigration policy (see Webber, 2001).

Legislative changes, such as the 1976 and 2000 Race Relations Acts, the 1998 Human Rights Act and the 2006 Equality Act, have shown the UK government's willingness to use anti-discrimination legislation to manage the 'problem' of diversity. However, this has been coupled with a growing emphasis on the importance of 'Britishness' and 'citizenship' by the current Labour government as it has attacked multiculturalism for promoting religious extremism (see Kundnandi, 2007). Furthermore, legislation such as the Human Rights Act, not only recognises individual and group rights but also the rights of multinational corporations and therefore further strengthens corporate power. Where rights are granted to individuals and groups, they are often qualified; for example, the 1995 Disability Discrimination Act places a duty on employers and businesses to only make 'reasonable adjustment' to accommodate the needs disabled people (Lawrence and Turner, 1999).

This chapter will focus, in particular, on the black and ethnic minority communities' challenge to both the explicit and institutional racism inherent in British society. It will focus on the 1970s when an inclusive radical black activism existed before it became more welfare focused and community based during the Thatcher period. This case study will act as an exemplar of the way in which certain sections of British society have been denied the opportunity of full citizenship and have been subject to widespread discrimination. It will start by providing a brief overview of 'race' and policy.

'Race' and policy

The 1948 British Nationality Act opened the door to those from new Commonwealth countries, giving them the right to work and settle with their families in the UK. The migrants who came from the Caribbean first, and then from Asia, were desperately needed by the UK economy to meet the widespread labour shortages of the post-war period, and generally found themselves in low-paid and menial jobs that white British workers did not want to fill. Certain employers such as London Transport even set up recruiting offices in the Caribbean to try to encourage immigration (see Mason, 2000). The former British colonies acted, as Sivanandan (1982) argues, as a 'reserve army of labour' to be used to free British workers for employment in better-paid and more desirable occupations. The newly arrived migrants were forced into poor housing in the most deprived areas of the large cities and exploited by landlords and employers. However, as capitalists gained from their exploitation of this cheap source of labour, tensions were rising:

> [T]he profit from immigrant labour had not benefited the whole of society but only certain sections of it (including some sections of the white working class) whereas the infrastructural 'cost' of immigrant labour had been borne by those in greatest need. That is not to say that immigrants (qua immigrants) had caused social problems – Britain, after all, was a country of net emigration – but that the forced concentration of immigrants in the deprived and decaying areas of the big cities high-lighted (and reinforced) existing social deprivation. (Sivanandan, 1982, pp 104-5)

It was these tensions that resulted in the 'race' riots during 1958 and forced the government to re-examine its open-door policy. The outcome was the 1962 Commonwealth Immigration Act, which introduced a voucher system that distinguished between those who had a firm job offer before coming to the UK and those who did not. For those who did not have a job, only those with specific skills would be allowed entrance. The 1968 Commonwealth Immigration Act further restricted the right to live and work in the UK to only those British passport holders who were 'born, adopted or naturalised in the UK' or who had a parent or grandparent 'born, adopted or naturalised in the UK' (Mason, 2000, p 27). This Act was introduced in order to limit the number of British Asians living in Kenya who wished to settle in the UK following the introduction of Kenya's Africanisation policy in 1967 (Sivanandan, 1982). Finally, the 1971 Immigration Act 'ended primary immigration' from the new commonwealth countries (Mason, 2000) and refocused British immigration policy back towards Europe. As Fryer (1984, p 381) argues, between 1958 and 1968 the UK government surrendered to racism and that 'step by step, racism was institutionalized, legitimized and nationalized'.

The open-door policy of the 1950s was very quickly was succeeded by a policy of increasing restriction on migration from the black and minority ethnic former colonies, which was coupled with the problematisation of 'race' relations. For Sivanandan (1982), this shift from open door to increasingly closed door was indicative of the accumulating costs to capital associated with 'racial' tensions. These costs also made it politically expedient to severely restrict immigration while simultaneously tackling the problem of 'racism' that made it no longer viable to use labour from the new Commonwealth.

The government's response was to pass a series of Race Relations Acts (1965, 1976, 2000) to manage the 'problem' of ethnic diversity, which had the consequence of transforming the black and minority ethnic communities into the problem rather than white racism.

Law (1999, pp 211-2) argues that, from the early 1990s, the application of 'new public management techniques' to the 'problem' of ethnic diversity in the UK represented a form of 'ethnic managerialism' that aimed:

> to construct 'consociationalism (Lijphart, 1977), where the liberal democratic state accommodates ethnic pluralism, simultaneously as attempts are being made to construct more ethnically exclusive criteria in the specification of citizenship in Britain and Europe. (Law, 1999, p 212)

Law argues that there are a number of negative consequences that result from the privileging of ethnicity under 'ethnic managerialism' not least the extension of 'racialised coding' that acts to emphasise the otherness of those from black and ethnic minority communities; an otherness that has been further strengthened by the UK government's handling of the issues of asylum and terrorism during the 1990s and 2000s. Both issues have been used to justify the need for greater management of the UK population through the issuing of biometric identity cards and increased sharing of information between government agencies. Although such cards will not stop terrorist attacks or those fleeing from persecution and violence coming to the UK, they will allow the government to manage entitlement. Entitlement has also been linked to an emphasis on integration and 'Britishness' as a necessary criterion for citizenship. This has amounted to an attack on the idea of multiculturalism. Rather than multiculturalism, New Labour has begun to emphasise the idea of 'community cohesion' (see Worley, 2005) as the foundation of its new race relations policy. The increasing use of the term 'community' as part of Labour's rhetoric has enabled the Westminster government to avoid identifying specific communities while suggesting that there needs to be increased levels of assimilation and integration of minority ethnic communities into mainstream 'British' society (Worley, 2005; Mooney and Neal, 2009). Following the riots in Bradford, Burnley and Oldham in 2001, politicians and the wider liberal establishment pointed to the isolation and ghettoisation of the Asian community in the UK as one of the primary causes of the disruption. The dangers of such isolation were underlined by the 9/11 attacks in the US and the July 7th bombings in London in 2005. Following these attacks, the political classes began to critique the policy of multiculturalism for promoting 'an over-tolerance of cultural diversity' that 'has allowed Asians in northern towns to "self-segregate", resulting in violent tensions' (Kundnani, 2007, p 26) building up between the Asian and white communities. Multiculturalism became a useful scapegoat for politicians since it enabled them to blame the communities themselves rather than the racism fuelled by their growing anti-immigration and anti-asylum political rhetoric that increased throughout the 1990s.

The attacks on multiculturalism strengthened as the war on terror constructed the Muslim as the terrorist in our midst. This led Sivanandan (2006, p 2) to argue that asylum and the war on terror have converged to produce a racism where all people from black and minority ethnic groups are seen as outsiders, illegal and potential terrorists:

> The war on asylum in fact predates the events of September 11. But after the London bombings of July 7, the two trajectories – the war on asylum and the war on terror – have converged to produce a racism which can not tell a settler from an immigrant, an immigrant from an asylum seeker, an asylum seeker from a Muslim, a Muslim from a terrorist. We are, all of us Blacks and Asians, at first sight, terrorists or illegals. We wear our passports on our faces, or lacking them, we are faceless.

Black and Asian movements

Unlike in the US where social movement theorists have written reams on the black civil rights movement, relatively little has been written on the black and ethnic minority communities' struggle against racism in the UK (Farrar, 2004). Despite this, those from the black and ethnic minority communities have been active in organising against the discrimination they experience in their everyday life. The newly arrived migrants during the 1950s and 1960s had to fight against not only widespread ignorance of their culture and religion but also a colonial attitude, a legacy of empire and a construction of those from black and ethnic minority communities as inferior (see Fryer, 1984). These racist beliefs were strengthened by a press-fuelled belief that migrants were getting more than they deserved and if not 'scrounging' they were, at the very least, taking jobs off the deserving white British. In policy terms, black and ethnic minority communities were constructed as a problem, exemplified in Enoch Powell's 1968 'Rivers of Blood' speech. This 'incitement to hatred' reinforced the widespread viewpoint that 'immigrants' were the problem rather than highlighting the mistaken and racist beliefs promoted by the tabloid press and fascist organisations such as the National Front, both of which actively promoted the notion of 'criminal' black youth presenting a major threat to the law-abiding white population (see Gilroy, 1987). Powell, despite being forced out of the Conservative Party and into the political wilderness, remained an important figure, not least because, as Miles and Phizacklea (1979, p 8) argue, he made 'racism more respectable'. It is against the backdrop of Powell's racist rhetoric and the growth of the far Right that during the 1970s there developed an inclusive radical struggle against racism, influenced by the rise of black power in the US.

The experience of the newly arrived migrant, as with successive generations of Irish migrants, was one of racism, discrimination and exploitation. Almost immediately the black and minority ethnic workers began fighting against the discriminatory treatment they received at the hands of their British employers. In many cases, these workers responded to the racism they experienced by quitting jobs, downing tools and in one instance a bus driver fed up with the abuse he suffered just abandoned his bus on the high street (Sivanandan, 1982). However, these individual acts of defiance were coupled with collective responses to both the abuse and the violence that black and minority ethnic communities experienced on the street and the discrimination they experienced in the workplace through their involvement in trade unions, the wider socialist movement and the setting up of their own workers' organisations. For example, the West Indian Association was formed in 1951 in an ordinance factory in Liverpool and in 1953 the Indian Workers' Association was founded. However, by the 1970s, a new militancy was growing and throughout the decade there were repeated confrontations between black and Asian youths and the authorities.

For Farrar (2004), the Mangrove trial represented an important turning point in the black and minority ethnic communities' fight back against the violence and the discrimination they experienced in their everyday lives. The Mangrove trial followed the arrest of nine black demonstrators who were protesting 'against police harassment of Frank Critchlow, the owner of the Mangrove Restaurant in Notting Hill' in August 1971 (Farrar, 2004, p 224). The arrests followed the police attempt to arrest members of the British Black Panthers who had turned up to support the demonstration. Despite very serious charges against the nine demonstrators, including 'incitement to riot and the attempted murder of a police officer', the nine were acquitted. The Mangrove restaurant confrontation was indicative of the growing concern about 'black power' and a fear of black youth that Gilroy (1987, pp 92-3) argues was fed even further by a 'sequence of bitter confrontations in and around other black cultural institutions – the dance-halls and clubs'. These confrontations between police and black youth during the 1970s, Gilroy (1987, p 93) argues, represented a new form of confrontation and organisation that was constructed around the defence of those arrested and which included protest both in and out of the courtroom:

> While the law was recognized as a repressive force there was no reluctance to use what constitutional and democratic residues it contained. The strategy that was devised sought to reveal and then exploit the political dimensions of the legal process by using the dock as a platform for the critical perspectives of the defendant while combining this legal struggle with popular, local agitation and organizing community support.... This combination of tactics and the synchronization of protest inside and outside the law, provided a model which has become central to the political repertoires of black activism.

Throughout the 1970s, these confrontations continued in Chapeltown in Leeds, Brixton and Notting Hill (see Gilroy, 1987; Farrar, 1999, 2004), to name a few, fuelled by the racist actions of the police and incitement to 'racial' hatred by a racist press that continually suggested that migrants were getting more than they deserved while the plight of the white working class was ignored. Typical of the banner headlines that supported the growing backlash against the black and minority ethnic communities during the 1970s was the *Sun* headline in 1976 of the 'Scandal of £600 a week immigrants' (Ramamurthy, 2006).

There was more to the anti-racism movement than these confrontations; for example, Asian workers, in particular, were likely to be involved in the trade union movement. However, Rex (1979, p 85) argued that there were significant differences between West Indian and Asian community politics, with Asian politics more closely aligned to British class politics:

> In many ways the Asian Community's politics differ from those of the West Indian. On the one hand they have a more anglicized mode of expression than the West Indian. The traditional national culture provides a leadership which fits easily into the paternalistic framework provided by the community Relations Commission (now reorganized into the Commission for Racial Equality) ... Indian labour and Marxist organizations help in some way to bring the Indian worker closer to the British.

The struggle of British Asian workers against their employers was exemplified by a number of high-profile and longlasting strike actions during the 1970s, most notably the strikes at the Leicester-based Imperial Typewriters in May 1974 and the nearly two-year struggle of predominantly Asian women at the Grunwick photographic factory in North London (see Farrar, 2004). These conflicts acted to create a sense of solidarity particularly among Asian and white trade unionists.

The 1970s also saw a resurgence of fascism. Growing support for the National Front led to an increase in racially motivated attacks on those from black and minority ethnic communities, even if the police seemed to be reluctant to admit that there was a racial dimension to these attacks. The National Front used the fear of black youths being constructed by the media reporting of 'mugging' to promote its brand of fascism (Nugent and King, 1979), which, mixed with the worsening economic crisis in the early 1970s, led to heightened tensions between sections of the white communities and the black and minority ethnic communities. In response to the rise of the National Front, the Left began to organise against this fascism and the racism it promoted through setting up of the Anti-Nazi League and Rock Against Racism that had been founded by supporters of the Socialist Workers Party in 1976. Rock Against Racism was a cultural challenge to rising levels of racism and the very public fascist and racist statements made by a number of rock stars. Rock Against Racism promoted its anti-racist message through the distribution of its fanzine *Temporary Hoarding*, first issued in 1977, and through a series of carnivals (see Gilroy, 1987).

While there was a clear solidarity between these movements and sections of the black and minority ethnic communities, there was also a growing gulf between white, black and Asian youths – a gulf provoked in part by the sense of alienation experienced, in particular, by African Caribbean youth and the developing sense of black cultural nationalism promoted in publications such as Notting Hill-based *Grassroots*. Farrar (2004, pp 227–8) argues that papers like *Grassroots* demonstrated an 'aspiration for a cultural and social life … quite separate from that of white citizens'. Influenced by the Rastarafarian movement, this growth of cultural nationalism was important because although it had 'little interest in the demonstrations, conferences and so on organised by the wider movement around "race", its influence on young black people was significant, because it expressed the deep alienation many felt within white society'. The influence of black power was also important for a generation of young British Asians who began to define themselves as politically black, recognising the common experience of racism shared by all people from black and minority ethnic groups. It was the political awakening of these youths along with the racially motivated murders of a number of Asians in particular during 1976 that led to the rise of the Asian youth movement in the second half of the 1970s.

The catalyst was the poor police response to the murder of Gurdip Singh Chaggar in Southall on 4 June 1976. The anger generated by this murder and the refusal of the police to admit that there was a racial dimension to the attack led Asian youths to mobilise, forming the Southall youth movement. The name was deliberately chosen to promote an inclusive struggle of all Southall youth against racism. The Southall youth movement inspired other Asian youths in cities across the UK to mobilise, for example the Indian Progressive Association formed in Bradford 1977, which was reformed the following year as the Bradford Asian youth movement. Like Asian youth in other cities, the Bradford Asian youth movement was a reaction to the sense of crisis felt by Asian youth during the 1970s. Influenced by black power, these youths sought common struggle with all members of the black and minority ethnic communities to defeat British racism. As Ramamurthy (2006, p 45) argues:

> They did not see black simply as a skin colour but as a political position; this was a standpoint reflected nationally across all the Asian Youth Movements. The term 'black' enabled a collective identity and solidarity to develop in the struggle against both the racism of the street and the institutional racism of immigration laws.

The message of the Asian youth movement was both inclusive and secular but during the 1980s this was undermined by increased government funding for minority ethnic communities following the publication of the Scarman Report on the 1981 Brixton riots (Scarman 1981; see also Barker and Beezer, 1983, for an excellent discussion of racism inherent in the Scarman Report). This funding acted to co-opt the leaders of the movement and channel their energies away from overtly political activities while at the same time engaging in a divide-and-rule strategy where specific communities received funds to work with their specific communities rather than working across all communities in a particular area (see Ramamurthy, 2006).

For Farrar (2004, p 232), the 1970s was an important decade during which 'a new social actor made its presence decisively felt in British society: black citizens found their militant voice, and the establishment was forced to make ad-hoc responses'. This response included the 1976 Race Relations Act and the setting up of the Commission for Racial Equality to fight against racial discrimination and promote equality. Farrar argues that four other consequences resulted from the militant black activism of the 1970s including: the recognition of a right of oppressed groups to 'autonomous self-organisation'; a 'cultural politics of everyday life' (to which Farrar argues the reclaim the street marches of the 1990s were indebted); a generation of white youths who 'admired black culture' and who recognised that 'race' was a constructed phenomenon; and because of this, 'multi-culturalism and anti-racism were losing their relevance in the everyday lives of young people living in the ethnically diverse cities of the UK' (Farrar, 2004, pp 232-3). While this might seem that Farrar is positing that by the end of the 1970s the UK had become an ethnically diverse utopia, he is not; instead, Farrar suggests that although the challenge against racism was uneven, the UK could no longer be characterised as 'universally racist'.

Farrar goes on to argue that, viewed through the work of Manuel Castells (see Chapters Three and Six), the 1970s radical black movement could be characterised as being successful in terms of 'their 'collective consumption' demands, over their 'identity' issues, and as 'citizens' movements' (Farrar 2004, p 236). However, like Ramamurthy (2006), Farrar recognises that the actions of the Conservative government following the 1981 riots in Birmingham, Bristol, Liverpool, London and Manchester among other towns and cities, undermined the radicalism of the movement and led to an increasingly fragmented, more reformist, community-based welfare-oriented black movement.

Ironically, the actions of the Conservative government during the 1980s may well have acted to create the insularity and alienation that has helped fuel religious extremism in recent years and did little to expose the institutional racism that incidences such as the Stephen Lawrence case demonstrated was still endemic in the UK. The debates on asylum have also furthered the sense of isolation among those from black and minority ethnic communities with those fleeing to the UK as a safe haven from political violence, ethnic cleansing and war being constructed as illegitimate by the media and increasingly by politicians. New Labour since coming to power in 1997 has continued to problematise the issue of asylum and the need to protect the UK from economic migrants disguised in refugee clothing. This has been combined with a newly invigorated policy of deportations throughout the European Union and target setting for deportations by the UK government (Fekete, 2005). However, global changes were also important in these youths' withdrawal into their own community as the US and Britain engaged in a war against Islamic fundamentalism while actively supporting Israel's continued oppression of the Palestinian people. This wider global situation, Ramamurthy (2006, p 57) argues, had significant consequences for how some former members of the Asian youth movement defined themselves:

> For most AYM [Asian youth movement] members, there was little contradiction between a black political identity and cultural and religious affiliations, such as Kashmiri and Sikh. Yet within a few years, the global situation had shifted with the rise of an Anglo-American Christian fundamentalism and its support for Zionism, the rise of Hindutva in India and the rise of Islamic organisations – partly fostered by American funding of Islamist groups during the Cold War. Muslims became the new scapegoat. By the 1990s, this had impacted on the way in which some ex-AYM members defined themselves.

In part, then, this shift is the response to a new religious- and cultural-based racism rather than one simply premised on colour. Islamophobia has become a major expression of racism in recent years and this has reinforced the sense of isolation felt by Muslim youth, an isolation that Sivanandan (2006, p 7) argues has resulted from the merging of the 'war on asylum' and the 'war on terror' and a changing focus of Western governments from a concern for the 'social welfare of the people' to a concern for the 'economic welfare of corporations'. This, Sivanandan argues, has had the effect of prioritising 'corporate values' at the expense of 'moral values' and it this shift in values that has led young Muslims to turn 'to Islam not just as a belief system but as a movement'.

Equality in the 21st century?

Rex (1979) argues that there exists considerable differences between the black movement in the US and that in the UK. For example, he argues that in the UK there has not been the development of an 'American-style' black civil rights movement with a national organisation such as the National Association for the Advancement of Colored People. The only British equivalent was the short-lived Campaign Against Racial Discrimination. In part, the difference between the US and UK may reflect differences in the political organisation of both countries, and in particular the political opportunities that the American constitution affords movements to legally challenge the infringement of their civil rights. Although social movements in the UK have had in the past limited opportunities to legally challenge the government through the process of judicial review and since 1966 through the European Court of Human Rights, it was not until the passing of the Human Rights Act in 1998 that the European Convention on Human Rights became incorporated into British law and offered social movements new opportunities to challenge discrimination. Not surprisingly, since coming into effect on 2 October 2000, there has been a plethora of legal cases from a diverse range of groups seeking to establish in law their civil rights.

However, while it might be the case that the Human Rights Act may be a useful tool for social movements, especially for challenging specific injustices such as illegal deportation of asylum seekers, there are some major flaws that limit its effectiveness. For example, one of the major drawbacks with the legislation, as Webber (2001) has argued, is that it accepts the notion that corporations have human rights, as if multinational corporations are as powerless as individuals and need even further government protection. Furthermore, the government maintains its right to discriminate whether it is against asylum seekers or individuals who the state mistakenly identifies as terrorists. While the Human Rights Act does provide a basic level of protection, for some groups this protection is very limited indeed:

> But, while corporations enjoy their freedom to print celebrity gossip and to advertise tobacco products in the name of freedom of expression, and receive compensation for adverse planning decisions in accordance with their 'human rights' of enjoyment of property, for the powerless groups in our society, those traditionally excluded and targeted by the police and immigration authorities, all indications are that the human rights ceiling is uncomfortably close to the floor. (Webber, 2001, p 92)

Conclusion

Migrants from the new commonwealth countries during the 1950s and 1960s not only had to contend with poor pay, working conditions and housing but also experienced widespread racism. The 'racial' tensions stoked by far Right movements, politicians and a racist press forced the UK government to revise its open-door policy and control new immigration while simultaneously trying to manage 'race' and 'race relations'. At the end of the 1960s and the start of the 1970s, the racist rhetoric of Enoch Powell, the rise of the fascist National Front and heavy-handed poling incited young black and Asian youth to fight back. These youths, inspired by 'black power' and the success and tactics of the American black civil rights movement, challenged the fascists and the racism inherent in UK society. They were joined by left-wing organisations such as the Anti-Nazi League and Rock Against Racism that sought to challenge the deteriorating situation in many of the UK's cities. Confrontations between these youths and the police continued throughout the 1970s, culminating in widespread disturbances in 1981. Following the Scarman Report on the 1981 disturbances, the Thatcher administration began a programme of community-based funding that acted to divide these youths into their respective communities and encouraged more welfare-oriented and less-radical community-based movements. However, despite legislation such as the 1998 Human Rights Act and the 2006 Equality Act, the problem of racism in the UK has not been overcome but rather the wars on asylum and terror in recent years have acted to incite both 'racial' and religious hatred and further alienate black and minority ethnic youth.

In terms of social movement theory, anti-discrimination movements such as the black and Asian movements, the women's movement and more recently the disability movement have successfully used a civil rights frame to legitimatise their demands on the state and transform their grievances into injustices. During the 1970s, this sense of injustice was exemplified in the confrontations between the police and black and Asian youth who were fed up of the constant police interference and harassment in their lives. These confrontations led to the construction of a new repertoire of contention by black activists who used the courtroom as a political platform to get their message heard in conjunction with protests outside the law courts. The law in this way became a weapon in the struggle against racism.

Castells' work on urban social movements is also useful for understanding the radical black movement of the 1970s. Not only did this movement construct an inclusive radical black cultural identity but it also challenged the dominant construction of black and Asian youth and their alienation from white society. Farrar (1999, 2004) has argued that the radical black movement of the 1970s was a successful urban social movement as defined by Castells, however, a process of cooption during the 1980s undermined the movement and turned the communities' focus inwards. This not only led to a growing gulf between Asian, black and white youth but also an increasing importance of religious identity within these communities.

Further reading

Two chapters by Max Farrar – 'Social movements in a multi-ethnic inner city: explaining their rise and fall over 25 years' in Bagguley and Hearn (Macmillan, 1999) and 'Social movements and the struggle over race' in Todd and Taylor (Merlin Press, 2004) – provide an excellent discussion of the Asian youth movement during the 1970s and early 1980s.

Staying Power: The History of Black People in Britain by Peter Fryer (Pluto Press, 1984) is a very good history of the post-war experience of black and minority ethnic migrants into the UK.

A Different Hunger: Writings on Black Resistance by Ambalavaner Sivanandan (Pluto Press, 1982) is a classic text on black resistance.

Useful websites

Equality and Human Rights Commission, which replaced the Commission for Racial Equality, the Equality Opportunity Commission and the Disability Rights Commission in 2007: *www.equalityhumanrights.com*

Muslim Council of Britain: *www.mcb.org.uk/*

Refugee Action, which works with refugees to help them build a new life in the UK: *www.refugee-action.org.uk*

Refugee Council: *www.refugeecouncil.org.uk*

Contesting the environment: eco-welfare movements

ten

Introduction: social movements and environmental welfare

This chapter aims to explore the contribution of environmentalism to the theory and practice of social welfare. It will begin by examining the evolution and impact of the environmental movement over the past few decades, before moving on to discuss the redefinition of social welfare as eco-welfare that is advanced by green social policy makers and academic commentators. An argument follows that the anti-roads protest movement of the 1990s constitutes a prime example of the ongoing struggle for eco-welfarism. A case study, utilising social movements theory, of the protest against the M77 motorway extension in Glasgow will show how social and environmental issues were brought together in an innovative manner to animate the practice of social movement activists from diverse critical political traditions. This type of practice it is argued is a prerequisite for the progressive greening of social welfare policy.

Environmentalism: the social movement and philosophy of our time?

As both a vibrant social movement and as a political ideology, environmentalism contains many competing and diverse strands (Pepper, 1996; Dobson, 1997). There is often disagreement and internal debate around tactics, strategy and organisation due to the sheer variety of political parties, pressure groups, conservation societies, non-governmental organisations, protest movements, single-issue protest campaigns, actors and activists that the movement contains. Most environmentalists nevertheless agree on a loosely defined common agenda that is centred, first, on a critique of the dominant Promethean rationality, and short-term prioritisation of profits and economic growth that has deformed the development of modern society and brought the Earth's eco-system into crisis, and second, on the need to reconstruct the human relationship with nature on a long-term sustainable basis that necessarily recognises the interconnectedness of all life.

In the early 21st century, the environmental movement remains the most high-profile and vigorous of the 'new' social movements to emerge from the radical insurgency of the late 1960s/early 1970s. The issues that give the environmental movement its raison d'être – pollution, resource depletion, species extinction, habitat destruction, population growth and global warming – have moved in the matter of a few decades from being marginal concerns on the periphery of the social and political stage to being ubiquitous reference points for contemporary culture and core concerns of world governance. By consistently raising these issues in the public sphere, green social movement activists have popularised a growing body of scientific knowledge regarding the negative environmental side-effects of the industrial economy and consumer capitalism (for both human and non-human life alike), and given impetus to new environmental sciences that suggest alternative more sustainable trajectories of social and economic development. Public awareness has been manifest in the adoption of green 'lifestyle choices' (recycling, energy efficiency and so on), which have been coupled with the development, marketing and consumption of an ever-widening range of 'environmentally friendly' products. It has also been manifest in the mushrooming of green literature, the fashion for environmental art and in the strong memberships of environmental movement organisations like the campaigning pressure groups Greenpeace and Friends of the Earth; and conservation lobby groups like the National Trust and the Royal Society for the Protection of Birds, which far outweigh that of the mainstream political parties (see Rootes, 2003).

In the political realm, concern with the environment has been translated into votes for the newly formed Green Parties of the 1980s, most notably in Austria, Germany, Sweden and the Benelux countries where they have achieved significant parliamentary representation. In Britain, the Green Party has faced a much more difficult task due to the 'first past the post' electoral system in General Elections (Rootes, 1992) – it has, however, scored limited success in elections to the European and Scottish Parliaments, which operate through systems of proportional representation and at local government level. Even in countries like Britain where national parliamentary representation has not been forthcoming, the environmental movement has succeeded in forcing the traditional parties to engage with

Green thinking as both New Labour and the (New) Conservatives green agendas attest to. This political engagement has had a knock-on effect in terms of government policy making at national and international levels as illustrated by the ever-expanding raft of environmental legislation that is designed to protect wildlife and the countryside, to control industrial pollution, waste and pesticide use, and to regulate greenbelt land development and planning applications. On a global scale, the Greens have also scored some limited successes – although ending in general disagreement and far from satisfactory from the green movement's point of view – the Earth Summits held in Rio (1992), New York (1997) and Johannesburg (2002) brought world leaders together to discuss ways of improving the world's environment; and in 2005 the Kyoto Protocol (agreed in 1997) came into effect whereby signatory states are committed to reducing CO_2 emissions to 1990 levels in order to address the problem of global warming.

The social movement theorists Dryzek et al (2003) argue that the significance of the environmental movement today is comparable to the great social movements of the past who managed to fuse their interests with core state imperatives and thus create seismic changes in the way that modern states and societies are constituted. They argue that just as the bourgeoisie challenged the feudal state to enable profit maximisation thus creating the liberal state; and just as the working class challenged the capitalist state to politically legitimate itself thus creating the welfare state, so the environmental movement is challenging 21st-century states to modernise both economically and politically through the adoption of a new core imperative of environmental conservation – for Dryzek et al this has the potential to create a historically new kind of state – the green state (see also Eckersley, 2004). Dryzek at al's argument is a statist variation on a common argument made by green-leaning social commentators that a process of ecological modernisation is under way across all sectors of society and especially in the economic realm (Young, 2000; Mol and Sonnenfeld, 2001).

Dobson (2003) views the radical strand of environmental thinking that is associated with ecologism as having the potential to create a new form of citizenship that supersedes traditional liberal rights-based and civic republican virtue-based conceptions. What he calls 'post-cosmopolitan' citizenship is a green form of global citizenship that extends rights and obligations beyond the traditional boundaries of the nation-state and extends the notion of citizenship itself beyond the confines of the public arena into the private realm of the family (paralleling feminism's emphasis on the personal being political; see also Dean, 2002, on eco-socialist citizenship). For other theorists, the contemporary prominence of the environmental movement signifies a shift towards 'a new stage in western culture' (Grove-White, 1997) that is variously conceived of as post-industrial, as post-modern or as constituting a risk society (Beck, 1992) or a network society (Castells, 2000).

One does not have to agree with these analyses to acknowledge the remarkable impact of the environmental movement over the past few decades and to recognise that environmental politics will play a key role in confronting what Beck (1992) has called the 'organised irresponsibility' of the capitalist system in the century ahead. Environmentalism has become an ideological master frame that all radical critiques of capitalism must refer to, as for example the strong green presence in the contemporary worldwide anti-capitalist movement attests to. For older movements (labour, feminism, urban and so on) frame realignment in line with the environmental master frame has become important for mobilisations in the contemporary era (Snow et al 1986). This significance is also indicated by the organised backlash against environmentalism led by a curious mixture of corporate interests and risk denying commentators (see for instance, Furedi, 2002; Taverne, 2005) who paradoxically reject overwhelming scientific evidence concerning human-made global warming and other forms of environmental degradation in the name of the Enlightenment (for critiques, see Rowell, 1996; Monbiot, 2006). John-Paul Sartre (2004), writing in the 1960s, described Marxism as 'the philosophy of our time' – the same can be said of environmentalism in the 21st century.

The greening of social welfare: towards eco-welfarism?

As previous chapters have shown, the post-war British welfare state was constructed around a conception of social welfare that put employment, education, health, housing and universal social security at its heart. Social movements – most notably the labour movement – fought for the creation of this welfare state as a mode of attaining a modicum of social justice and then sought to both deepen its reach and extend its boundaries through social policy legislation during the 1950s and 1960s. However, by the late 1960s/early 1970s, the welfare state and its traditional conception of welfare was increasingly deemed inadequate. The 'new' social movements of the period argued that both the state's welfare provision and its conception of social welfare were too narrow. The feminist movement and the various movements for minority rights maintained that the much-lauded universal welfare state was far from universal in that it privileged white, male heterosexual workers and discriminated against women and minority ethnic groups, while its mass nature meant that it was remote, bureaucratic, inflexible and controlling. Contemporary environmentalism adds a further multidimensional critique that centres on the argument that the conception of social welfare that underpins traditional social policy is impoverished because it fails to properly recognise:

- the importance of quality of life issues to social welfare. From this perspective, social welfare is too often reduced to simple economic well-being and access to consumer goods. Quality of life widens the conception of welfare out to encompass an individual's sense of social, physical and psychological well-being – this is of course dependent on that individual's ability to meet basic needs (and the ability of the community they are living in to do likewise) but also to develop personal attributes, pursue life goals, form relationships and to generally enjoy life. Access to a healthy built and natural environment is an integral aspect of having a good quality of life (Cahill, 2002).
- the need for sustainability in relation to the provision of social welfare services, health, housing, education and social security. Sustainability is famously defined in a much-quoted passage from the Brundtland Report (United Nations, 1987, p 8) as development that 'meets the needs of the present, without compromising the ability of future generations to meet their own needs'.
- the benefits of an integrated approach to social welfare (that stands in contrast to the compartmentalisation of the traditional approach). Greens argue that a perspective on social welfare that recognises social policy areas as mutually determining is essential. Barry and Doherty (2002, pp 126-7) give a good example of how this type of conceptualisation operates: 'housing policy is related to transport policy and health (including mental health) policies, since housing affects health. The building of new housing stock is often affected by transport policy, road building programmes and land use and planning, as well as having a significant impact on individual health and well being and on the natural world'.
- the potential opportunities for advancing social welfare provided by decentralising welfare provision and empowering local communities through the enhancement of forms of participatory democracy, third sector engagement and social enterprise ownership. Local autonomy is a key feature of green political theory and there is much internal debate as to how far processes of devolution of power should go. The famous green slogan to 'act locally and think globally' reflects this commitment while at the same time pointing to ideas of global interconnectedness. As Hoggett (2002, p 145) argues, the vision of the good society contained in the idea of 'eco-welfarism' is one where 'well being resides in the quality of relations between people and between people and nature' – an idea that

can only be operationalised if power is decentralised in a democracy that is far more thoroughgoing than the dominant representative form.

For green social scientists and environmentalists working within the field of social welfare policy, the theory and practice of social welfare needs to be redefined as 'eco-welfarism': a holistic conception of human and planetary welfare that puts sustainability, quality of life and participatory democracy alongside the traditional welfare commitment to social justice at its centre.

One prominent example of how the environmental movement has influenced welfare policy making in a concrete manner is through Local Agenda 21, which was agreed as part of the ambitious Agenda 21 blueprint for global sustainable development agreed by signatory states at the 1992 Rio Earth Summit. Local Agenda 21 embodies eco-welfarist themes when it states that:

> All States and all people shall cooperate in the essential task of eradicating poverty as an indispensable requirement for sustainable development, in order to decrease the disparities in standards of living and better meet the needs of the majority of the people of the world. (United Nations, 1992, p 10 [Principle 5])

Furthermore:

> Environmental issues are best handled with the participation of all concerned citizens, at the relevant level. At the national level, each individual shall have appropriate access to information concerning the environment that is held by public authorities, including information on hazardous materials and activities in their communities, and the opportunity to participate in decision-making processes. States shall facilitate and encourage public awareness and participation by making information widely available. Effective access to judicial and administrative proceedings, including redress and remedy, shall be provided. (United Nations, 1992, p 11 [Principle 10])

There are clear emphases in these principles (and in the other 25 that underpin Local Agenda 21) on joining up policy making on tackling poverty, improving life quality, enhancing democratic accountability and community control of local environments to promote the overall goal of sustainable development. Of course, there is only nominal commitment by signatory states to these principles but the environmental movement nevertheless views this commitment as significant because it shows some recognition by world governments of the need to at least begin to acknowledge the importance of sustainable development, while also providing a benchmark that the movement can campaign around. The aim of the environmental movement with regard to the outcomes of the Rio Summit and subsequent summits and international environmental treaties is to force states to close the gap between rhetoric and reality.

Within the Local Agenda 21 document there is also an important commitment whereby 'Each local authority should enter into a dialogue with its citizens, local organizations and private enterprises and adopt "a local Agenda/21"' (United Nations, 1992, p 402). Local Agenda 21 commits local authorities to 'consultation and consensus-building' and learning 'from citizens and from local, civic, community, business and industrial organizations' to 'acquire the information needed for formulating the best strategies' for sustainable development (United Nations, 1992, p 403). The document goes on to state that:

> The process of consultation would increase household awareness of sustainable development issues. Local authority programmes, policies, laws and regulations to achieve Agenda 21 objectives would be assessed and modified, based on local programmes adopted. Strategies could also be used in supporting proposals for local, national, regional and international funding. (United Nations, 1992, p 403)

In the wake of the Rio Summit, Local Agenda 21 was particularly influential in UK local government, where the stress on local authority programmes was naturally welcomed and there is a tradition linking social and environmental issues that reaches back to the public health campaigns of the 19th century. In fact, it is arguable that the modern environmental movement has its roots in the conservation societies and local authority public health campaigns of the Victorian era. In England, the Commons Preservation Society was founded in 1865 as the first national environmental conservation organisation – its aims were to preserve public access to open land and green spaces, primarily so that the urban working class would have an enhanced quality of life (Rootes, 2008). Each UK local authority has to a greater or lesser extent engaged with Local Agenda 21 with the aim of integrating social and environmental policy. This is a process that involves raising community awareness of sustainability issues, environmental auditing and working in partnership with community representatives and third sector organisations to tackle poverty and improve environmental amenity (see Cahill, 2002, pp 20-45).

There are of course numerous structural obstacles that stand in the way of successful reconstitution of welfare as anything resembling eco-welfare – the most salient being systemic economic imperatives for economic growth and related infrastructural development. Hence, for example, during the 1990s when on the one hand local authorities were busily trying to implement Local Agenda 21, on the other hand they were also charged by central government with presiding over the largest expansion of the road and motorway system for a generation as outlined in the 1989 White Paper *Roads for Prosperity*. This £23 billion construction programme was to be implemented in a manner that ran in a diametrically opposite direction to Local Agenda 21 – it would degrade and pollute local built environments and green spaces, remove access to amenities and divide communities. Moreover, road-building programmes have a tendency to penalise the poorest communities because urban routes are often planned through those communities, and because the poor do not possess the vehicles to use the roads and motorways when constructed. Rather, new roads and motorways benefit car-owning commuters and the business interests who lobby for them, while even according to the government's own scientific analysis they induce more traffic that in turn generates demand for yet more new roads and motorways (SACTRA, 1994).

Defending environmental welfare: the anti-roads protest movement

> The mobilisation of local communities in defence of their space, against the intrusion of undesirable uses, constitutes the fastest-growing form of environmental action, and one that perhaps most directly links people's immediate concerns to broader issues of environmental deterioration....While the movement is local, it is not necessarily localistic, since it often affirms residents' rights to the quality of their life in opposition to business and bureaucratic interests. What is questioned by these movements is, on the one hand, the bias of undesirable materials or activities towards low income communities and minority inhabited areas, on the other hand the lack of transparency in decision making about the use of space. (Castells, 1997, p 115)

Given the upsurge in public consciousness of environmental issues following the Rio Summit and local authority emphasis on community empowerment in line with Local Agenda 21, it is not surprising that in the mid-1990s the government's massive road- and motorway-building programme sparked a wave of protests across the UK. What is perhaps surprising though is the way that these protests developed into the most confrontational and indeed successful challenge to government policy since opposition to the Poll Tax in the late 1980s. In 1992, at the M3 construction site on Twyford Down in Hampshire, events occurred that were to be pivotal in setting the tone for anti-roads protests over the next few years. For the first time, after lengthy planning and legal processes had been exhausted, significant numbers of 'respectable' local objectors joined together with radical eco-activists to engage in collective non-violent direct action (NVDA) protests that involved tree sitting, obstruction of machinery and group trespasses, which flouted the law and led to physical confrontation with security guards and mass arrests from the police. These events made headline news and brought an intense media presence to the construction site, which served to positively publicise the objectors' case and to inspire related protests over the next few years (Porritt, 1996). High-profile protests on the model of Twyford occurred in the Wanstead and Leyton areas of London (1994, M11 link road), in Bath (1994, A36 Batheaston bypass), Glasgow (1994-95, M77 extension), Newbury (1995-97, A34 bypass) and Fairmile (1996-97, A30 Honiton bypass), as well as at numerous smaller protests of a similar nature at road construction sites across the UK. Such protests encapsulate in a very dramatic manner the type of polarisations and issues concerning quality of life, democracy, planning, poverty and sustainability that are embodied in the eco-welfare perspective and which Castells pointedly articulates in the passage quoted above.

At the protest movement's height in the mid-1990s, there were approximately 300 objectors' groups affiliated to the national anti-roads umbrella organisation Alarm UK. Because Alarm UK took a stance against all road-building and unequivocally supported NVDA, it played a key bridging role in facilitating dialogue and building solidarity between the local objectors' groups and the militant eco-activists who were often associated with the newly formed British wing of the environmental 'disorganisation' Earth First! and the green anarchist group Reclaim the Streets (McNeish, 2000). Both of these radical groups emerged in and through the anti-roads movement to operate as important actors in coordinating direct action protests.

Few protests were successful in their own right – Oxleas Wood (1993, East London River Crossing, A2 to A13) is probably the most significant victory and it was won by the threat of mass direct action before construction work was begun. However, in 1997, the deeply unpopular Conservative government, under political pressure due to an approaching General Election, and under fiscal pressure to cut public spending, slashed its roads budget by more than two thirds to £6 billion. Under New Labour's Roads Review, which it announced on taking office, this figure was cut still further while a Road Traffic Reduction Bill, which aims to cut traffic by 10% by 2010, became law in 1998. A few controversial schemes remained (for example, the Birmingham Northern Relief Road, which was completed in 2003, and the M74 extension in Glasgow, which is currently under construction and being opposed by the JAM74 (Joint Action against the M74 coalition); but is arguable that in the late 1990s the anti-roads protest movement had at least temporarily won the war – so much so that Alarm UK was folded in 1999. The anti-roads protest movement had mobilised just at the right time – when the political opportunity structure (Tarrow, 1994) was relatively open to a radical green challenger. It would appear though that, like previous Conservative governments, New Labour has succumbed to pressure from the powerful roads lobby (which is deeply embedded in the Confederation of British Industry) with plans announced through the early 2000s for a huge future expansion of the UK's road and motorway system and big budget increases for the Highways Agency. This is likely to re-galvanise the anti-roads protest movement with veterans of the 1990s protests already lobbying government and threatening renewed direct action opposition (Sadler, 2006).

Case study: eco-welfarism in practice – protesting against the M77 extension

> At this moment in time we believe the ecological holocaust facing our lands and wider environment to be so great, that it is our right, our duty, to throw off such forms of government that allow such evils to continue, and provide for our future security. We take this step with great reluctance and it is our intention to maintain peaceful relations with Her Majesty's government of the United Kingdom and Strathclyde Regional Council. Nevertheless it is our view that the undemocratic activities of these two institutions, through the proposed Criminal Justice and Public Order Act and M77 motorway extension are so unpopular, destructive and oppressive and their behaviour so unreasonable in the face of our appeals for mercy that we face no choice but to separate and determine our own future.

Declaration of Independence from the People of Pollok Free State (20 August 1994) (PFS, 1994)

The 25-year campaign to stop the £53 million M77 motorway extension from being built through the south side of Glasgow reached its climax between January and March 1995 when local people from the surrounding council estates joined with eco-activists based at the Pollok Free State eco-encampment in taking various forms of mass direct action to resist the motorway's construction. During those few cold months, police and security guards fought running battles with the protesters, mass arrests were made and the Scottish media went into a feeding frenzy debating the issue, conducting opinion polls and making heroes and villains out of individuals in the pro and anti lobbies alike. This was Scotland's first taste of the militant environmentalism surrounding the government's roads programme that had swept across other parts of the UK in the wake of the protests at Twyford Down. The M77 extension is undoubtedly the most controversial in Scotland's history in that quite apart from the vehement local hostility it engendered, it split Glasgow's ruling Labour Party down the middle by pitting the district council against the regional council while also becoming something of an international environmental *cause célèbre* due to its route, which not only infringes upon a number of deprived council estates but also cuts through the edges of the historically important and greenbelt-designated Pollok Estate. Sir John Maxwell had given the 1,118-acre estate to the people of Glasgow in 1939 to be held 'in perpetuity' for the enhancement of their environment, and its conservation was to be managed by the National Trust of which Maxwell was the founder in Scotland. The Estate contains Pollok Mansion House, Pollok Country Park and the world-famous Burrell collection of fine art and archaeological artefacts.

Plans for the M77 extension had first been mooted in the *Highway Plan for Glasgow* (Corporation of the City of Glasgow, 1965) (although the idea of a major roadway through the south side of Glasgow towards Ayrshire has its origins in the Clyde Valley Regional Plan in 1946) and opposition initiated during the 1970s by community activists from the Corkerhill council estate challenging the removal of a right of way to Pollok Park (Corkerhill's only major amenity) on the grounds of social justice. Opposition grew during the 1980s through the formation of new alliances with city-wide environmental, amenity and public transport activists who exhausted legal remedies through the Public Local Inquiry that was held in 1988. The Reporter to the Public Local Inquiry that was held in 1988 said: 'Corkerhill has a high unemployment rate, poor housing and associated illnesses, and few community facilities' and yet its 'environment would be substantially worsened by the (M77) Ayr

Road Route' (SRC, 1988, p 65). Indeed, Corkerhill would suffer from each of the five negative effects that a road can have on a community: noise, air pollution, visual obstruction, visual intrusion and obstruction to movement (SRC, pp 114-16). The Reporter nevertheless found in favour of the motorway. The final phase of opposition culminated in the 1994 formation of the STARR (Stop the Ayr Road Route) Alliance, an umbrella body totalling 20 different community councils, environmental organisations, amenity societies and public transport pressure groups. What had begun in the 1970s as a small, low-key community campaign with a primarily social justice orientation had mushroomed into a major conflict where social issues became to be framed through the wider prism of the environment. Arguably, a process of frame realignment took place over time as the mobilisation moved through different phases and new activists, social movement organisations and lobby groups joined the protest campaign (Snow et al, 1986; Snow and Bedford, 1992; also see Chapter Three).

The Pollok Free State operated as the hub of the No M77 extension campaign during its final phase. It had been set up by Glasgow Earth First! activists in association with local anti-motorway campaigners in the STARR Alliance during June 1994 as a fortified encampment that lay directly in the path of the planned route. This role it combined with one of highly visible defiance to the 1994 Criminal Justice and Public Order Act, which contained among its draconian clauses serious restrictions on the right to party, protest, demonstrate and pursue unconventional lifestyles, as well as the removal of the right to silence upon arrest.

On 20 August, after a couple of months of 'digging in', constructing defences and building living quarters, the activists at the Free State provocatively declared independence from the British state (see extract above), and began issuing passports to all who shared the 'beliefs, ideals and aspirations to come to the defence of this new domain' from 'the threat to our environment and liberty by this road and legislation which is incompatible with sustainable environmental use and any notion of democracy' (PFS, 1994, p 1). During the next few months, over 1,000 passports were issued, and the Free State became a hive of creative oppositional activity where people from across Scotland, the UK, and even small numbers from Europe and other parts of the world, came to take part in training in NVDA and the practices of 'ecotage' in order to prepare for the final 'showdown' with the state and the building contractors over the motorway. In doing so, they also inevitably joined in, and added to, the ferment of ideas generated by the ongoing political, ideological and environmental debate and discussion between a socially diverse range of activists from organisations affiliated to the STARR Alliance, radical left-wing political groupings (most prominently Scottish Militant Labour

– the forerunner of the Scottish Socialist Party) that had strong roots in the surrounding estates, and environmentalists of all shades of green (most prominently Earth First!), which became a regular feature of Free State life. This dialogue involved the clash of an eclectic pot-pourri of critical ideological stances with currents of anarchism and deep ecology, being articulated by the Free State's resident eco-activists, and different variants of socialism being propagated by the working-class local community activists and left-wing groupings. The activists' Declaration of a Peoples Free University of Pollok 'where degrees are offered in living' is an apposite testament to the type of cross-fertilising communicative dialogue that the Free State facilitated (Habermas, 1987b).

Throughout January 1995, rumours were rife among the protesters and press alike that construction work was about to begin and that the Free State and four smaller outposts that it had sprouted were about to be evicted. The protesters based in the camps and their supporters from the surrounding estates began to prepare for the final 'battle' by 'spiking' trees to inhibit chainsaws and creating barricades, elevated walkways and fortified treehouses. Look-outs were posted along the route as an early warning system that would enable a rallying call to be sent out, thereby marshalling protesters to counteract the contractors plans. Laing (1995), writing critically of the protesters' plans in the *The Herald*, reported that:

> The moment the construction crews move in the demonstrators' jungle drums will beat a muster call and within hours there will be as many as 200 on the scene. Spectacular direct action is predicted and the Glasgow based groups have been promised a helping hand from English activists who were involved in the Newbury protest. The anti-M77 action, even in its death throes, seems set to become the event of the 1995 campaign calendar. It will be the unseemly and unpleasant face of environmental protest.

However, it was not until early February that the first serious clashes between the protesters and contractors occurred. The construction firm Wimpey had engaged the security firm Securiguard to protect its project and on 2 February, 12 of its guards fought a running battle with protesters in an area of woodland known locally as 'Pollok Castle' near the Newton Mearns end of the extension. Here protesters chained themselves to tree-fellers' equipment, vehicles and to the treefellers themselves in order to halt the work and Wimpey was forced to retreat. In this first serious confrontation, police were not involved and the security presence was relatively small – thus, the protesters were victorious. Wimpey was, however, to learn from this mistake and use large numbers of both police and security guards in the future. Two days later though the campaign scored another victory when Scottish Office Minister Allan Stewart, the Conservative MP for Eastwood, confronted a group of protesters brandishing a pick-axe in a threatening manner. A complaint was made to the police about his behaviour and he was forced to resign his ministerial post on 7 February. From this point onwards, direct actions to hinder construction work intensified, arrests began and protesters began to make regular appearances in Glasgow Sheriff Court where they either agreed to bail conditions banning them from approaching, obstructing or interfering with Wimpey's workmen, or refused them and were remanded in custody in Barlinnie prison until trial. Over time, these actions by the state authorities proved highly effective in draining the direct action campaign of many of its leading activists.

On 14 February, highly controversial incidents occurred at the Pollok Free State after columns of 200 police (backed by a helicopter), 150 yellow-jackets (security guards) and bulldozers moved in to attempt to clear the site. The protesters defending the Free State were caught off guard and as arrests began to be made it seemed as though they would be overwhelmed by the sheer weight of opposing forces. However, just as all seemed lost, over 100 school children from the nearby Bellarmine secondary school streamed from over a hill and surged forward to unfurl banners proclaiming 'NO M77!' and obstruct the bulldozers. As a result, the contractors were once again forced to retreat and 26 security guards deserted, one being quoted as saying 'Ah'm no here tae hit weans'. The regional council, various 'morally outraged' MPs and members of the public condemned the actions of the school children in the media and demanded that they be dealt with appropriately by the school authorities (Bell, 1995). They also accused leading members of Scottish Militant Labour (SML) of encouraging a 'children's crusade'. In a research interview, Tommy Sheridan (former leader of the Scottish Socialist Party [SSP] and former SSP Member of the Scottish Parliament) who was at the time a SML councilor, denied any such encouragement by either himself or any other SML member and explained the school children's actions as follows:

> The true story is that the local school Bellarmine Secondary for many years has won first prizes in environmental awards for environmental awareness, and there have been courses run in it in the school. So the school students have been given all sorts of plaudits for their excellent environmental work but of course when they try and involve themselves in saving the environment they are condemned. Most of them were senior students who heard what was happening at the camp and

left of their own volition to assist the protest and I've got to say that if they hadn't done that then the felling would have taken place because there wasn't enough people there to stop it – their intervention was crucial to delaying the felling and a continuation of the campaign. Now although it was hysterical nonsense that the media printed, it got national news, opened it up and raised the arguments about the road once again. People asked me on the record 'do you condemn these school students?' and I said 'why should I condemn them for trying to take part in shaping their lives?' – I mean we're all too quick to condemn them for pumping their veins full of shit, slashing each other and vandalising – here they are trying to save the environment and they want to condemn that as well ... it's just garbage. (Sheridan, 1997)

The actions of the Bellarmine students inspired school students from other schools in the area to follow suit, staging strikes, demonstrations and walkouts in support of the campaign, and they became a regular presence at the Free State's 'Free University' and at ongoing skirmishes along the route. Key events over the next few weeks included the creation of 'Carhenge' by protesters on the weekend of 18 February, which consisted of a number of upended old cars symbolically embedded in concrete in the motorway's route, and the STARR Alliance's demonstration from George Square in central Glasgow, where the city council headquarters are located, to the Free State on 25 February, which involved approximately 2,000 people.

The beginning of the end for the direct-action campaign began with the clearance of the Free State's outposts along the motorway route. The contractors' new tactic of cordoning off areas of trees to be felled with steel fencing and police support proved to be highly productive. Over the next few weeks, thousands of trees were cut down despite the increasingly desperate efforts of protesters. On 22 March, the last major action of the campaign occurred when 16 protesters were arrested for public order offences during an operation involving 250 police officers near the Pollok Free State. This last battle was on the day that Wimpey announced that its tree-felling programme had been completed. Smaller isolated protests and actions against construction work continued to occur sporadically after this point but after the trees had been felled a palpable rationale no longer existed for continuing the direct-action campaign. The main eco-camp of Free State remained, however, defiantly undefeated because the contractors had decided that a showdown with the protesters living there was not worth the time and effort. Instead, a planned exit route for the motorway was moved. Pollok Free State continued to operate as a meeting place for environmental activists and as an environmental resource and education centre until November 1996. The M77 motorway extension was opened in December 1996.

Conclusion: roads protest, environment and eco-welfare

From the beginning, the protest campaign against the M77 extension brought social and environmental issues together in a manner that can be conceptualised as a struggle for eco-welfare. First, the protests were about a defence of local democracy and the rights of a community to determine its own environment. The motorway was being imposed by national government and the regional council in the interests of jobs and the economy, despite strong objections from the local communities, community councils, local councillors, MPs and Glasgow District Council. Second, the protests were about defence of a modicum of quality of life that was already impoverished because of multiple deprivation. The motorway would have serious negative effects on the working-class communities it impinged upon in terms of health and amenity – there was an implicit acknowledgement in the findings of the Reporter at the 1988 Public Local Inquiry that communities like Corkerhill would be sacrificed in the name of the wider aim of economic growth. Third, the protests were about the negative impact of the motorway on environmental sustainability. Where the route infringes upon the Pollok Estate, the natural environment would be degraded by the construction process and once built the motorway itself would induce more traffic, thereby generating more pollution. Equally, its construction would encourage further commercial developments on greenbelt land and detract from the usage of rail services in its environs. Smith (2001, p 163) summarises the nature of protests surrounding road-building when he says:

> [W]e are witnessing a confrontation between two quite different ethical architectures, two different ways of shaping the ethical field. Where the roads' advocates couch their arguments and tactics in abstract terms of economic utilitarianism and legal rights, the protesters emphasise the specific ecology and ethos of the locality they defend, its uniqueness, special qualities, and associated traditions.

The protesters' struggle is a struggle for eco-welfare – the holistic integration of social and environmental goods, which form the basis of a sustainable and socially just society.

The impact of the anti-roads protest movement of the 1990s has extended much wider than simply on the government's road-building programmes. The protest movement produced radical new organisations like Alarm UK, Earth First! and Reclaim the Streets who not only challenged the road developers but also the 'environmental establishment' of large environmental movement organisations by stimulating a diverse range of informal do-it-yourself environmental activist networks outside the mainstream (McKay, 1998). These networks have evolved and diversified to create new overlapping organisations that embrace eco-welfarist causes that lie at the heart of struggles as diverse as those surrounding airport expansion (for example the current high-profile campaign against a third runway at Heathrow), housing, retail, incinerator, phone mast and related infrastructure developments through to opposition to genetically modified agriculture and traditional enemies such as nuclear power and nuclear arms (see, for example, Law and McNeish, 2007). At the level of activist practice, the anti-roads protest movement popularised a 'repertoire of contention' (Tarrow, 1994) that involved and evolved NVDA tactics such as tree-sitting, camp fortification, locking-on, trespassing and other innovative modes of obstruction and disruption, many of which lead either directly or indirectly to law breaking. Arguably, the anti-roads protest movement normalised this repertoire so that it has become a widely adopted approach to protest that animates all social movements active in the contemporary period (see the wider discussion of resource mobilisation and political process theories in Chapter Three).

At a more abstract theoretical level, Habermas's (1981, 1987b) analysis of 'new' social movements in relation to the theory of communicative action points to a way of understanding the emancipatory potentials of the anti-roads protest movement, the wider environmental movement and the struggle for eco-welfare. For Habermas, the emancipatory potentials of the 'new' (contemporary) movements stem from their disposition to create alternative institutions and practices that run counter to the dictates of the state and capital, their encouragement of participatory forms of democracy, which is vital for the revival of communicative reason, their defence of the lifeworld from System intrusion, and their exemplar function of providing examples and prototype models for a new society predicated on equality, universal rights and radical democracy. Multi-organisational eco-welfare protests where social and environmental issues are drawn together like the M77 campaign, in many respects fulfil each of Habermas's positive criteria. For example, in creating a social space where a culture of solidarity and dialogue stands in opposition to the social alienation that is the norm; in law breaking NVDA, which exposes the repressive power of the state; in a grassroots participatory orientation; and in a refusal to abide by the state's repressive laws or planning decisions. In fulfilling these criteria, eco-welfare protests like the M77 campaign not only bring to light policy decisions that run counter to universal interests of sustainability but more importantly they also open up those decisions and indeed other wider related issues to critical debate and political action in the public arena (McNeish 1999; see also the wider discussion of new social movements theory in Chapter Three).

Further reading

There are two very readable introductions to green political thought: *Modern Environmentalism: An Introduction* by David Pepper (Routledge, 1996) and *Green Political Thought* by Andrew Dobson (Routledge, 1997). Dobson's (2003) book on green citizenship *Citizenship and the Environment* is a substantial contribution to contemporary debates on the subject.

Michael Cahill's book *The Environment and Social Policy* (Routledge, 2002) and his collaboration with Tony Fitzpatrick to produce the edited collection *Environmental Issues and Social Welfare* (Blackwell, 2002) are both useful additions to the growing body of literature concerning the greening of social policy.

Brian Doherty et al's edited collection *Direct Action in British Environmentalism* (Routledge, 2000) gives a good flavour of contemporary debates concerning the evolution of the environmental movement in the UK, while Chris Rootes looks comparatively at *The Environmental Movement in Western Europe* (Oxford University Press, 2003).

Earth First! and the Anti-Roads Movement by Derek Wall (Routledge, 1999) shows how social movements theory can be applied to analyse and understand the evolution of this particular strand of environmental protest.

The journal *Environmental Politics* is available online at www.ingentaconnect. com/content/routledg/ep;jsessionid=a3uskuza5tb.alexandra

Useful websites

Earth First!: *www.earthfirstjournal.org/*

Friends of the Earth: *www.foe.co.uk/*

George Monbiot's website: *www.monbiot.com/*

Greenpeace: *www.greenpeace.org.uk/*

Reclaim the Streets: *http://rts.gn.apc.org/*

eleven

Contesting neoliberalism: global social justice movements

Introduction: key questions and tensions

> [T]ens of thousands of committed activists at the nexus of a global political movement embracing tens of millions of people. Just over a decade after the fall of the Berlin Wall and the 'End of History' promised by Francis Fukuyama ... there is a growing sense that global capitalism is once again fighting to win the argument....The new wave of activism has coalesced around the simple idea that capitalism has gone too far. It is as much a mood as a movement, something counter-cultural. It is driven by the suspicion that companies, forced by the stock markets to strive for ever greater profits, are pillaging the environment, destroying lives and failing to enrich the poor as they promised. And it is fuelled by the fear that democracy has become powerless to stop them, as politicians are thought to be in the pockets of companies and international political institutions are slaves to a corporate agenda. (Harding, 2001)

The global financial crisis that exploded in 2008, the worst economic crisis since the great crash of 1929, has refocused attention in ways that relatively few could have predicted on the failures of international banking and financial systems – and has brought with it an abrupt answer to the repeated claims of the past three decades that the way of the market was the only way to organise the global economy. The financial earthquake has not only seriously undermined one of the key pillars of the globalised economy, in the process it has also provided more ammunition for those who have struggled against 'globalisation', as was seen in the protests against the G20 summit in London in early April 2009.

'Resistance to globalisation' has become a significant feature of the global political landscape over the past two decades. The 'anti-globalisation movement', to use the term that seems to have found favour with large sections of the media and in political commentary, has also in turn generated a significant volume of literature, resources that can be deployed across different forms of resistance, much of it provided through a rich and diverse range of websites, on blogs and in other forms of e-media. Some of this derives from key moments of opposition, such the protests at the World Trade Organization (WTO) in Seattle in 1999, which we highlighted in the introductory chapter, or from regular resistance events such as the World Social Forum and other national and transnational fora at which opponents of globalisation have sought to develop new ways of challenging 'globalisation'. As we have seen in the chapters in Part One of this book in particular, but a theme that runs through this entire volume, is that the label 'social movement' has historically covered a varied, rich and heterogeneous set of struggles, forms of resistance and oppositions. While this has raised significant conceptual and theoretical difficulties, again as we have seen, arguably the issue of opposition to globalisation/global capitalism has propelled such definitional conceptual and theoretical disputes to new levels.

The main aim of this chapter is to introduce some of the key debates and issues that relate to the issue of global social movements, of movements for social justice. In particular, we seek to consider some of the ways in which the development of resistance to globalisation has re-ignited long-standing controversies around social movements concerning their internal dynamics, organisational forms and relationships to other sources of protest and mainstream political parties. How has this affected our understanding of social movements in the world today?

The chapter will also consider some of the important, for want of a better term, 'tensions' that inform and shape our understanding of global social movements. For example, what is the anti-globalisation movement (a term we appreciate is problematic and we will return to this) actually 'against'? What is it 'anti', in other words? For some sections of the media, indeed, the 'anti-globalisation movement' was, simply, an 'anti-movement'. An alternative approach and the one that informs this chapter is that the anti-globalisation movement so-called is not anti-globalisation per se, but instead seeks to build and articulate alternative globalisations founded on ideas of social justice, eco-welfare and equity, that another globalisation might be possible!

A related tension concerns the extent to which we can see global social movements primarily (or even entirely) as reactive forces and forms of opposition, or as generative of new ways of doing, of living and of organising economic and social life. For those with a particular interest in social welfare this is a particularly important issue, with the possibility of new forms of welfare and social policy making, progressive methods of meeting welfare needs, of participation and of building new forms of community and solidarity produced through the debates, activities and resistance that have preoccupied social movements operating within and across national contexts in recent years. In no small part this is also fuelled by growing and widening campaigns that are concerned with questions and issues of environmental protection and sustainability (see also Chapter Ten). Thus, we can talk of a global justice movement – a movement organising against corporate globalisation, organising for equality of distribution, fair trade and for the global solidarity of all peoples.

There are, however, further tensions and disputes: what is the relationship between recently emerged social movements that operate globally and 'traditional' movements of labour, or working-class movements? And closely related to this is the question of the relationship between the Left, however defined, and some of the 'new' social movements that have developed around the world in recent times. As we have discussed already in this book, such issues have long informed the debate around social movements (see Chapters Two and Three), the complex relationship between class mobilisation and social movements in the urban context, for instance, helping to inform the discussion in Chapter Six. But once again, arguably, such issues are taken to qualitatively different levels as a result of the development of global social justice movements.

Already such issues alert us that the question of the nature of globalisation and the pursuit of global social justice have re-ignited long-standing disputes and controversies in the understanding and analysis of social movements. The objective here is to offer an accessible introduction to some of the main issues surrounding questions of global justice and forms of resistance as well as considering why this matters for our understanding of social welfare. We begin by setting the global 'scene'. What is it about our world and the organisation of global economic and social life that has driven the development of diverse social movements?

Global inequality, global injustices and the pursuit of global social justice

Our world is a world of inequality. We live on a planet that is divided and unequal to a historically unprecedented degree (see Callinicos, 2000,

2003; Ferguson et al, 2002; Harvey, 2005; Glynn, 2006; Milanovic, 2005, 2007; Greig et al, 2007; Held and Kaya, 2007; Yeates, 2008a; Wilkinson and Pickett, 2009). Leaving aside the many definitional, conceptual and methodological disputes that inform the analysis and understanding of such inequalities (see Ridge and Wright, 2008), there is considerable evidence that points to a world where wealth and affluence co-exist alongside acute poverty, want and hunger. World Bank economist Branko Milanovic (2007, p 40) notes that:

> [T]he top 5 per cent of highest earners in the world receive one-third of the world income, whereas the bottom 5 per cent receive only 0.2%. Consequently, the ratio of the top 5 per cent to the bottom 5 per cent is 165 to 1. Differently, the top 10 per cent of people in the world get around one-half of world income, leaving the remaining 90 per cent of the world population the other half of the global income.

Such figures point to a picture of global inequality in terms of income, but what about wealth? Given the propensity of the global rich to hide much of their wealth and its sources, abetted by governments across the world (including the UK government!), in 'off-shore' tax-havens, the degree of inequality here is more difficult to estimate. However, Thomas Pogge (2007, p 132) reminds us that:

> [I]nequalities in the wealth are much greater (than inequalities in income), because the wealth of affluent people is typically greater than their annual income while the wealth of poor people is typically smaller than their annual income. In fact, the investment income of a few dozen of the world's richest people exceeds the total income of the world's poor.

In the early 21st century, the top 10% of adults own 85% of global wealth while the lowest 50% of the world's adults own only 1% of global wealth (Yeates, 2008a, p 95). This is the stark reality of inequality today.

These inequalities are patterned across the world: they occur at many different although overlapping and interrelated levels: between different parts of the world, the global South and the global North and between different countries and regions within the global South and global North. However, the focus on income and wealth inequalities, important that this is, does not begin to capture the different and multiple ways in which such inequalities both underpin yet also reflect massive inequalities in life changes for people across the globe.

Highlighting the income and wealth divide or 'gap' between rich and poor is crucially important but taken in isolation from an understanding of the multidimensional, dynamic and far-reaching implications of such inequalities and their routes in global relations of exploitation and oppression cannot capture what this might mean for those tens of millions who struggle to survive – and many do not manage to survive – on a daily basis. In 2007-09 the world has been gripped by yet another major food crisis, affecting many people in different poor countries in the global South – as well as in parts of the global North. While media and political attention might have been largely focused on the global financial and credit crisis at this time, the human costs of economic turmoil are only too evident: hunger, malnutrition, starvation and death.

Within countries as well as between them there are major inequalities. The affluent enclaves, 'gated communities' and zones of pleasure for the global rich in cities such as Dubai, in what Davis and Monk (2007) refer to as the 'dreamworlds' and 'evil paradises' of neoliberalism, stand in stark contrast to the misery facing many others who, while residing in similar urban locations, effectively inhabit different parallel urban worlds (see Neuwirth, 2006).

According to estimates produced by UN-Habitat (2003, 2006), approximately one sixth of the world's population – one billion people – live in slums, shantytowns and squatter settlements across the planet, with an additional 400 million people projected to be living in slums across the world by 2020 – some 1.4 billion people. In Delhi, India, it is estimated of the 500,000 people who migrate to the city each year, 400,000 end up living in slums, leading one Indian planning expert to comment that 'if such a trend continues unabated, we will have only slums and no cities' (quoted in Davis, 2006, p 18). Such *'favela-isation'*, *favelas* being the shantytowns that are to be found in most large Latin American cities, is one of the many transnational and global trends that signify the growing inequalities and divisions that so characterise the world in the early years of the 21st century.

At the same time, it is important that we remember that while all the available evidence points to one conclusion – a growing gulf or economic and social polarisation between rich and poor – the world has never seen so much wealth nor has it ever enjoyed the capacity that it does now to feed, clothe and provide shelter, indeed to provide for all the needs of the population of Earth. It takes under two weeks for the world to produce in the early 2000s what it took a year to produce in 1900. The world is wealthier and healthier than in the past. Yet such economic capacity, immense productivity and prosperity is marked by inequality, not only continuing inequality, but growing inequality and new forms of inequality, for instance, the so-called 'digital divide' between the 'information rich' and the 'information poor'. And yet, again, we fail to capture the extent of such inequality. For many their standard and quality of life has worsened. Indeed, it has been accepted by global organisations such as the International Monetary Fund (IMF) that one in five of the world's population has gone backwards in economic terms in recent decades (Greig et al, 2007, p 5).

In the words of renowned global economist, Amartya Sen, this is a world of 'unprecedented opulence' and 'remarkable deprivation' (quoted in Greig et al, 2007, p 5). However, the story of rising and deepening global inequality is accompanied by an growing awareness that the pursuit of wealth accumulation, affluence and unregulated economic growth is leading to climate change, and more frequent ecological and environmental catastrophes from Indonesia to Bangladesh to centres of the global North such as New Orleans (see http://understandingkatrina.ssrc.org/), where the devastation wrought by Hurricane Katrina in August 2005 brought home in the starkest possible terms that it is poor people *the world over* who pay the enormous costs of such change. Pollution is affecting climate change, altering the ecological system, which is also under threat from the growing use of genetically modified crops, deforestation, agri-business and intensive farming, the erosion of peat bogs, urbanisation, increasing use of petrol-driven vehicles and so on.

We appreciate that there are many other processes and factors that are working across the planet to deepen and widen the growing sense of insecurity and risk that hundreds of millions of people experience on a daily basis. Poverty, environmental degradation, food shortages and inequality can be understood as 'social harms': these are socially created problems with collective and society-wide consequences (see Newman and Yeates, 2008a; Cochrane and Walters, 2008). The growing awareness of social harms and of the kinds of global 'problems' that we have highlighted here, though of course to reiterate these are not experienced each and everywhere in the same way nor by all groups in a similar fashion, has brought questions of how such social injustices are to be addressed. How do we create a world in which there is greater human safety, security and equality? How do we address fear, risk and uncertainty?

Such questions are entangled with questions of social justice, of universal human rights, of citizenship – of global citizenship. A world of such profound social injustices raises important questions of equality and of social justice, of global social justice (see Callinicos, 2003; Mayo, 2005; Craig et al, 2008; Newman and Yeates, 2008a, 2008b). But these questions are also inseparable from questions of how we understand the causes of such injustices, the driving force that underpins rising inequalities. This brings us directly to the question of what it is that 'anti-globalisation' social movements are struggling against.

Globalisation or neoliberal globalisation?

There is now a general appreciation that the concept of 'globalisation' is, to put it mildly, 'contested'. 'It' has long been the subject of dispute and debate, which need not detain us here. At its most simplest, and perhaps this even invites critique, globalisation is generally taken to refer to the ways in which the world, and economic, social, political and cultural organisation, is increasingly interconnected – or enmeshed – in diverse and unequal ways. While many in the anti-globalisation movement use the label 'globalisation' uncritically – or perhaps more often interchanging it with other labels such as the 'globalisation movement' – nonetheless, it is now widely appreciated and understood that the term 'anti-globalisation' is both very limited and negative, and which fails to capture the diversity, richness or the rich and sophisticated understandings of the kinds of global problems that we highlighted above – or of the diversity of 'the movement' itself (to which we return later). One point that needs to be highlighted immediately is of course that the global social movement, global justice movement or the movement for global democracy and/or citizenship – to highlight only some of the many labels that have been used – is not anti-global per se. It seeks to organise globally – or transnationally. The global social justice movement seeks to be a *global movement*, although some researchers suggest that a coherent global movement may not exist (see Cumbers et al, 2008). In terms that do not begin to capture the heterogeneity of participants, ideas, tactics, strategies and objectives, it is for a different kind of globalisation: sometimes an 'alternative globalisation', 'alterglobalisation', 'deglobalisation', 'anti-neoliberal globalisation', 'anti-corporate globalisation', or 'anti-capitalism'. As Desai and Said (2001, p 51) comment on the nature of the movement: 'protestors rarely attack globalisation as such, targeting instead corporate globalisation, global capitalism, the neoliberal order, multinational companies, international financial institutions, and trade agreements'.

As we will see, following the Seattle protests in 1999, significant sections of the global social justice movement recognised that anti-globalisation, in the narrow sense of this term, and a pro-internationalist/pro-global agenda did not sit easily together. Instead, the growing understanding that what was being pursued was an alternative form of globalisation. As Naomi Klein (2002, p 4) noted in the aftermath of the protests against the WTO in Seattle in 1999:

> [O]ne thing is certain: the protestors in Seattle are not anti-globalisation; they have been bitten by the globalisation bug as surely as the trade lawyers inside the official meetings. Rather, if this new movement is 'anti' anything, it is anti-corporate, opposing the logic that what's good for business – less regulation, more mobility, more access – will trickle down into good news for everybody else.

The possibility of the emergence of a new kind of internationalism was constructed – is being constructed – on a number of different platforms, including campaigns against Third World debt, which understand these as part of the overall distribution of economic and other resources across the world. Other members of the social justice movement argue for new forms of solidarity and support between those involved in resistance across the planet – that there are interconnections between struggles against the supermarket domination of the market for food in the UK and the plight of small farmers in the global South – as well as many of those in the UK itself. New forms of internationalism are also reflected in long-standing support for displaced peoples whether, for instance, those affected by and protesting against many of the dam projects that are being developed in many poor countries as we write, or those affected by war and military interventions. Arguments are advanced for a different kind of globalisation where welfare and need come first. This welfare globalisation is sharply juxtaposed against the workings of capitalist globalisation, which in prioritising profit and private accumulation threaten welfare provision across the world.

Global opposition to environmental degradation and renewed struggles to promote biodiversity and sustainability have also generated ideas for a new kind of globalisation (see Chapter Ten). Among the most important elements of these newer forms of global solidarity and resistance has been opposition to war and to imperialism (see Harvey, 2003b, 2005; Hubbard and Miller, 2005). In particular, the wars in Iraq and Afghanistan have been important in sustaining key elements of the global justice movement who in turn draw important links between such wars, the new imperialism of the US and the interests of global big business, transnational corporations and the institutional architecture of neoliberal governance in the shape of the IMF, World Bank and WTO.

As such there has been a greater sense that the target of the global justice movement is not 'globalisation' – but neoliberal globalisation as a particular phase in the development of global capitalism, which, among other dimensions, offers a celebration of the untrammelled market, which prioritises the profit-making activities and objectives of corporations and business, promotes free trade and argues for minimum state intervention in economic activity (although not in terms of military intervention nor with regard to issues of crime, social order and the management and control of problem populations across the globe) (see Callinicos, 2003; Prempeh, 2007). Further, proponents of neoliberalism interpret inequality as a natural outcome of the operations of a free economy, and poverty and want in terms that often speak of individual, group or communal failure, lacking or inadequacy. The target of protestors has been the key institutions that form the backbone of the neoliberal political project such as the World Bank and WTO.

Globalisation 'from above' ... or 'from below'!

This recognition has also extended to the understanding of neoliberal globalisation as a project of the rich and powerful – of transnational corporations, global oil and big business backed by transnational organisations, for instance, the IMF and WTO, and by powerful states such as the US. In this regard, it makes sense to speak of globalisation 'from above', that is, as the project of what Sklair (2001) has termed the 'transnational capitalist class'. This is an important point for us as it enables an understanding that there is a 'social movement for global capitalism' (Miller and Dinan, 2008, p 81). The transnational class comprises interrelated global elites supported by the institutions of transnational corporate power, for instance the North American Free Trade Agreement (NAFTA) established in 1994, which enabled American corporations to plunder the low-cost labour and other resources of Mexico. The activities of what Farnsworth (2008) terms 'global business interest associations' have been instrumental in shaping policy outcomes in ways that favour the interests of the corporations, for instance in the UK, Europe and elsewhere, in forcing open the markets in healthcare, education and other key 'heartland' areas of social welfare provision. 'Privatisation' and 'marketisation' represent the more visible outcomes of an entangled web of global business interests. But such interests are also entwined in diverse – and often obscured – ways with the activities of intergovernmental organisations such as the European Commission, or the Organisation for European Co-operation and Development (OECD).

By contrast, opponents of neoliberal globalisation have argued for a form of 'globalisation from below', which is premised on a vision of a global unity between people North and South and is driven by a concern with social justice, citizenship and human rights, security, environmental concerns, gender, 'race', ethnic and cultural equality, and opposition to war and oppression, inequality, poverty and social harms of the kind that we have flagged above. But importantly, and again to return to a theme that was flagged in the Introduction, it is important to see such alternative globalisations as more than defensive or 'conservative' reactions to movements from above. While such defensive opposition and resistance is only too important, we also want to highlight that in the process new ways of doing and organising has been thrown up. Defence of this kind may be, in other words, transformative, generating new ideas and ways of thinking, new partnerships, relationships and global interconnections – and of course new goals, new objectives and new aspirations. Such has been the vitality of the global justice movement.

A movement of many movements?

Seattle, USA, 30 November 30 1999: demonstrators against the WTO and the Multilateral Agreement on Investment were successful in disrupting the WTO meeting scheduled to take place in the city and through a concerted campaign of civil disobedience the city was brought almost to standstill. The 'Battle of Seattle', 29 November to 2 December 2000, marked for many observers a turning point in the struggle against global capitalism (see Smith, 2000; Bircham and Charlton, 2001). This is the home town of Microsoft, Starbucks and at the time also of military and civil aviation giant, Boeing. All were important, key symbols of much that protestors were demonstrating against. Seattle was seen as a watershed in the global opposition to free trade and neoliberal globalisation. Writing in the immediate aftermath of Seattle, Marxist geographer Neil Smith (2000, p 2) noted:

> Seattle is already widely perceived as an ideological turning point. The corporate globalization rhetoric of the late 1980s and 1990s never went unchallenged, but its sponsors did enjoy some success in passing globalization off as a natural result of economic evolution, free-trade as the essence of democracy and human rights. Seattle wrote the obituary for that self-serving fiction. It was aided and abetted by simultaneous protests in various cities around the world.... After Seattle, free trade, globalization, and neoliberalism are unmasked as social and political projects with decisive agendas, masquerading as economic inevitabilities.

Seattle has been pinpointed as the key event in the history of global resistance movements where the radical ideas came to interplay with concrete forms of protest and real social movements. However, as Nicola Yeates (2008b) reminds us, 'anti-globalisation' movements have a much longer and noteworthy history, for instance the anti-slave trade movement, 1787-1807. In the period prior to Seattle there were, for example, global social movement protests against the WTO in Geneva in 1993 and again in 1998 and in New Delhi in both 1994 and 1998, against the G8/G7 group of rich and powerful countries at Munich in 1998 and Cologne in 1999. The 1990s also witnessed other events that were to be influential on the fledging global justice movement: the armed rising in the state of Chiapas in South-Eastern Mexico in January 1994 by the Zapatista Army of National Liberation, which denounced NAFTA as it removed peasants' right of access to common land, and the French public sector strikes in late 1995. Non-governmental organisations (NGOs) were also active during this decade in helping to encourage the emergence of activist movements that campaigned against injustices such as sweatshop labour and Third World debt. While Seattle itself was characterised by a considerable degree of spontaneity, many long and diverse roads led to Seattle and from that the global social justice movement took on a new impetus. Seattle was followed by global 'days of action' in Genoa, Gleneagles and in numerous other countries and cities against neoliberalism and the institutions of neoliberal governance, such as the IMF, World Bank and WTO but also against free trade in general.

The notion of 'a movement of many movements' was coined by well-known anti-globalisation writer Naomi Klein in 2001 (Klein, 2001). In some ways this helps to capture the sheer diversity of the anti-globalisation movement, the extent to which these are mobile and fluid, overlapping and dynamic with new movements forming as others collapse or move on to other things. In addition, such social movements comprise a wide range of different coalitions, which span trade unions and community associations, human rights groups, environmentalists, left-wing organisations, women's organisations, indigenous peoples' organisations, anti-racism and anti-imperialism groups and associations, anarchists, socialists, greens, consumer groups, peace groups, animal rights groups, NGOs, social justice and pro-democracy movements, anti-poverty and anti-war movements.

As we have highlighted in other chapters, such movements frequently seek to relate struggles taking place in particular territories to much broader and transnational and global networks of struggle and resistance. In turn this is leading to the development of new networks of resistance – some of it enabled by web-based communications and the explosion in global events such as the World Social Forums and European Social Forums, which provide for the sharing of ideas and practices – and for the airing of many disputes and disagreements over tactics and practices.

In particular, one such dispute stood out and has come to be a key point of disagreement and tension in the global justice movement – whether the organisations that constitute the institutional framework of neoliberal globalisation – the IMF, World Bank and WTO – could be reformed – or should be abolished. In other words, could 'globalisation' be tamed or even 'humanised'.

To briefly illustrate these controversies, we highlight two issues of contention that emerged in the aftermath of Seattle. First, social clauses. Trade unions in the US argued that 'social clauses' protecting child labour and union rights would improve the conditions of workers in third wWorld countries, and would work to limit the ability of multinationals to cut labour costs and attack working conditions. The ideas of 'No Sweats' and 'Fair Trade' have been key to campaigns by other organisations, for instance student and consumer boycott protests, for many years now. However, critics have argued that such clauses can be circumvented by the large corporations while appearing also to cover up the worst aspects of the business methods of the big multinationals. Others argue that this misses the key issue that is at the heart of the relationship between workers and multinational corporations wherever they are located: that this is a relationship of class exploitation that is beyond reform. Another issue that emerges here is that among the voices heard in the debates around social clauses were from those who argued that what was required was some form of protection for indigenous firms, thereby increasing their ability to compete with the multinationals. Such a position was also criticised for effectively justifying exploitation by Third World firms.

The second example we wish to flag here relates to the issue of Third World debt. Debt Campaigns such as Jubilee 2000 were forceful in arguing for a cancellation of Third World debt by 2000. Jubilee 2000 – 'mobilisation for debt relief' – was a transnational coalition movement, drawing support from people of all and no faiths, academics, politicians, trade unions, NGOs and an assortment of international music and sports stars. Importantly, it was also organised at both a national and a transnational level with important connections between activist networks in the North and South. Organisations such as Jubilee 2000 were important in drawing attention to the huge transfers of money from the poorest countries to the world's leading banks and financial institutions on a yearly basis (see Mayo, 2005). However, and in similar ways to the debate around social clauses, the issue that provoked most controversy was whether such debts should either be reduced or cancelled or whether the entire global system of finance trade, that is, the activities of the large banks and multinationals and their respective national governments supported by the IMF and so on, as well as the wider relationships between First and Third World countries, were at fault and that *simply* calling for debt relief neglected such systems and therefore were not a solution in the longer term but would lead to further and growing problems for already impoverished countries.

Such arguments, and similar controversies, have featured across a wide range of issues that have been central to the campaigns and protests of global protestors, have both come to shape the global justice movement but are also derived from it – and in particular emerge from the very diversity that is for most one of the key strengths of the movement. It also raises fundamental questions about the entire basis of the global justice movement and its ability to effect real and concrete change.

The global justice movement: what kind of social movement is it?

The global justice movement is generally characterised in the media and in political commentary as large mobilisations and protests in opposition to global summits of international government organisations such as the WTO or in terms of opposition policy fora. However, as we have seen, one of the most striking features of the global justice movement is its diversity. As part of this heterogeneity, we can see the convergence – although by no means a problem-free coming-together of previously disparate groups and protests – of the 'old' kinds of social movements, for instance of labour, nuclear disarmament and peace campaigns, together with the 'new' forms of women's, indigenous peoples', human rights, citizenship and environmental protest movements. This has been immortalised in a slogan first aired at Seattle, 'Teamsters and turtles: together at last', which has been used since to both reflect and to invoke the growing awareness between previously disparate movements that there is a shared enemy in the form of neoliberal globalisation.

The activities of the movement for global social justice encompass – as we might expect – a wide range of forms of protest and resistance: strikes, pickets, demonstrations, consumer boycotts, defacing billboards, letter and email writing campaigns, legal actions, invasions of corporate spaces, airports and transport hubs, taking control of urban streets, occupying military bases and destroying military and other hardware and software, street theatre, sit-downs, mass cycle protests that lead to street gridlocks and riots and other forms of violence protest and action. Some of these might be considered as 'traditional' forms of protest – others new, enabled in part by new developments in information and communication technology (ICT), which has enabled knowledge transfer across countries (see Mayo, 2005), an issue to which we return shortly. In these ways, the campaigns and global social movements operate and organise across different geographical scales.

Social movement theorists Della Porta and Tarrow (2005) are among those who have sought to draw on the conceptual frameworks and insights developed through generations of social movement analysis to develop an understanding of the new forms of transnational politics and social activism that have emerged over the past two decades (see also the chapters in Part One of this book). They claim that there are three main processes that provide for an understanding of the dynamics of the global justice movements:

- *diffusion*: this refers to transnational connections, partnerships and forms of cooperation as well as the sharing of organisational methods. Della Porta and Tarrow illustrate this by referring to the 'sit–in', which spread from the US civil rights movements in the 1960s to Western Europe. Furthermore, and importantly, this process allows for the identification of opponents that may be targeted from different campaigns in different parts of the world. Diffusion also refers to the dissemination of the experiences of success – and of failures. This is much enhanced through the spread of ICT and the increasing use of the internet as a weapon of protest;
- *internalisation*: this refers to playing out in national or domestic contexts and territory, conflicts that may have an external origin. This 'domestication' might involve protests against international organisations;
- *externalisation*: this refers to the activities of social movement organisations (SMOs) that come to operate at transnational or supranational levels. NGOs are particularly adept at targeting international organisations for accessing resources that can be used domestically.

Taken together these processes contribute to the kinds of transnational collective action involving campaigns of activists against states, multinational corporations, global financial and business organisations and international institutions that have been highlighted in this chapter. It also raises important questions about the ability of 'traditional' social movement theories to engage with and offer an analysis and understanding of the new forms of global movements that have emerged in recent times. Does the distinction between 'old' and 'new' social movements hold any meaning in the dynamic and shifting contexts of the 1990s and 2000s?

For some it is the way in which different protests have come together that makes it 'new' – coalescing different traditions, ideologies, ways of organising. Protests and organisations may maintain their own visibility and identity but also in the process contribute to the development of a larger protest movement. However, this in turn raises yet another set of issues. The emergence and development of these new 'transnational geographies of resistance' (Featherstone, 2005, p 252) brings into sharp relief long-standing points of contention around the pursuit of particularist or universalist objectives. This question has long been of concern to those who are concerned with social welfare objectives and processes of inclusion, exclusion and questions of recognition and voice in social welfare policy making (see Lister, 2008; Young, 2008). Arguably, universalist goals and aspirations have generally been attributed to old social movements, for instance trade unions and parties of the Left. By contrast, particularist aspirations are associated with newer forms of social movement, such as the women's movement, black people's movements and also with other movements based on identity politics that developed significantly in the last few decades of the 20th century and which were instrumental in developing critiques of the failures of universalist politics and policy making (see Laclau and Mouffe, 1985).

Harvey (2001) has sought to think of ways of reconciling particular and universal through Raymond Williams' concept of 'militant particularism' (Williams, 1989). Williams used this idea to make sense of the ways in which particular working-class struggles in particular localities – 'place-bound politics' – could be connected with general struggles and universal (and indeed global) imaginaries and ambitions. This necessitates looking beyond localised protests and forms of struggle, and local solidarities, thereby 'ideals forged out of the affirmative experiences of solidarities in one place get generalised and universalised' (Harvey, 2001, p 172). Heterogeneous and fragmented movements, such as the global resistance movement, need a common language and political discourse if they are to challenge neoliberal globalisation effectively. For Harvey, this means that we need to look beyond a rigid division between universal and particular and that:

> universality always exists in relation to particularity: neither can be separated from the other even though they are distinctive moments within our conceptual operations and practical engagements. The notion of social justice, for example, acquires universality through a process of abstraction from particular instances and circumstances, but, once established as a generally accepted principle or norm, becomes particular again as it is actualised through particular actions in particular circumstances. (Harvey, 2001, p 194)

Such an argument has been controversial and does not fit easily with all the different political and theoretical traditions that comprise the global justice movement. Evoking universal principles is in particular likely to present a direct challenge to those who have been involved in identity politics and who have built claims around identity. However, neoliberal globalisation is now itself understood as a totalising or universalising process, which links issues and processes once thought to be separate, and this provides the opportunity for the reaffirming of universal principles such as opposition to war and social and environmental justice.

This does not mean that differences and disagreements in the global justice movement will or can be overcome. It has led to a challenging and to a questioning of the rigid distinction between local/particular and global/universal. The multiple intersections and interconnections that form the life blood of the social justice movement can give rise to new ways of thinking and doing – and an understanding of this dynamism is vital to an appreciation of social movements as they organise transnationally and globally today.

Webs and networks of resistance: new forms of technopolitics

Resistance and protest have always required some kind of media outlet and way of publishing causes – for example, in the form of underground presses in the 1950s and 1960s – or now in the 1990s and 2000s through the use of ICTs such as mobile phones, personal digital assistants and more significantly the personal computer. The development and spread of the world wide web has enabled not only the dissemination of information almost instantly, it also allows for the interconnections of different individuals and groups involved in a myriad of campaigns, struggles and forms of resistance. The web is also interactive, facilitating debate and argument, and supporting the flow of information, images, films, photographs and a vast assortment of other cultural forms of resistance that can be shared by a vast array of social movements. In this way, importantly, it provides a platform for those voices that are ignored and marginalised by the mainstream media (see Kellner, 2003).

Cyberspace has become a key arena in the battle for ideas and in the struggles around different aspects of corporate globalisation. The irony here is that the global internet and global forms of communication have been central to 'globalisation' itself – they are now also major weapons in the war against such globalisation. Such 'electronic activism' was also central to the call for protests at Seattle, Genoa and in other large protest events. As Yeates (2002, p 133) among others has observed, 'thus, the technology that enables economic globalisation is also used to oppose it'. Web-based campaigns against global corporations such as Nike have involved hackers attacking websites, replacing corporate phraseology with alternative messages promoting resistance and global solidarity (see Klein, 2000). Other 'hacktivists' locate information about corporate operations and government policies that such organisations would prefer to remain hidden while also working to create forms of software that are freely available to all, thereby undermining attempts by corporations and governments to regulate and control the web.

Other forms of web-based resource allow for the development of radical alternative media (see, for example, www.Indymedia.org) and have been used to counter claims from mainstream media and national and transnational government agencies that global justice movement protestors are, to use some of the terminology deployed, violent Trotskyists, anarchists, criminals and troublemakers, thereby denying legitimacy to the protests. Global protests have therefore generated new forms of media, giving rise to a potent anti-corporate globalisation culture, which in turn is supporting and widening other protest movements. The technologies of resistance and insurrection that have been developed in recent times are now indispensable to social movements the world over.

Corporate responses to global justice movements: the relevance for social welfare

> Structural adjustment in the 1980's dismantled the elaborate system of public agencies that provided farmers with access to land, credit, insurance inputs, and cooperative organization. The expectation was that removing the state would free the market for private actors to take over these functions – reducing their costs, improving their quality, and eliminating their regressive bias. Too often, that didn't happen. In some places, the state's withdrawal was tentative at best, limiting private entry. Elsewhere, the private sector emerged only slowly and partially – mainly serving commercial farmers but leaving smallholders exposed to extensive market failures, high transaction costs and risks, and service gaps. Incomplete markets and institutional gaps impose huge costs in forgone growth and welfare losses for smallholders, threatening their competitiveness and, in many cases, their survival. (World Bank, 2008, p 138)

From the World Bank this represents a very blunt and realistic assessment of the impact that the policies that it and other institutions have developed, central to rolling forward neoliberal globalisation in recent decades have had on poor and disadvantaged groups, here small farmers. This is not out of place with the kinds of critique that global justice movements have been making, and in important respects reflects the recognition by the World Bank and other related transnational organisations that there may be a contradiction between policies that pursue economic growth and the 'social' outcomes of such policies in terms of rising levels of inequality. As opposition to neoliberalism has grown, it has become impossible for international governmental organisations to ignore the arguments that have been made by the protestors. This has led to some rethinking around issues such as human welfare, poverty, water and food supply. Ignoring protests is no longer an option.

There is certainly greater awareness that global social welfare issues need to be addressed. The Millennium Development Goals announced by the United Nations in 2000 included ambitious targets that by 2015, for example, child mortality would be reduced by two thirds, extreme poverty and hunger would be eradicated, universal primary school education would become a fact of life for children the world over, gender equality would be enhanced and environmental sustainability improved (www.un.org/millenniumgoals; see Greig et al, 2007, p 7). Critics have argued that this represents merely a set of aspirations, little else.

Another illustration of such a change in thinking at the level of global government is the G8 summit in Gleneagles in Scotland in the summer of 2005. Here the New Labour leadership of Tony Blair and Gordon Brown called for the G8 to lead a global campaign to cancel debt for the poorest countries, supported by a broad and varied alliance of transnational NGOs such as, but by no means only, Oxfam, and media celebrities such as Bob Geldoff and Bono. Underlying such developments and the greater awareness of the need for global institutions and governments to respond to social welfare issues is the view that the global market can be made to work in ways that are 'fairer', that reform is possible and that a 'softer' or 'social' neoliberal approach can be developed but one which, crucially, does not hinder competitiveness and profitability. In other words, growth and equality can be married together in ways that benefit all. This is also accompanied by a growing interest in ideas of corporate social responsibility, that companies can and should contribute to wider social and community needs, and that there should be systems of voluntary and self-regulation in place so that companies police themselves in ways that moderate the worst excesses of the marketplace and which also mean that the private and public/state sectors can work together in promoting environmental sustainability and a more 'inclusive' global economy (see Farnsworth, 2008, p 85-90).

This is also accompanied by changes in social policy making at a transnational and global level, which have seen a growing convergence between social policies and the needs of business. 'Active' social policies that promote individual development and self-improvement are supported while redistributive taxation is rejected as deterring the take-up of work. Across many countries in the West the greater role of the market sector in the delivery of social welfare as well as the far bigger involvement of private financial institutions in financing capital expenditure in 'heartland' areas of welfare have become much more pronounced in recent decades. Market 'liberalisation' and restricting state provision have become committed objectives of organisations such as the World Bank.

Critics in the global justice movement have argued that policies such as these continue to prioritise the interests of business and the powerful in ways that only pay lip service to the needs of the global poor. The idea that a global social democracy can be built on the premises of neoliberal globalisation has been widely attacked by those who argue that reform is not possible (see Prempeh, 2007). Filipino sociologist and activist Walden Bello (2000, 2004) is one of the more notable critics who say that reform of neoliberal globalisation is not possible, based as it is on the pursuit of economic growth, capital accumulation and wealth. This brings us back to the key tension that runs through the movement – an ongoing debate reflecting the different strands and traditions, ideologies and movements that have come together in the global justice movement: reform or revolution?

Conclusion: *Ya basta* – enough is enough!

Despite the difficulties and disagreements that feature in the global justice movement, there is a shared view that, in the slogan of the Zapatista movement, '*Ya basta*' – enough is enough! The emergence of a global justice movement, or the movement against neoliberal globalisation, has re-energised long-term debates and arguments around social movements. Our understanding of social movements has been deepened through the rich and ongoing studies of different protests and protest movements that are ongoing as this is written in late 2008. We are living through just such protests, which both adds to the appreciation of its dynamism, as well as to its weaknesses, (although this closeness can in some ways also make our appreciation and analysis of this more difficult).

There are some important points of caution that emerge from our discussion. While it is seductive to see novelty and newness in each and every aspect of the global justice movement, many of the organisations that are centrally involved have been around for a long time. Arguably, their targets have also been long-term targets. Studying global social movements/the global justice movement is about appreciating continuity and change: in tactics and strategies, in ideas, in the arguments, disagreements, controversies that are a feature of social movement protests – but also in terms of the potential for unity and for challenging neoliberal globalisation in ways that are diverse and which are both potent and new. This brings us back to an important issue that was raised in Chapter Three concerning claims made in new social movement theories about the discontinuity between old and new social movements. In many respects, arguably, global social movements are more in tune with the radical aims of the new social movements, rejecting the 'older' organisational structures and ways of doing.

However, in many other respects the global justice movement is both 'old' and 'new' – or more helpfully, through the term we deploy in Chapter Three, it is contemporary: the diverse, dynamic, developmental and radical nature of this movement renders any simple distinction between old and new as redundant. Further, to return to an earlier theme of this chapter, challenging neoliberal globalisation is not *simply* a reactive process. As we have seen in the example of the Zapatista revolution, it is possible to construct new knowledges, new ways of organising, new forms of welfare and of meeting need – concrete practices that embody the belief that 'another world is possible' (see Fisher and Ponniah, 2003). But other movements for global justice do call on 'older' forms of protest and organisation, albeit shaped by contemporary global developments and other forms of protest.

Chapter Three also introduced and raised other important questions that emerged from debates between American and European social movement theorising. How do the differing approaches of American resource mobilisation theory (RMT) and the European new social movements perspective help us understand the dynamics and organisational aspects of global social movements? The short response is that they offer only limited insights. As we argued in Chapter Three, RMT tends to understand social movements as single-issue protests and campaigns, protests that seek to forge alliances with mainstream organisations whose ultimate aim is political inclusion and accommodation with the status quo. In many respects, global social movements are more in tune with the radical aims of the new social movements, rejecting the 'older' organisational structures, mainstream approaches and ways of doing politics. However, both approaches fail to capture the richness and diversity of the movements and forms of protests that contribute to the fight for global social justice.

There is much in this chapter that is central to our understanding of social welfare and social policy: how it is increasingly being shaped by global economic agendas and the needs of global big business, and the recognition that economic growth and social (and environmental) justice are (unlikely) partners. But there are struggles taking place across the world around social welfare needs and the failures of states and transnational governmental organisations to meet these. It is reasonable to argue that neoliberal globalisation has further enabled protestors in disparate movements to draw links between struggles taking place in different parts of the world. As we will see in the final chapter, it is through this process that once again the meaning of citizenship is being contested as a key issue across global capitalism.

Further reading

Live Working or Die Fighting by Paul Mason (Harvill Secker, 2007) is an excellent and readable discussion of the parallels between the struggles of the global working class and labour movement in the late 19th and the early 20th century and the global resistance movement today.

In *The Global Resistance Reader* (Routledge, 2005), Louise Amoore brings together a diverse range of authors involved in global protests to provide a comprehensive collection of studies of many different aspects of the global justice movement.

The collection *Understanding Global Social* Policy edited by Nicola Yeates (The Policy Press, 2008), which is also part of The Policy Press/Social Policy Association 'Understanding Welfare' series, offers a very accessible and comprehensive exploration of the ways in which 'globalisation' and the global is increasingly important for our understanding of the construction of social welfare policy today.

Social Justice, Welfare, Crime and Society edited by Janet Newman and Nicola Yeates (Open University Press, 2008) provides a thoughtful discussion of the idea of social justice and how this has become more central to social welfare in recent times.

Useful websites

European Social Forum: *www.fse-esf.org*

Globalise resistance: *www.resist.org.uk*

Indymedia: *www.indymedia.org.uk*

Union Island (trade union, virtual world Second Life): *www.slunionisland.org*

World Development Movement: *www.wdm.org.uk*

World Social Forum 2008: *www.wsf2008.net*

Conclusion

A New Deal for social welfare movements?

As the worst global financial crisis for 80 years broke over the heads of national governments in 2008, some commentators lamented the absence of a social movement in a position to forcefully pose alternative solutions. Where were the forces today that would pressure governments and banks to mend their ways? Which mobilisations would prepare the conditions for an alternative to neoliberal social welfare in the way that struggles around unemployment, poverty, sickness, housing and education prepared the ground for the Beveridgean welfare state (see Part Two)? In the past, the labour movement largely preformed that role. It had focused its efforts on the strategic power of the state as the medium for social reform. Through long and difficult struggles, a major plank of its programme was realised with the foundation of the welfare state (see Chapters One and Two). Its influence was further acknowledged in the post-war institutional collaboration between state, labour and capital known as corporatism (Harris, 1972).

In earlier periods of economic crisis, such as the Depression of the 1930s, class and state were the locus for emerging mass solidarities (Chapter Four). Some contemporary commentators see an 'uncanny' parallel with the 1930s, with important historical lessons for today.

> The Roaring Twenties that preceded the crash of 1929 was the first great age of consumer and corporate debt – and the last 10 years was the second. In the darkest days, people buried their money in coffee cans in the back garden, while workers from

the northeast of England marched on London in what came to be called the Jarrow Crusade. (Parker, 2008, p 75)

A further parallel has been drawn between the 'recapitalisation' of the banks in October 2008 and the New Deal (see below) in the US of the 1930s. In both cases, the previously sacrosanct principles of the free market were unceremoniously abandoned. Another ominous parallel is the return of the spectre of mass unemployment. By 1933, anything between one quarter to one third of the US labour force were out of work (Galbraith, 1961). The resulting social collapse was graphically captured in John Steinbeck's novel and, later, John Ford's film, *The Grapes of Wrath*. Against this a new social movement of unemployed labour materialised. Twenty thousand veterans who had fought in the First World War marched on Washington in 1932 to demand that a service bonus be paid now that they found themselves in dire need, only to be brutally attacked by the army.

With the election in 1933 of Franklin D. Roosevelt, a series of progressive reforms know as the New Deal was implemented to help stabilise the economy and alleviate the suffering of the poor and the unemployed. As part of what is called Keynesian demand management, the New Deal created public works that allowed the unemployed to earn an income that they can then spend and in this way help to reflate a depressed economy. Better this, the managers of state and capital thought, than their rebellion turning into a revolution. Political mobilisation and sit-down strikes against lay-offs also played their part in the creation of the New Deal. In many parts of the country the concessions represented by the New Deal further incited desperate people to help themselves. Unemployed councils were set up all over America. As one writer at the time described unemployed activism in 1932:

> If an unemployed worker has his gas or his water turned off because he can't pay for it, to see the proper authorities; to see that the unemployed who are shoeless and clothesless get both; to eliminate through publicity and pressure discriminations between Negroes and white persons, or against the foreign born, in matters of relief ... to march people down to relief headquarters and demand that they be fed and clothed. Finally to provide legal defense for all unemployed arrested for joining parades, hunger marches, or attending union meetings. (quoted in Zinn, 2001, p 394)

Hence, the example of the American New Deal has a contemporary resonance. For instance, the pattern of financial crisis that has engulfed

Argentina since 1995 has been followed with an ascending curve of protest and collective action among the unemployed (Garay, 2007).

Nevertheless, the forces that prepared the conditions for the New Deal or the Beveridgean welfare state do not represent a model for the revival of social movements everywhere and at all times. There remains an ongoing need for detailed empirical studies and rethinking of social policy in the light of an interrelated understanding of social movements, mobilisation and social reform.

The contribution of social movements to state welfare

Understanding Social Welfare Movements has attempted to overcome evolutionary, ahistorical and inadequate accounts of the relationship between social movements and social welfare. Social movements have made a significant direct and indirect contribution to both how social welfare is understood and how state welfare is utilised. Welfare movements emerge to dispute or issue claims about some particular aspect of social policy. What all the campaigns, events, groups, protests and values share in common is that, perforce, they enter into a conflictual relationship with the state at different levels – local, regional and national level – and, as Chapter Eleven shows, global scales. In some cases, movement leaders can end up as a collaborator rather than an opponent of state policy. Such assimilation happened to labour leaders during the post-war phase of corporatism and, later, to movements around sexuality, gender or 'race' movements in the equal opportunities industry (see Chapters Eight and Nine).

A further hallmark of social welfare movements is that they also contest the authority of expert knowledge (Chapter Five). Again, this is viewed as a particular characteristic of new movements. What this obscures is that many earlier movements contested both the legitimacy and the veracity of authorised experts. Campaigns with regard to unemployment frequently dispute what counts as adequate social security and the institutional arrangements for redistributing resources (Chapter Four). Elite educationalists were challenged by the broad movement for comprehensive schooling, within which the labour movement played a considerable part (Chapter Seven). On the other hand, new social movements are also said to mobilise considerable expert forms of alternative knowledge in their own right (Law, 2008). This can take the form of protests on the basis of public health against scientific expertise, as in the case of research by two of us into recent campaigns against the public health hazards represented by mobile phone masts (Law and McNeish, 2007).

Again, there is nothing especially new in this. In the case of health, for instance, the National Health Service (NHS) was only established after the ideological and legitimating conditions were established by the activities in the 1930s of radical medical pressure groups such as the Committee Against Malnutrition and the Socialist Medical Association. Here, medical experts used their knowledge and positions to advance the case for socialised medicine to alleviate unnecessary working-class suffering. The Committee Against Malnutrition organised large public meetings in the 1930s while the Socialist Medical Association, operated mainly within the Labour Party as a pressure group, whose ideas would form the ideological and medical conditions for the creation of the NHS (Stewart, 1999). That it later changed its name to the Socialist Health Association in 1981 indicates the shifting emphasis after the 1960s, not least under the impact of feminism (Chapter Five), from a medical model to a more socially oriented model of health and well-being.

What appears astonishing about welfare movements is that their action alters the familiar arrangement of things. Reforms are enacted, professional practices are changed, bureaucratic procedures are simplified, new values are adopted, closure programmes are stopped, or resources are more fairly redistributed. Individuals are released from their fate to be passive, submissive, obedient, grateful objects of social policy to become more active, confident, articulate agents of political, institutional and professional change. Welfare movements have an invigorating effect on state welfare. Such an open-ended approach to social movements means that the emergence of a radical culture of challenge to failing economic conditions cannot be precluded now as in the past, as was the case, inter alia, in Glasgow in 1915 (Chapter Six), in South Wales in 1935 (Chapter Four) and in Seattle in 1999, Genoa in 2001 and Edinburgh in 2005 (Introduction and Chapter Eleven).

Does this then lend support for Piven and Cloward's (1979) claim that poor people's movements only win reforms when they are spontaneous, innovative and disorganised, directed at tangible local targets? Our examples in this book do *not* generally support Piven and Cloward's central contention about the bureaucratic demobilisation of poor people's movements. In Chapter Four, for instance, we saw how the National Unemployed Workers' Movement (NUWM) constituted itself in a highly organised fashion, with conferences, rules, subscriptions, newspapers and paid officials and it remained a catalyst for protest in the form of the hunger march, pavement sleep-ins, building occupations, street battles and vandalism. When the National Unemployed Workers' Committee Movement (NUWCM) dropped the word 'committee' from its name to become the NUWM it tried to move away from autonomous activist-led branches of the early 1920s. But NUWM centralisation was always partial and subject to the initiatives of the local activists (Croucher, 1987, p 104; Flanagan, 1991, p 167). In any case, the unemployed were impelled by events to collective action in their material interest to defend or improve relief levels without waiting on instructions from a centralised leadership.

In some ways, the example of unemployed protest supports the claims of resource mobilisation theory (RMT) (Chapter Three). First, the NUWM harnessed the material incentives that the unemployed had for engaging in collective action. The fight by the unemployed for adequate subsistence was clearly 'a politics of the belly'. It was rational for the unemployed to take whatever action they could to improve or defend benefit levels. Second, although the unemployed seemed to lack material resources, especially funds, in fact the leading unemployed activists, the 'movement entrepreneurs' if you like, possessed considerable organisational resources; many of them were experienced socialists, unemployed syndicalists and ex-shop stewards. Crucial here is the active external role of left-wing cadres in providing organisational and ideological resources that 'the unemployed' did not spontaneously possess. Again, something similar occurred in the role of labour movement activists in anti-racism struggles and campaigns for health, housing and education (Chapters Five, Six, Seven and Nine).

In still other ways, however, RMT fails to capture adequately the vibrancy and idealism of welfare struggles. Of course, such movements fought over immediate material needs. But, in so doing, they transcended the fight over this or that benefit cut, a mean-spirited regulation, or specific local grievances. These struggles were never purely strategic and instrumental. Every demand for social justice always contains an ethical dimension. As Perry (2007, p 5) acknowledges for the struggles of the unemployed:

> Unemployed protest is in the first instance a struggle for recognition. The demand for adequate government provision for the unemployed was a call for respect and acknowledgement. It was based upon the premise that the unemployed suffered from a plight not of their own making.

Moreover, where analysis is restricted to the struggles of immediate milieu, say in particular benefit offices, hospital wards or urban spaces, it presents an incomplete and foreshortened picture. Protest is prematurely confined to only one stage, the most immediate and direct, neglecting the longer cycle of the wider and more circuitous route of the reform process. Movement influence has an uneven temporal dimension, from immediate struggles through to the effects that reverberate at a later stage when the whole set of circumstances have changed. Here the struggles of the 1930s and the 1940s helped to define ('Never Again!') the post-war political landscape. The struggle of the civil rights movements of the 1960s and 1970s challenged the ideal of universal civil rights when so many groups were being denied equal rights – women, disabled people, national, ethnic and religious minority groups. This was encapsulated by the Derry Housing Action Committee protesting against anti-Catholic discrimination in housing allocations in Northern Ireland, whose banner placed a question mark against the 1968 celebrations as the United Nations' 'Year of Human Rights?' Meanwhile, as noted in the Introduction, the world of today continues to feel the after-effects of Seattle ('Ya basta!') as capitalism displays grave difficulties in maintaining itself as a system for organising socioeconomic resources. By preparing the conditions for welfare reform, social welfare movements express epoch-making shifts in national social policy; in the 1940s, this was on the basis of universal politics of social rights rather than discretionary charity (Chapter Seven); in the 1980s, this was on the basis of a politics of cultural difference rather than discrimination (Chapters Nine and Eleven). Demands for social justice challenge the distributive mechanism of the free market, which had once seemed to be an inviolable law of nature. While the vast majority of welfare users are not politically active, neither are they exactly 'free-riders', sitting it out at no cost to themselves while the militant minority inside a passive majority takes all the risks and pay the costs.

The mosaic of protest: state, class, identity

This book has amply shown that no social movement operates in conditions of its own choosing. Movements are not simply a matter of voluntarism, of pure will exercised over inopportune circumstance. Movements are circumscribed and inhibited by a whole range of structural and institutional factors. Chapter Three introduced the idea of a 'political opportunity structure' as one way of adjudicating the relationship between collective action and the political environment. A crucial factor is the nature of the state that movements face in the balance it strikes between coercion and consent. As we saw in Chapter One, in accounts like T.H. Marshall's (1950), the British state was gradually persuaded to grant its people, first, civil rights, then political rights and, finally, social rights. Clearly, the process of arriving at the classical welfare state was much more messy than this suggests. It had at its heart the struggle of ordinary people in urgent conditions of meeting the need for everyday necessities. Some of the historical contours of this struggle were indicated in Chapter Two, although much more could have been said about the historically variable interrelationship between mobilisations from below, the role played by intermediaries, and the changing nature of the state itself. That is a job not for a single book but for an entire series of empirical studies of specific movements and theoretical reflection.

One way to compensate for the gaps and silences of the social movements that it proved impossible to accommodate in a single volume is to convey a sense of what is at stake in the debates over social movements. Each substantive chapter has sought to provide answers to the question of how to theorise movements introduced at the end of Chapter Three. You may have noticed that the chapter titles in Part Two all begin with 'Fighting....' while in Part Three they begin with 'Contesting....'. This reflects the subtle shift in vocabulary around new social movements, displacing the more confrontational language of the earlier movements with the vaguer discourses of the later ones. In the latter case, oppositional language and practices do of course occur. One of the main threads of our empirical studies has been the question of just how 'new' are the new social movements covered in Part Three compared to the supposedly 'old' social movements in Part Two. Any attempt to hold on to a dichotomy of old versus new movements risks submerging the material aspects as the precondition of struggles over welfare provision. The redistributive politics of class threatens to be displaced with the cultural politics of difference and the economics of inequality by the politics of civil society (Powell, 2007). Contrariwise, 'old' movements based on class, above all the labour movement, can be condescendingly dismissed as lacking a concern with identity, culture, dignity and recognition. Hence, the 'moral protest' emphasised by new social movement theory, if not practice, can have an air of disdain towards supposedly amoral working-class movements.

By neglecting the skein of class society, 'post-materialist' accounts of social movements seem to express what Bourdieu (1984) called the cultural capital of middle-class theorists, elevated above the vulgar, undignified business of the crude fight for material necessities. It could be argued that post-materialism is a skilful mark of class distinction rather than an accurate reflection of the disappearance of class as a locus of political struggle. Perhaps as global capitalism retrenches under the impact of economic crisis and recession, a less superior attitude will be taken to the strategic kind of collective grievance emphasised by RMT (see Chapter Three).

In practice, alliances are formed between direct-action protest, the 'movement entrepreneurs' as social movement theory calls them (Chapter Three), socialist groups and working-class communities. Chapter Ten demonstrated such an alliance in the case of the anti-roads protest in the so-called Pollok Free State. Chapter Nine situated the case of anti-racism struggles within the changing political, cultural and economic conditions of working-class life in post-war Britain, including the galvanising role played by members of small, left-wing parties such as the Socialist Workers Party in initiating the Anti-Nazi League and Rock Against Racism. Chapter Eleven showed how in the case of Seattle and the 'global social justice movement' an often fragile alliance can be built between labour activists and environmentalists, between Teamsters and Turtles in that vivid case. In our Introduction, we also briefly discussed the past decade or so of popular protest in France in order to indicate the confluence of forces contending around state welfare and how they cooperate, learn to frame their grievances and adopt tactics from each other in struggle.

At the other end of the debate, particularly on the question of poverty where crude materiality predominates, resistance to professional power and expertise can often take forms that stand apart from the contentious politics of formal social movement organisations (SMOs) as we have conceived them. Like the equal opportunities apparatus, a poverty infrastructure has also emerged that encompasses intermediaries, professionals, bureaucrats and functionaries. Pressure groups such as the Child Poverty Action Group form part of a pressure group lobby that attempts to highlight the unacceptable levels of impoverishment and deprivation in society and influence government policy. Within health, a blurring of boundaries is also apparent between user groups and voluntary sector organisations (see Chapter Five; Barnes et al, 2007). Others such as benefit rights workers and Citizen's Advice Bureaux and represent the interests of poor people in negotiating their way through the quagmire of benefit rules and regulations to claim entitlements. Such intermediaries necessarily substitute for the self-activity of their clients. Institutional changes in entitlement processes, especially the removal of discretionary powers, have altered the political opportunity structure for claimants themselves to organise collectively.

Protest unbound?

Some have largely discounted the unemployed or the labour movement of the 21st century from ever again mounting any challenge to mass unemployment, insecurity or diswelfare (see Bagguley, 1991). Since the 1970s, institutional restructuring and bureaucratic centralisation have all but closed down the spaces that provide a focus for discontent and make possible mass solidarities and cultures of challenge. Claiming on an individual basis at a remote distance from decision makers has made self-organisation among the unemployed much more difficult compared to the 1970s let alone the 1930s (Bagguley and Hearn, 1999). The Unemployed Workers and Claimant Unions active in the 1970s stressed their autonomy, participative structures and ideological opposition to the forced take-up of low-paid employment (Jordan, 1999); characteristic of new social movements perhaps but also self-consciously modelled after the NUWM of the 1930s. Moreover, their alternative culture and radical nature can be exaggerated. Many Claimants Unions were preoccupied with the day-today business of advocacy and casework without combining it with agitation and direct action as earlier movements had done.

But even the ideological and organisational space for this type of culture of challenge to market orthodoxy has been curtailed over the past 30 years. After all, and notwithstanding the massive Anti–Poll Tax campaign, Jordan (1999, p 217) has argued that 'Public protests or campaigns are rather easily suppressed; if miners and printers failed, why should unemployed people believe they can succeed, especially in the absence of support from trade unions or political parties?'. Instead of looking to the structures of the welfare state for redress through their own organised collective action, the unemployed can find individual solutions to their predicament by opportunistically working in the informal economy while claiming, strategic separation of couples, begging, petty crime and busking rather than complying with state parsimony and regulation.

Such everyday 'weapons of the weak' appear to some activist-academics like Jordan and Piven and Cloward as a form of resistance that frustrates the market-led policies of the state. They invert the negative connotations of the 'underclass' discourse and valorise the recalcitrant quality of the more informal cultures of the poor. This has been given further theoretical ballast in Hardt and Negri's (2004) idea of 'the multitude'. Instead of confronting the authority of the state directly through collective organisation, resistance by 'the multitude' is preoccupied with micro-level, guerrilla tactics of 'nomadic' struggle of anonymous masses on the move, above all migrants, that can swarm the chaotic, lumbering structures of the Empire and subvert it at any point. Such a curiously intangible and vague notion as that of 'the multitude' did have a short-lived appeal for some among the Seattle generation. In such ways, direct action can sanction an abstract voluntarism, glamourising the theory of the deed over praxis, the political process of mutual reasoning that comes from the close interweaving of theory and practice.

Against unidirectional explanations of social reform and mobilisation, an important lesson of this book is that the possibilities for resurgent social movements should never be entirely discounted. The very process of organising can open up spaces of resistance where perhaps none seemed to exist before (see Chapter Four). This is what gives movements their astonishing or miraculous character (see Introduction). Even where conditions seem unpropitious, movements can emerge; it is only retrospectively that they appear to be an inevitable outgrowth of their times. Even in the 1930s, social movements differed radically from each other according to the national context. In Germany, all independent social movements were physically annihilated after the Nazis came to power in 1933. In France, the radicalisation of protest in 1936 brought lasting reforms to the social security system that even now right-wing governments such those of Chirac and Sarkozy challenge at their peril.

In contrast to the more favourable political climate of New Deal America, the unemployed movement in Britain faced a deeply hostile national political environment. The NUWM was demonised by the press and even the official labour movement, which sought to demobilise the unemployed. Activists braved considerable personal risks, including imprisonment, police violence, victimisation and loss of benefit. The gains that were made for millions of people in these years were a direct result of the action of the active unemployed minority itself rather than sympathetic politicians. This hostile national political context in Britain indicates the limits to the idea of a 'political opportunity structure' introduced in Chapter Three as a necessary precondition for collective action. In the face of widespread political hostility, determined collective action by a sizable militant minority of the unemployed itself helped to reshape the political context. Importantly, they were only able to effect this due to a localised focus on Boards of Guardians and Public Assistance Committee (PACs). The local state, in other words, provided a tangible political opportunity structure for recurrent mobilisation at a level beneath the centralised national state (see Chapter Six; Bagguley, 1991).

But by the first decade of the 21st century, so the argument goes, declassed new social movements on the one hand and the market-driven politics of the neoliberal state on the other has left a vacuum of political legitimacy for collectivist politics. Class, it is claimed, has been de-centred from its former position at the centre of the political universe (see Chapters Three and Eleven). Since the late 1960s, the working class has been comprehensively restructured and fragmented by upward social mobility, service sector employment and the international division of labour. In response to the earlier crisis of the mid-1970s, the state has progressively removed from the free play of market forces much of the apparatus of national protectionism and social welfare. Into the breach stepped the new social movements, expressing concerns with trans-class or 'post-materialist' problems of identity, culture, feelings, values and ethics, or 'militant particularism' (Chapters Three and Eleven). Moreover, standing in between the state and social movements are the incorporated but dependent forces of pressure groups, lobby organisations, partnerships and organised policy forums (Barnes et al, 2007). While we warned against making a fetish of rigid definitions in the Introduction, intermediate social and political forces between the state and welfare users ought *not* to be considered social welfare movements. For us they lack the oppositional politics of contention that are the hallmark of any social welfare movement.

Where now?

Understanding Social Welfare Movements has shown the continuing relevance of social movements to struggles over welfare. It has done this *historically*, allowing a richer sense of the discontinuities and similarities between old and new movements. The proliferation of movements contending around welfare rights in recent decades – over gender, environment, 'race', disability, sexuality – should not be either entirely subsumed to social class but neither should their intimate relationship to class society be gainsaid. The book has also *theoretically* outlined competing perspectives for *understanding* social movements and social welfare. How movements emerge, organise, endure and decline has a certain pattern to it, perhaps best captured by Tarrow's idea of a 'cycle of protest' (Chapter Three). Here, the material dimensions of grievance and organisational resources remain indispensable preconditions for the incentives and means of welfare mobilisations.

We have also presented *empirical* evidence in the substantive chapters of Parts Two and Three on social welfare movements. As the case studies repeatedly show, even the debate between American and European theory (Chapter Three) can become too one-dimensional for understanding the dialectics of mobilisation. Ideas, values and recognition *and* material interests and organisational resources are important grounds for mobilising around the claims of entitlement that citizenship embodies. This is far from the politics of the symbolic gesture that is supposed to characterise distinctively *new* social movements. Social welfare movements are always related to concrete struggles over immediate demands for resources in one form or another. Social movements and the contentious politics of social welfare will be continually replenished by renewed patterns of economic recession and new rounds of mass unemployment and welfare austerity. It is therefore imperative that social movements are more adequately absorbed into our understanding of the essentially contested nature of contemporary social policy.

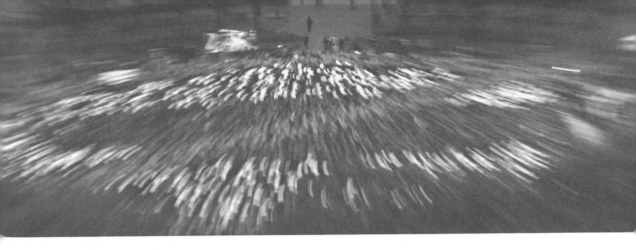

Bibliography

Allan, C. (2008) *Housing Market Renewal and Social Class*, London: Routledge.

Allen, J. (1999) 'Cities of power and influence', in J. Allen, D. Massey and S. Pile (eds) *Unsettling Cities*, London: Routledge, pp 181-227.

Allsop, J., Jones, K. and Baggott, R. (2005) 'Health consumer groups in the UK: a new social movement?', in P. Brown and S. Zavestoki (eds) *Social Movements in Health*, Oxford: Blackwell, pp 57-76.

American Psychiatric Association (1968) *Diagnostic and Statistical Manual of Mental Disorders: Second Edition: DSM II*, Washington, DC: American Psychiatric Association.

Amoore, L. (ed) (2005) *The Global Resistance Reader*, London: Routledge.

Anderson, B. (1991) *Imagined Communities: Reflections on the Origin and Spread of Nationalism*, London: Verso.

Annetts, J. and Thompson, B. (1992) 'Dangerous activism', in K. Plummer (ed) *Modern Homosexualities: Fragments of Lesbian and Gay Experience*, London: Routledge, pp 227-36.

Arnot, M., David, M. and Weiner, G. (1999) *Closing the Gender Gap: Post-War Education and Social Change*, Cambridge: Polity Press.

Auchmuty, R. (2004) 'Same-sex marriage revived: feminist critique and legal strategy', *Feminism Psychology*, 14 (1): 101-26.

Baggott, R., Allsop, J. and Jones, K. (2005) *Speaking for Patients and Carers: Health Consumer Groups and the Policy Process*, Basingstoke: Palgrave Macmillan.

Bagguley, P. (1991) *From Protest to Acquiescence? Political Movements of the Unemployed*, London: Macmillan.

Bagguley, P. (1992) 'Social change, the middle class and the emergence of "new social movements"', *Sociological Review*, 40 (1): 27-48.

Bagguley, P. and Hearn, J. (eds) (1999) *Transforming Politics: Power and Resistance*, London: Macmillan.

Barber, M. (1994) *The Making of the 1944 Education Act*, London: Cassell.

Barker, C. (1999) 'Empowerment and resistance: "collective effervescence" and other accounts, in P. Bagguley and J. Hearn (eds) *Transforming Politics: Power and Resistance*, London: Macmillan, pp 11-31.

Barker, K. (1998) 'A ship upon a stormy sea: the medicalization of pregnancy', *Social Science & Medicine*, 47 (8): 1067-76.

Barker, M. and Beezer, A. (1983) 'The Language of racism: an examination of Lord Scarman's report on the Brixton riots', *International Socialism*, 18 (108): 108-25.

Barnes, C. (2007) 'Disability action and the struggle for change: disability policy and politics in the UK', *Education, Citizenship and Social Justice*, 2 (3): 203-21.

Barnes, C., Newman, J. and Sullivan, H. (2007) *Power, Participation and Political Renewal*, Bristol: The Policy Press.

Barry, J. and Doherty, B. (2002) 'The Greens and social policy: movements, policy and practice?', in M. Cahill and T. Fitzpatrick (eds) *Environmental Issues and Social Welfare*, Oxford: Blackwell, pp 119-39.

Beck, U. (1992) *Risk Society*, London: Sage Publications.

Bell, D. (1960) *The End of Ideology*, New York, NY: Free Press.

Bell, G. (1995) 'The real battle of Pollok Free State commences', *The Herald*, 15 February.

Bello, W. (2000) *Why Reform of the WTO is the Wrong Agenda*, Bangkok: Focus on the Global South.

Bello, W. (2004) *Deglobalization: Ideas for a New World Economy*, London: Zed Books.

Benato, R., Clarke, A., Holt, V. and Lack, V. (1998) 'Women and collective general practice: the Hoxton experience', in L. Doyal (ed) *Women and Health Services*, Buckingham: Open University Press, pp 201-12.

Benyon, J. and Solomos, J. (eds) (1987) *The Roots of Urban Unrest*, Oxford: Pergamon Press.

Berger, B. and Berger, P.L. (1983) *The War over the Family: Capturing the Middle Ground*, London: Hutchinson.

Beveridge, W. (1909) *Unemployment: A Problem of Industry*, London: Longman and Co.

Beveridge, W. (1942) *Social Insurance and Allied Services* (The Beveridge Report), Cmnd 6404, London: HMSO.

Beveridge, W.H. (1944) *Full Employment in a Free Society: Misery Breeds Hate*, London: George Allen & Unwin.

Bircham, E. and Charlton, J. (eds) (2001) *Anti-Capitalism: A Guide to the Movement*, London: Bookmarks.

Black, D., Morris, J.N., Smith, C. and Townsend P. (1991) 'The Black Report', in P. Townsend, M. Whitehead and N. Davidson (eds) *Inequalities in Health*, Harmondsworth: Penguin, pp 29-213.

Blackledge, P. and Kirkpatrick, G. (2002) *Historical Materialism and Social Evolution*, London: Palgrave Macmillan.

Block, F. and Somers, M. (2003) 'In the shadow of Speenhamland: Social policy and the Old Poor Law', *Politics & Society*, 31 (2): 283-323.

Board of Education (1944) *Report of the Committee on Public Schools* (the Fleming Committee), London: HMSO.

Borkenau, F. (1962) *World Communism: A History of the Communist International*, Ann Arbor, MI: University of Michigan Press.

Bottomore, T. (1992) 'Citizenship and social class, forty years on', in T.H. Marshall and T. Bottomore (1992) *Citizenship and Social Class*, London: Pluto Press.

Bourdieu, P. (1984) *Distinction: A Social Critique of the Judgement of Taste*, Cambridge, MA: Harvard University Press.

Bourdieu, P. (1998) 'The protest movement of the unemployed, a social miracle', in P. Bourdieu, *Acts of Resistance: Against the Tyranny of the Market*, Cambridge: Polity Press.

Bourdieu, P. (2003) 'For a European social movement', in P. Bourdieu, *Firing Back: Against the Tyranny of the Market 2*, London: Verso.

Bourdieu, P. (2008) 'An upsurge of action by the unemployed', in P. Bourdieu, *Political Interventions: Social Science and Political Action*, London: Verso.

Bradley, Q. (nd) *The Birth of the Council Tenants Movement: A Study of the 1934 Leeds Rent Strike*, available at http://freespace.virgin.net/labwise.history6/1934.html

Bradley, Q. (1997) *The Leeds Rent Strike of 1914: A Re-Appraisal of the Radical History of the Tenants Movement*, Leeds: HNC Housing Studies Research Project, available at http://freespace.virgin.net/labwise.history6/rentrick.htm

Branson, N. (1979) *Poplarism, 1919-1925: George Lansbury and the Councillors Revolt*, London: Lawrence and Wishart.

Briggs, A. (1962) *Fabian Essays*, London: George Allen & Unwin.

Brown, P. and Zavestoski, S. (2005) 'Social movements in health: an introduction', in P. Brown and S. Zavestoki (eds) *Social Movements in Health*, Oxford: Blackwell, pp 1-16.

Brown, P., Zavestoski, S., McCormick, S., Mayer, B., Morello-Frosch, R. and Altman, R.G. (2004) 'Embodied health movements: new approaches to social movements in health', *Sociology of Health and Illness*, 26 (1): 50-80.

Bruce, M. (1968) *The Coming of the Welfare State*, London: Batsford.

Bryant, B. (ed) *Twyford Down, Campaigning and Environmental Law*, London: Chapman and Hall.

Burn, D. (1972) *Rent Strike: St Pancras 1960*, London: Pluto Press, available at www.whatnextjournal.co.uk/Pages/History/Rentstrike.html

Bush, J. (2007) *Women Against the Vote: Female Anti-Suffragism in Britain*, Oxford: Oxford University Press.

Butterfield, Sir H. (1932) *The Whig Interpretation of History*, www.eliohs.unifi.it/testi/900/butterfield

Byrne, P. (1997) *Social Movements in Britain*, London: Routledge.

Cahill, M. (2002) *The Environment and Social Policy*, London: Routledge.

Cahill, M. and Fitzpatrick, T. (eds) (2002) *Environmental Issues and Social Welfare*, Oxford: Blackwell.

Calder, A. (1969) *The People's War: Britain, 1939-45*, London: Pimlico.

Calhoun, C. (1993) 'New social movements of the early nineteenth' century', *Social Science Journal*, 17 (3): 385-427.

Callinicos, A. (2000) *Equality*, Cambridge: Polity Press.

Callinicos, A. (2003) *An Anti-Capitalist Manifesto*, Cambridge: Polity Press.

Campbell, B. (1984) *Wigan Pier Revisited: Poverty and Politics in the 80s*, London: Virago.

Canel, E. (1992) 'New social movement theory and resource mobilisation theory: the need for integration', in W.K. Caroll (ed) *Organising Dissent*, Canada: Garamond Press, pp 22-51.

Castells, M. (1977a) *The Urban Question: A Marxist Approach*, London: Edward Arnold.

Castells, M. (1977b) 'The class struggle and urban contradictions', in J. Cowley, A. Kaye, M. Mayo and M. Thompson (eds) *Community or Class Struggle?*, London: Stage One, pp 36-52.

Castells, M. (1978) *City, Class and Power*, London: Macmillan.

Castells, M. (1983) *The City and the Grassroots*, London: Edward Arnold.

Castells, M. (1997) *The Power of Identity: The Information Age, Economy, Society and Culture, Vol 2*, Oxford: Blackwell.

Castells, M. (2000) *The Rise of the Network Society: The Information Age, Economy, Society and Culture, Vol 1*, Oxford: Blackwell.

Castells, M. (2006) 'Changer la Ville: a rejoinder', *International Journal of Urban and Regional Research*, 30 (1): 219-23.

Charlton, J. (1997) *The Chartists: The First National Workers' Movement*, London: Pluto Press.

Charlton, J. (2000) 'Talking Seattle', *International Socialism*, 86: 3-18.

Charlton, J. (2003) 'The pre-history of social movements: from Newport to Seattle', in K. Flett and D. Renton (eds) *New Approaches to Socialist History*, Cheltenham: New Clarion Press, pp 9-17.

Chesters, G. and Welsh, I. (2006) *Complexity and Social Movements: Multitudes at the Edge of Chaos*, Oxford: Routledge.

Christian Institute (2002) *Counterfeit Marriage: How Civil Partnerships Devalue Marriage*, Newcastle Upon Tyne: Christian Institute.

Chun, L. (1995) *The British New Left*, Edinburgh: Edinburgh University Press.

City: Analysis of Urban Trends, Culture, Theory, Policy, Action (2006) Special themed issue on urban social movements, 10 (3).

Clarke, J. and Langan, M. (1993) 'Restructuring welfare: the British welfare regime in the 1980s', in A. Cochrane and J. Clarke (eds) *Comparing Welfare States: Britain in International Context*, London: Sage Publications.

Cochrane, A. and Walters, R. (2008) 'The globalisation of social justice', in J. Newman and N. Yeates (eds) *Social Justice: Welfare, Crime and Society*, Maidenhead: Open University Press, pp 163-79.

Cockburn, C. (1977) *The Local State*, London: Pluto.

Cohen, J.L. (1985) 'Strategy or identity? New theoretical paradigms and contemporary social movements', *Social Research*, 52 (4): 663-716.

Cole, M. (2007) 'Re-thinking unemployment: a challenge to the legacy of Jahoda et al.', *Sociology*, 41 (6): 1133-49.

Committee of the Secondary School Examinations Council (1943) *Curriculum and Examinations in Secondary Schools* (Norwood Report), London: HMSO.

Committee on Higher Education (1963) *Higher Education* (Robbins Report), London: HMSO.

Committee on Scottish Health Services (1936) *Report* (Cathcart Report), Cmd 5204, London: HMSO.

Consultative Committee on Secondary Education (1938) *Secondary Education with Special Reference to Grammar Schools and Technical High Schools* (Spens Report), London: HMSO.

Cook, H. (2004) *The Long Sexual Revolution: English Women, Sex & Contraception 1800-1975*, Oxford: Oxford University Press.

Cook, I. (2004) 'National day of action', *Ouch! 'that site for disabled people'*, 11 March, www.bbc.co.uk/ouch/news/btn/action_day.html

Cook, M., Mills, R., Trumbach, R. and Cocks, H.G. (2007) *A Gay History of Britain: Love and Sex between Men since the Middle Ages*, Santa Barbara, CA: Greenwood World Publishing.

Coote, A. and Pattullo, P. (1990) *Power and Prejudice: Women and Politics*, London: Weidenfeld and Nicolson.

Corporation of the City of Glasgow (1965) *A Highway Plan for Glasgow*, Glasgow: Scott, Wilson, Kirkpatrick and Partners.

Cotgrove, S. (1982) *Catastrophe or Cornucopia: Environment and the Politics of the Future*, London: Wiley & Sons.

Cotgrove, S. and Duff, A. (1980) 'Environmentalism, middle class radicalism and politics', *Sociological Review*, 28 (2): 333-51.

Cowden, S. and Singh, G. (2007) 'The "user": friend, foe or fetish? A critical exploration of user involvement in health and social care', *Critical Social Policy* 27: 5-23.

Craig, G., Burchardt, T. and Gordon, D. (eds) (2008) *Social Justice and Public Policy: Seeking Fairness in Diverse Societies*, Bristol: The Policy Press.

CRFR (Centre for Relationship and Family Research) (2002) *Research Briefing*, Number 3, Edinburgh: Centre for Relationship and Family Research.

Crick. B. and Robson, W. A. (eds) (1970) *Protest and Discontent*, London: Pelican.

Crook, S., Pakulski, J. and Waters, M. (eds) (1992) *Postmodernisation: Change in Advanced Society*, London: Sage Publications.

Crossley, N. (2002) *Making Sense of Social Movements*, Milton Keynes: Open University Press.

Crossley, N. (2003) 'Even newer social movements? Anti-corporate protests, capitalist crises and the remoralisation of society', *Organisation*, 10: 287-305.

Crossley, N. (2006) *Contesting Psychiatry: Social Movements in Mental Health*, London: Routledge.

Croucher, R. (1987) *We Refuse to Starve in Silence: A History of the National Unemployed Workers' Movement*, London: Lawrence and Wishart.

Croucher, R. (1990) 'Communist unemployed organisations between the wars: international patterns and problems', *Archiv für Sozialgeschichte*, 30: 584-95.

Cumbers, A., Routledge, P. and Nativel, C. (2008) 'The entangled geographies of global justice networks', *Progress in Human Geography*, 32 (2): 183-201.

D'Anieri, P.D., Ernst, C. and Kier, E. (1990) 'New social movements in historical perspective', *Comparative Politics*, 22 (4): 445-58.

Dale, R. (1989) *The State and Education Policy*, Milton Keynes: Open University Press.

Dalton, R.J., Keuchler, M. and Burklin, W. (1990) 'The challenge of the new movements', in R.J. Dalton and M. Keuchler (eds) *Challenging the Political Order*, Cambridge: Polity Press, pp 3-20.

Daly, G., Mooney, G., Poole, L. and Davis, H. (2005) 'Housing stock transfer in the UK: the contrasting experiences of two UK cities', *European Journal of Housing Policy*, 5 (3): 327-41.

Damer, S. (1980) 'State, class and housing, Glasgow, 1885-1919', in J. Melling (ed) *Housing, Social Policy and the State*, London: Croom Helm, pp 73-112.

Damer, S. (2000) 'The Clyde rent war? The Clydebank rent strike of the 1920s', in M. Lavalette and G. Mooney (eds) *Class Struggle and Social Welfare*, London: Routledge, pp 71-95.

Danaher, K. and Burbach, R. (eds) (2000) *Globalize This! The Battle Against the World Trade Organization and Corporate Rule*, New York, NY: Common Courage Press.

Davis, M. (2002) *Late Victorian Holocausts: El Nino Famines and the Making of the Third World*, London: Verso.

Davis, M. (2006) *Planet of Slums*, London: Verso.

Davis, M. (2009) 'The betrayed generation', *Socialist Review*, January.

Davis, M. and Monk, D.M. (eds) (2007) *Evil Paradises*, London: Verso.

DCH (Defend Council Housing) (2003) *The Case for Council Housing* (second edition), London: DCH.

De Certeau, M. (1984) *The Practice of Everyday Life*, Berkeley and Los Angeles: University of California Press.

De Souza Santos, B. (2008) 'The world social forum and the global left', *Politics and Society*, 36 (2): 247-70.

Deacon, A. (1981) 'Unemployment and politics in Britain since 1945', in B. Showler and A. Sinfield (eds) *The Workless State: Studies in Unemployment*, Oxford: Martin Robertson.

Dean, H. (2002) 'Green citizenship', in M. Cahill and T. Fitzpatrick (eds) *Environmental Issues and Social Welfare*, Oxford: Blackwell, pp 22-37.

Deleuze, G. (1973) 'Nomad thought', in D.B. Allison (ed) (1985) *The New Nietzsche*, New York, NY: MIT Press, pp 142-9.

Della Porta, D. and Diani, M. (2006) *Social Movements: An Introduction*, Oxford: Blackwell.

Della Porta, D. and Tarrow, S. (eds) (2005) *Transnational Protest and Global Activism*, Oxford: Rowman and Littlefield.

Desai, M. and Said, Y. (2001) 'The new anti-capitalist movement: money and global civil society', in M. Anheier, M. Gasius and M. Kaldor (eds) *Global Civil Society 2001*, Oxford: Oxford University Press, pp 51-78.

Dobson, A. (1997) *Green Political Thought*, London: Routledge.

Dobson, A. (2003) *Citizenship and the Environment*, Oxford: Oxford University Press.

Doherty, B., M. Paterson and B. Seel (eds) (2000) *Direct Action in British Environmentalism*, London: Routledge.

Dowse, L. (2001) 'Contesting practices, challenging codes: self, advocacy, politics and the social model', *Disability & Society*, 16 (1): 123-41.

Doyal, L. (1985) 'Women and the National Health Service: the carers and the careless', in E. Lewin and V. Olesen (eds) *Women, Health & Healing: Towards a New Perspective*, London: Tavistock, pp 236-69.

Doyal, L. (1994) 'Changing medicine? Gender and the politics of health care', in J. Gabe, D. Kelleher and G. Williams (eds) *Challenging Medicine*, London: Routledge, pp 141-60.

Doyal, L. (1998) *Women and Health Services*, Buckingham: Open University Press.

Dryzek, J., Downes, D., Hunold, C., Schlosberg, D. and Hernes, H.-K. (2003) *Green States and Social Movements*, Oxford: Oxford University Press.

Dunphy, R. (2000) *Sexual Politics: An Introduction*, Edinburgh: Edinburgh University Press.

Durham, M. (1991) *Sex and Politics: The Family and Morality in the Thatcher Years*, Basingstoke: Macmillan.

Eckersley, R. (2004) *The Green State: Rethinking Democracy and Sovereignty*, Boston, MA: MIT Press.

Eder, K. (1993) *The New Politics of Class*, London : Sage.

Engel, S.M. (2001) *The Unfinished Revolution: Social Movement Theory and the Gay and Lesbian Movement*, Cambridge: Cambridge University Press.

Eyerman, R. and Jamison, A. (1991) *Social Movements: A Cognitive Approach*, Cambridge: Polity Press.

Faludi, S. (1992) *Backlash: The Undeclared War Against Women*, London: Chatto & Windus.

Farnsworth, K. (2008) 'Business and global social policy formation', in N. Yeates (ed) *Understanding Global Social Policy*, Bristol: The Policy Press, pp 73-99.

Farrar, M. (1999) 'Social movements in a multi-ethnic inner city: explaining their rise and fall over 25 years', in P. Bagguley and J. Hearn (eds) *Transforming Politics: Power and Resistance*, Basingstoke: Macmillan, pp 87-105.

Farrar, M. (2004) 'Social movements and the struggle over race' in M.J. Todd and G. Taylor (eds) *Democracy and Participation: Popular Protest and New Social Movements*, London: Merlin Press, pp 218-47.

Farrell, M. (1980) *Northern Ireland: The Orange State*, London: Pluto Press.

Featherstone, D. (2005) 'Towards the relational construction of militant particularisms: or why the geographies of past struggles matter for resistance to neoliberal globalisation', *Antipode*, 37 (2): 250-71.

Fekete, L. (2005) 'The deportation machine: Europe, asylum and human rights', *Race and Class*, 47 (1): 64-91.

Ferguson, I., Lavalette, M. and Mooney, G. (2002) *Rethinking Welfare*, London: Sage Publications.

Firestone, S. (1979) *The Dialectic of Sex: The Case for Feminist Revolution*, London: Women's Press.

Fisher, W.F. and Ponniah, T. (eds) (2003) *Another World is Possible*, London: Zed Books.

Flanagan, R. (1991) *'Parish-Fed Bastards': A History of the Politics of the Unemployed in Britain, 1884-1939*, New York, NY: Greenwood Press.

Foucault, M. (1977) *Language, Counter-Memory, Practice*, Ithaca, NY: Cornell University Press.

Foucault, M. (1979) *The History of Sexuality*, Vol 1, London: Penguin.

Frankel, B. (1987) *The Post-Industrial Utopians*, Cambridge: Polity Press.

Fraser, D. (1984) *The Evolution of the Welfare State*, London: Macmillan.

Fryer, P. (1984) *Staying Power: The History of Black People in Britain*, London: Pluto Press.

Furedi, F. (2002) *Culture of Fear: Risk Taking and the Morality of Low Expectation*, London: Continuum International Publishing.

Galbraith, J.K. (1961) *The Great Crash, 1929*, Boston, MA: Houghton Mifflin.

Gallagher, W. (1978) *Revolt on the Clyde* (4th edition), London: Lawrence & Wishart.

Gamson, W. (1975) *The Strategy of Social Protest*, Homewood, IL: Dorsey Press.

Gamson, W. (1995) 'Constructing social protest', in H. Johnston and B. Klandermans (eds) *Social Movements and Culture*, London: UCL Press, pp 85-106.

Garay, A. (2007) 'Social policy and collective action: unemployed workers, community associations and protest in Argentina', *Politics & Society*, 35 (2): 301-2.

Garraty, J.A. (1978) *Unemployment in History, Economic and Thought and Public Policy*, London: Harper & Row.

Giddens, A. (1987) *The Consequences of Modernity*, Cambridge: Polity Press.

Gilroy, P. (1987) *There Ain't No Black in the Union Jack: The Cultural Politics of Race and Nation*, London: Hutchinson.

Ginsburg, N. (2005) 'The privatization of council housing', *Critical Social Policy*, 25 (1): 115-35.

Glyn, A. (2006) *Capitalism Unleashed: Finance, Globalization and Welfare*, Oxford: Oxford University Press.

Godber, G. (1988) 'Forty years of the NHS: the origins and early developments', *British Medical Journal*, 297: 37-43.

Goldner, M. (2005) 'The dynamic interplay between Western medicine and the complimentary and alternative medicine movement: how activists perceive a range of responses from physicians and hospitals', in P. Brown and S. Zavestoki (eds) *Social Movements in Health*, Oxford: Blackwell, pp 31-56.

Goldthorpe, J. (1982) 'On the service class, its formation and future', in A. Giddens and G. Mackenzie (eds) *Social Class and the Division of Labour*, Cambridge: Cambridge University Press, 162-85.

Goodwin, J. and Jasper, J.M. (eds) (2003) *The Social Movements Reader: Cases and Concepts*, New York, NY: Blackwell.

Gouldner, A. (1979) *The Future of Intellectuals and the Rise of the New Class*, Oxford, USA: Oxford University Press.

Graham, H. (1985) 'Providers, negotiators and mediators: women as the hidden carers' recipients', in E. Lewin and V. Olesen (eds) *Women, Health & Healing: Towards a New Perspective*, London: Tavistock, pp 53-85.

Gramsci, A. (1971) *Selections from the Prison Notebooks*, London: Lawrence & Wishart.

Grassic Gibbon, L. (1934) *Grey Granite: A Scots Quair, Part III*, Edinburgh: Polygon (2006).

Greenwood, W. (2004) *Love on the Dole*, London: Vintage.

Greig, A., Hulme, D. and Turner, M. (2007) *Challenging Global Inequality*, London: Palgrave Macmillan.

Griffiths, S. and Bradlow, J. (1998) 'Involving women as consumers: the Oxfordshire health strategy' experience', in L. Doyal (ed) *Women and Health Services*, Buckingham: Open University Press, pp 213-20.

Grove-White, R. (1997) 'Environment, risk, democracy' in M. Jacobs (ed) *Greening the Millennium: The new politics of the environment*, Oxford: Blackwell.

Gurr, T.R. (1970) *Why Men Rebel*, Princeton, NJ: Princeton University Press.

Gusfield, J.R. (1963) *Symbolic Crusade: Status Politics and the American Temperance Movement*, Urbana, IL: University of Illinois Press.

Gusfield, J. (1986) *Symbolic Crusade: Status Politics and the American Temperance Movement* (2nd edition), Chicago, IL: University of Illinois Press.

Habermas, J. (1976) *Legitimation Crisis*, London: Heinemann.

Habermas, J. (1981) 'New social movements', *Telos*, 49: 33-7.

Habermas, J. (1987a) *The Philosophical Discourse of Modernity*, Oxford: Blackwell.

Habermas, J. (1987b) *The Theory of Communicative Action*, Vol 2, London: Beacon Press.

Hallas, D. (1985) *The Comintern*, London: Bookmarks.

Halsey, A.H. (2004) *A History of Sociology in Britain*, Oxford: Oxford University Press.

Halsey, A.H., Heath, A.F. and Ridge, J.M. (1980) *Origins and Destinations: Family, Class and Education in Modern Britain*, Oxford: Clarendon Press.

Hanley, L. (2007) *Estates: An Intimate History*, London: Granta.

Hannington, W. (1979) *Unemployed Struggles: 1919-1936*, London: Lawrence & Wishart.

Harding, J. (2001) 'Globalisation's children strike back', *Financial Times*, 11 September.

Harding, R. (2007) 'Sir Mark Potter and the protection of the traditional family: why same sex marriage is (still) a feminist issue', *Feminist Legal Studies*, 15: 223-34.

Hardt, M. and Negri, A. (2000) Empire, London: Harvard University Press.

Hardt, M. and Negri, A. (2004) *Multitude*, London: Hamish Hamilton.

Harman, C. (1998) *The Fire Last Time: 1968 and After*, London: Bookmarks.

Harris, B. (2004) *The Origins of the British Welfare State: Society, State and Social Welfare in England and Wales, 1800-1945*, Basingstoke: Palgrave.

Harris, N. (1972) *Competition and the Corporate Society: British Conservatives, the State and Industry, 1945-64*, London: Methuen.

Harrison, M. and Reeve, K. (2002) 'Social welfare movements and collective action: lessons from two UK housing cases', *Housing Studies*, 17 (5): 755-71.

Harvey, D. (2001) *Spaces of Capital*, Edinburgh: Edinburgh University Press.

Harvey, D. (2003a) 'The right to the city', *International Journal of Urban and Regional Research*, 27 (4): 939-41.

Harvey, D. (2003b) *The New Imperialism*, Oxford: Oxford University Press.

Harvey, D. (2005) *A Brief History of Neoliberalism*, Oxford: Oxford University Press.

Held, D. and Kaya, A. (eds) (2007) *Global Inequality*, Cambridge: Polity Press.

Hennessey, P. (1992) *Never Again: Britain, 1945-51*, London: Jonathan Cape.

Hewitt, M. (1993) 'Social movements and social need: problems with postmodern political theory', *Critical Social Policy*, 37: 52-74.

Hickman, R.M. (2004) *M74 Special Road: Report of Public Local Inquiry into Objections*, accessed online at www.scotland.gov.uk/Publications/2005/03/20752/53462

Hilton, M. and Hirsch, P. (eds) (2000) *Practical Visionaries: Women, Education and Social Progress 1790-1930*, Harlow: Pearson Education.

Hobhouse, L.T. (1922) *Elements of Social Justice*, London: Allen & Unwin.

Hobsbawm, E.J. (1984) *Worlds of Labour: Further Studies in the History of Labour*, London: Weidenfeld & Nicolson.

Hobsbawm, E.J. (1990) *Industry and Empire*, London: Penguin.

Hobsbawm, E.J. (2007) 'Karl Marx and the British labour movement', in *Revolutionaries*, London: Abacus.

Hobsbawm, E.J. and Rude, G. (1969) *Captain Swing*, London: Lawrence & Wishart.

Hoggett, P. (2002) 'Democracy, social relations and ecowelfare', in M. Cahill and T. Fitzpatrick (eds) *Environmental Issues and Social Welfare*, Oxford: Blackwell, pp 140-58.

Howkins, A. and Saville, J. (1979) 'The nineteen thirties: a revisionist history', in R. Miliband and J. Saville (eds) *The Socialist Register 1979: A Survey of Movements and Ideas*, London: Merlin Press.

Howson, A. (1999) 'Cervical screening, compliance and moral obligation', *Sociology of Health and Illness*, 21 (4): 401-25.

Hubbard, G. and Miller, D. (eds) (2005) *Arguments Against G8*, London: Pluto Press.

IJURR (*International Journal of Urban and Regional Research*) (2003) Symposium on urban movements, *International Journal of Urban and Regional Research*, 27 (1).

IJURR (2006) Debate on urban politics and social movements, *International Journal of Urban and Regional Research*, 30 (1).

Illich, I. (1995) 'The epidemics of modern medicine' in B. Davey, A. Gray and C. Seale (eds) *Health and Disease: A Reader*, Buckingham: Open University Press, pp 237-42.

Inglehart, R. (1977) *The Silent Revolution: Changing Values and Lifestyles amongst Western Publics*, Princeton, NJ and London: Princeton University Press.

Inglehart, R. (1990) *Culture Shift in Advanced Society*, Princeton, NJ: Princeton University Press.

Jacobs, M. (ed) (1997) *Greening the Millennium: The new politics of the environment*, Oxford: Blackwell.

Jahoda, M., Lazarsfeld, P. and Zeisel, H. (2002) *Marienthal: The Sociography of an Unemployed Community*, New Jersey, NJ: Transaction Publishers.

Joffe, C.E., Weitz, T.A. and Stacey, C.L. (2004) 'Uneasy allies: pro-choice physicians, feminist health activists and the struggle for abortion rights', *Sociology of Health & Illness*, 26 (6): 775-96.

Johnson, A. (2000) 'The making of a poor people's movement: a study of the political leadership of poplarism, 1919-1925', in M. Lavalette and G. Mooney (eds) *Class Struggle and Social Welfare*, London: Routledge, pp 96-116.

Johnston, H. and Klandermans, B. (eds) (1995) *Social Movements and Culture*, London: UCL Press.

Johnstone, C. (2000) 'Housing and class struggle in post war Glasgow', in M. Lavalette and G. Mooney (eds) *Class Struggle and Social Welfare*, London: Routledge, pp 139-54.

Johnstone, C. and Mooney, G. (2007) '"Problem" people, "problem" places? New Labour and council estates', in R. Atkinson and G. Helms (eds) *Securing An Urban Renaissance*, Bristol: The Policy Press, pp 125-39.

Jordan, B. (1999) 'Collective action and everyday resistance', in R. van Berkel, H. Coenen and R. Vlek (eds) *Beyond Marginality: Social Movements of Social Security Claimants in the European Union*, Aldershot: Ashgate, pp 202-19.

Kelleher, D. (1994) 'Self-help groups and medicine', in J. Gabe, D. Kelleher and G. Williams (eds) *Challenging Medicine*, London: Routledge, pp 104-17.

Kelleher, D., Gabe, J. and Williams, G. (1994) 'Understanding medical dominance in the modern world', in J. Gabe, D. Kelleher and G. Williams (eds) *Challenging Medicine*, London: Routledge, pp x-xxviii.

Kellner, D. (2003) 'Globalisation, technopolitics, and revolution', in J. Foran (ed) *The Future of Revolutions: Rethinking Radical Change in the Age of Globalization*, London: Zed Books, pp 180-94.

Kenny, M. (1995) *The First New Left: British Intellectuals After Stalin*, London: Lawrence & Wishart.

Kettle, M. and Hodges, L. (1982) *Uprising: The Police, The People and the Riots in Britain's Cities*, London: Pan Books.

Keynes, J.-M. (1936) *General Theory of Employment Interest and Money*, New York, NJ: Harvest Books (1964).

Khagram, S., Riker, J. V. and Sikkink, K. (eds) (2002) *Restructuring World Politics: Transnational Social Movements, Networks and Norms*, Minneapolis, MN: University of Minnesota Press.

King, E. (1993) *Safety in Numbers*, London: Cassells.

Kingsford, P. (1982) *The Hunger Marches in Britain, 1920-1939*, London: Lawrence & Wishart.

Klandermans, B. (1984) 'Mobilization and participation: social-psychological expansion of resource mobilization theory', *American Sociological Review*, 49 (October): 583-600.

Klandermans, B. (1992) 'The social construction of protest and multiorganizational fields', in A.D. Morris and C.M. Mueller (eds) *Frontiers in Social Movement Theory*, New Haven, CT: Yale University Press, pp 77-103.

Klandermans, B., Kriesi, H. and Tarrow, S. (eds) (1988) *From Structure to Action*, New York, NY: JAI Press.

Klein, N. (2000) *No Logo*, London: Flamingo.

Klein, N. (2001) 'Reclaiming the Commons', *New Left Review*, 9: 81-9.

Klein, N. (2002) *Fences and Windows*, London: Flamingo.

Klein, R. (2001) *The New Politics of the NHS*, Harlow: Pearson.

Knott, J. (1986) *Popular Opposition to the 1834 Poor Law*, London: Palgrave Macmillan.

Kolker, E. (2004) 'Framing as a cultural resource in health social movements: funding activism and the breast cancer movement in the US 1990-1993', *Sociology of Health & Illness*, 26 (6): 820-44.

Kornhauser, A. (1959) *The Politics of Mass Society*, New York, NY: Free Press.

Kouvelakis, S. (2006) 'France: from revolt to the alternative', *International Socialist Tendency Discussion Bulletin*, 8: 3-11, www.istendency.net/pdf/IST_Discussion_Bulletin_8.pdf

Kundnani, A. (2007) 'Integrationism: the politics of anti-Muslim racism', *Race & Class*, 48 (4): 24-44.

Kynaston, D. (2007) *Austerity Britain 1945-51*, London: Bloomsbury.

Laclau, E. and Mouffe, C. (1985) *Hegemony and Socialist Strategy: Towards a Radical Democratic Politics*, London: Verso.

Laing, A. (1995) 'Beginning of the bitter end', *The Herald*, 7 January.

Lake, R.W. (2006) 'Recentering the city', *International Journal of Urban and Regional Research*, 30 (1): 194-7.

Land, V. and Kitzinger, C. (2007) 'Contesting same-sex marriage in talk-in-interaction', *Feminism Psychology*, 17 (2): 173-83.

Laughlin, S. (1998) 'From theory to practice: the Glasgow experience', in L. Doyal (ed) *Women and Health Services*, Buckingham: Open University Press, pp 221-37.

Lavalette, M. and Mooney, G. (eds) (2000) *Class Struggle and Social Welfare*, London: Routledge.

Law, A. (2008) 'The elixir of social trust: social capital and cultures of challenge in health movements', in J. Brownlie, A. Greene and A. Howson (eds) *Researching Trust and Health*, New York, NY, and Abingdon: Routledge.

Law, A. and McNeish, W. (2007) 'Contesting the irrational actor model: a case study of mobile phone mast protest', *Sociology*, 41 (3): 439-56.

Law, A. and Mooney, G. (2005) 'Urban landscapes', *International Socialism Journal*, 106: 89-101.

Law, I. (1999) 'Modernity, anti-racism and ethnic managerialism', in P. Bagguley and J. Hearn (eds) *Transforming Politics: Power and Resistance*, Basingstoke: Macmillan, pp 206-28.

Lawrence, E. and Turner, N. (1999) 'Social movements and equal opportunities work', in P. Bagguley and J. Hearn (eds) *Transforming Politics: Power and Resistance*, Basingstoke: Macmillan, pp 183-205.

Le Bon, G. (1995) *The Crowd*, New Brunswick, NJ: Transaction Publishers.

Lefebvre, H. (1968/1996) 'The right to the city', in *Writings on Cities*, Oxford: Blackwell, pp 63-184.

Lenin, V.I. (1903) *What is to be Done?* Harmondsworth: Penguin (1989).

Leontidou, L. (2006) 'Urban social movements: from the 'right to the city' to transnational spatialities and Flaneur activists', *City*, 10 (3): 259-68.

Lewis, G. (ed) (1998) *Forming Nation, Framing Welfare*, London: Routledge.

LEWRG (London Edinburgh Weekend Return Group) (1980) *In and Against the State*, London: Pluto.

Lijphart, A. (1977) *Democracy in Plural Societies: A Comparative Exploration*, New Haven, CT: Yale University Press.

Lister, R. (2008) 'Recognition and voice: the challenge for social justice', in G. Craig, T. Burchardt and D. Gordon (eds) *Social Justice and Public Policy: Seeking Fairness in Diverse Societies*, Bristol: The Policy Press, pp 105-22.

Lo, C. (1992) 'Communities of challengers in social movement theory', in A.D. Morris and C.M. Mueller (eds) *Frontiers in Social Movement Theory*, New Haven, CT: Yale University Press, pp 224-48.

Local Economy (2004) Special issue on cultural policy and urban regeneration, *Local Economy*, 19 (4).

Lovenduski, J. and Randall, V. (1993) *Contemporary Feminist Politics: Women and Power in Britain*, Oxford: Oxford University Press.

Lowe, R. (1988) *Education in the Post-War Years: A Social History*, London: Routledge.

Lowe, S. (1986) *Urban Social Movements*, London: Macmillan.

Lucas, I. (1998) *OutRage! An Oral History*, London: Cassell.

Lupton, D. (1999) *Risk*, London: Routledge.

Lyotard, J.F. (1984) *The Postmodern Condition*, Manchester: Manchester University Press.

McAdam, D. (1982) *Political Process and the Development of Black Insurgency, 1930-1970*, Chicago, IL: University of Chicago Press.

McAdam, D. (1996) 'Conceptual origins, current problems, future directions', in D. McAdam, J.D. McCarthy and M.N. Zald (eds) *Comparative Perspectives on Social Movements: Political Opportunities, Mobilizing Structures, and Cultural Framing*, Cambridge: Cambridge University Press, pp 23-40.

McAdam, D., McCarthy, J.D. and Zald, M.D. (1988) 'Social movements', in N.J. Smelser (ed) *Handbook of Sociology*, Newbury Park, CA: Sage Publications, pp 695-737.

McCarthy, J.D. and Zald, M.N. (1973) *The Trend of Social Movements in America: Professionalisation and Resource Mobilisation*, Morristown, New Jersey, NJ: General Learning Press.

McCarthy, J.D. and Zald, M.N. (1977) 'Resource mobilisation and social movements: a partial theory', American Journal of Sociology, 82 (6): 1212-41.

McClymont, K. and O'Hare, K. (2008) '"We're not NIMBYs!": contrasting local protest groups with idealised conceptions of sustainable communities', *Local Environment*, 13 (4): 321-35.

McCoy, L. (1998) 'Education for Labour: social problems of nationhood', in G. Lewis (ed) *Forming Nation, Framing Welfare*, London: Routledge, pp 93-138.

McCrae, M. (2003) *The National Health Service in Scotland: Origins and Ideals, 1900-1950*, East Linton: Tuckwell Press.

MacDonald, K. (2006) *Global Movements: Action and Culture*, Oxford: Blackwell.

MacDougall, I. (1990) *Voices from the Hunger Marches: Personal Recollections by Scottish Hunger Marchers of the 1920s and 1930s, Volume I*, Edinburgh: Polygon.

MacDougall, I. (1991) *Voices from the Hunger Marches: Personal Recollections by Scottish Hunger Marchers of the 1920s and 1930s, Volume II*, Edinburgh: Polygon.

Macintyre, S. (1980) *Little Moscows: Working Class Militancy in Interwar Britain*, London: Croom Helm.

Macintyre, S. (1986) *A Proletarian Science: Marxism in Britain, 1917-1933*, London: Lawrence & Wishart.

McKay, G. (ed) (1998) *DIY Culture: Party and Protest in Nineties Britain*, London: Verso.

McKee, L. and Bell, C. (1986) 'His unemployment, her problem: the domestic and martial consequences of male unemployment', in S. Allen, A. Watson, K. Purcell and S. Wood (eds) *The Experience of Unemployment*, Basingstoke: Macmillan.

McKenzie, J. (2001) *Changing Education: A Sociology of Education since 1944*, Harlow: Pearson.

McKie, L. and Cunningham-Burley, S. (eds) *Families in Society: Boundaries and Relationships*, Bristol: The Policy Press.

McKie, L., Cunningham-Burley, S. and McKendrick, J.H. (2005) 'Families and relationships: boundaries and bridges', in L. McKie and S. Cunningham-Burley (eds) *Families in Society: Boundaries and Relationships*, Bristol: The Policy Press, pp 3-18.

Macmillan, H. (1938) *The Middle Way*, London: Macmillan.

McNeish, W. (1999) 'Resisting colonisation: the politics of anti-roads protesting, in P. Bagguley and J. Hearn (eds) *Transforming Politics: Power and Resistance*, London: Macmillan, pp 67-86.

McNeish, W. (2000) 'The vitality of local protest: Alarm UK and the British anti-roads protest movement', in B. Seel, M. Patterson and B. Doherty (eds) *Direct Action in British Environmentalism*, London: Routledge, pp 183-98.

McShane, H. (1933) *Three Days that Shook Edinburgh: Story of the Thirties Scottish Hunger March*, Edinburgh: AK Press (1994).

McShane, H. and Smith, J. (1978) *No Mean Fighter*, London: Pluto Press.

Maffesoli, M. (1996) *The Time of the Tribes*, London: Sage Publications.

Maines R. (1999) *The Technology of Orgasm: Hysteria, the Vibrator & Women's Sexual Satisfaction*, Baltimore, MD: John Hopkins Press.

Marshall, J. (1983) 'The medical profession', in B. Galloway (ed) *Prejudice and Pride: Discrimination against Gay People in Modern Britain*, London: RKP, pp 165-93.

Marshall, T.H. (1950) 'Citizenship and social class', in T.H. Marshall and T. Bottomore (1992) *Citizenship and Social Class*, London: Pluto Press.

Marshall, T.H (1972) 'Value problems of welfare-capitalism', *Journal of Social Policy*, 1 (1): 18-32.

Marshall, T.H. and Bottomore, T. (1992) *Citizenship and Social Class*, London: Pluto Press.

Martin, G. (2001) 'Social movements, welfare and social policy: a critical analysis', Critical Social Policy, 21: 361-83.

Marx, K. (1976) *Capital: Critique of Political Economy, Volume 1*, Harmondsworth, Penguin.

Mason, D. (2000) *Race and Ethnicity in Modern Britain*, Oxford: Oxford University Press.

Mason, P. (2007) *Live Working or Die Fighting*, London: Harvill Secker.

Mayer, M. (1995) 'Social movement research in the United States: a European perspective', in S.M. Lyman (ed) *Social Movements: Critiques, Concepts, Case Studies*, London: Macmillan, pp 168-98.

Mayer, M. (2006) 'Manuel Castells' *The City and the Grassroots*', *International Journal of Urban and Regional Research*, 30 (1): 202-6.

Mayo, M. (2005) *Global Citizens*, London: Zed Books.

Melling, J. (1983) *Rent Strikes*, Edinburgh: Polygon.

Melucci, A. (1980) 'The new social movements: a theoretical approach', *Social Science Information*, 19 (2): 199-226.

Melucci, A. (1988) 'Getting involved: identity and mobilisation in social movements', in B. Klandermans, H. Kriesi S. Tarrow (eds) From Structure to Action, New York, NY: JAI Press, pp 329-48.

Melucci, A. (1989) *Nomads of the Present: Social Movements and Individual Needs in Contemporary Society*, London: Hutchinson Radius.

Merton, R.K. (1957) *Social Theory and Social Structure*, Glencoe, Ill: Free Press.

Miceli, M. (2005) 'Morality politics vs. identity politics: framing processes and competition among Christian Right and gay social movement organizations', *Sociological Forum*, 20 (4): 589-612.

Milanovic, B. (2005) *Worlds Apart: Measuring International and Global Inequality*, Princeton, NJ: Princeton University Press.

Milanovic, B. (2007) 'Globalisation and inequality', in D. Held and A. Kaya (eds) *Global Inequality*, Cambridge: Polity Press, pp 26-49.

Miles, R. and Phizacklea, A. (1979) 'Some introductory observations on race and politics in Britain', in R. Miles and A. Phizacklea (eds) *Racism and Political Action in Britain*, London: RKP, pp 1-27.

Miliband, R. (1972) *Parliamentary Socialism: A Study in the Politics of Labour*, London: Merlin Press.

Miller, B. (2006) 'Castells' *The City and the Grassroots*: 1983 and today', *International Journal of Urban and Regional Research*, 30 (1): 207-11.

Miller, D. and Dinan, W. (2008) *A Century of Spin*, London: Pluto.

Miller, F.M. (1979) 'The British unemployment assistance crisis of 1935', *Journal of Contemporary History*, 14: 329-52.

Mills, C.W. (1959) *The Sociological Imagination*, New York, NY: Oxford University Press.

Ministry of Health (1920) *Interim Report on the Future Provision of Medical and Allied Services* (Dawson Report), London: HMSO.

Ministry of Health (1944) *A National Health Service*, London: HMSO.

Ministry of Reconstruction (1944) *Employment Policy*, Cmnd 6527, London: HMSO.

Mishra, R. (1981) *Society and Social Policy: Theories and Practice of Welfare*, London: Macmillan.

Mol, A.P.J. and Sonnenfeld, D. (eds) (2001) *Ecological Modernisation Around the World: Perspectives and Critical Debates*, London: Routledge.

Monbiot, G. (2006) *How to Stop the Planet Burning*, London: Allen Lane.

Mooney, G. (2008) '"Problem" populations, "problem" places', in J. Newman and N. Yeates (eds) *Social Justice: Welfare Crime and Society*, Maidenhead: Open University Press, pp 97-128.

Mooney, G. and Fyfe, N. (2006) 'New Labour and community protests: the case of the Govanhill swimming pool campaign, Glasgow', *Local Economy*, 21 (2): 136-50.

Mooney, G. and Law, A. (eds) (2007) *New Labour/Hard Labour?*, Bristol: The Policy Press.

Mooney, G. and Neal, S. (eds) (2009) *Community: Welfare, Crime and Society*, Maidenhead: Open University Press.

Mooney, G. and Poole, L. (2005) 'Marginalised voices: resisting the privatisation of council housing in Glasgow', *Local Economy*, 20 (1): 27-39.

Moore, R. (2004) *Education and Society: Issues and Explanations in the Sociology of Education*, Cambridge: Polity Press.

Moore, S.E.H. (2008) 'Gender and the new paradigm of health', *Sociology Compass*, 2 (1): 268-80.

Morgen, S. (2002) *Into Our Own Hands: The Women's Health Movement in the United States, 1969-1990*, London: Rutgers University Press.

Mynott, E. (2002) 'From a shambles to a new apartheid: local authorities, dispersal and the struggle to defend asylum seekers', in S. Cohen, B. Humphries and E. Mynott (eds) *From Immigration Controls to Welfare Controls*, London: Routledge, pp 106-125

Neuwirth, R. (2006) *Shadow Cities*, London: Routledge.

Newman, J. and Yeates, N. (eds) (2008a) 'Making social justice: ideas, struggles and responses', in J. Newman and N. Yeates (eds) *Social Justice: Welfare, Crime and Society*, Maidenhead: Open University Press, pp 1-28.

Newman, J. and Yeates, N. (eds) (2008b) *Social Justice: Welfare, Crime and Society*, Maidenhead: Open University Press.

Norris, P. (2002) Democratic Phoenix, New York, NY: Cambridge University Press.

Nugent, N. and King, R. (1979) 'Ethnic minorities, scapegoating and the extreme Right', in R. Miles and A. Phizacklea (eds) *Racism and Political Action in Britain*, London: RKP, pp 28-49.

Oakley, A. (1993) *Essays on Women, Medicine and Health*, Edinburgh: Edinburgh University Press.

Offe, C. (1984) *Contradictions of the Welfare State*, London: Hutchinson.

Offe, C. (1985) *Disorganised Capitalism: Contemporary Transformations of Work and Politics*, Cambridge: Polity Press.

Olesen, V. and Lewin, E. (1985) 'Women, health and healing: a theoretical introduction', in E. Lewin and V. Olesen (eds) *Women, Health & Healing: Towards a New Perspective*, London: Tavistock, pp 1-24.

Oliver, M. (1990) *The Politics of Disablement*, Basingstoke: Macmillan.

Olson, M. (1965) *The Logic of Collective Action*, Cambridge: Harvard University Press.

Orwell, G. (1937) *The Road to Wigan Pier*, London: Book Club Associates (1981).

Pahl, J. (1979) 'Refuges for battered women: social provision or social movement?', *Nonprofit and Voluntary Sector Quarterly*, 8: 25-35.

Paine, T. (1791) *The Rights of* Man, available at www.ushistory.org/paine/rights/index.htm

Pakulski, J. (1995) 'Social movements and social class: the decline of the Marxist paradigm', in L. Maheu (ed) *Social Movements and Social Classes*, London: Sage Publications, pp 55-86.

Parekh, P. (2000) *Rethinking Multiculturalism: Cultural Diversity and Political Theory*, London: Palgrave Macmillan.

Parker, S. (2008) 'Will it really be that bad?', *Sunday Herald*, 26 October, pp 74-5.

Parkin, F. (1968) *Middle Class Radicalism*, Manchester: Manchester University Press.

Payne, S. (1998) '"Hit and miss": the success and failure of psychiatric services' in L. Doyal (ed) *Women and Health Services*, Buckingham: Open University Press, pp 83-99.

Pepper, D. (1996) *Modern Environmentalism: An Introduction*, London: Routledge.

Perry, M. (2000) *Bread and Work: Social Policy and the Experience of Unemployment, 1918-39*, London: Pluto Press.

Perry, M. (2005) *The Jarrow Crusade: Protest and Legend*, Houghton-le-Spring: Business Education Publishers.

Perry, M. (2007) *Prisoners of Want: The Experience and Protest of the Unemployed in France, 1921-45*, Aldershot: Ashgate.

PFS (Pollok Free State) (1994) *Passport and Declaration of Independence*, Campaign Leaflet.

Phillips, R. (2003) 'Education policy, comprehensive schooling and devolution in the disunited kingdom: a historical "home international" analysis', *Journal of Education Policy*, 18 (1): 1-17.

Pickvance, C. (2003) 'From urban social movements to urban movements: a review and introduction to a symposium on urban movements', *International Journal of Urban and Regional Research*, 27 (1): 102-9.

Piratin, P. (1978) *Our Flag Stays Red*, London: Lawrence & Wishart.

Pittas, G. (2009) 'Letter from Greece', *Socialist Review*, January.

Piven, F.F. and Cloward, R.A. (1979) *Poor People's Movements: Why they Succeed, How they Fail*, New York, NY: Pantheon Books.

Plummer, K. (1999) 'The lesbian and gay movement in Britain: schisms, solidarities, and social worlds', in B.D. Adam, J.W. Duyvendak and A. Krouwel (eds) *The Global Emergence of Gay and Lesbian Politics*, Philadelphia, PA: Temple University Press, pp 133-57.

Pogge, T. (2007) 'Why inequality matters', in D. Held and A. Kaya (eds) *Global Inequality*, Cambridge: Polity Press, pp 132-47.

Polanyi, K. (1944) *The Great Transformation: The Political and Economic Origins of Our Time*, Boston, MA: Beacon Press (2002).

Pollock, A.M. (2004) *NHS plc: The Privatisation of our Health Care*, London: Verso.

Porritt, J. (1996) 'Twyford Down – the aftermath', in B. Bryant (ed) *Twyford Down, Campaigning and Environmental Law*, London: Chapman and Hall, pp 297-310.

Portaliou, E. (2007) 'Anti-global movements reclaim the city', *City*, 11 (2): 165-75.

Potts, L. K. (2004) 'An epidemiology of women's lives: the environmental risk of breast cancer', *Critical Public Health*, 14 (2): 133-47.

Powell, F. (2007) *The Politics of Civil Society: Neoliberalism or Social Left?*, Bristol: The Policy Press.

Prempeh, E.O.K. (2007) *Against Global Capitalism*, Aldershot: Ashgate.

Pring, R. and Walford, G. (1997) *Affirming the Comprehensive Ideal*, London: Falmer Press.

Pugh, M. (2000) *Women and the Women's Movement in Britain*, London: Macmillan.

Purvis, J. (2005) 'Viewpoint: a lost dimension ? The political education of women in the suffragette movement in Edwardian Britain', in C. Skelton and B. Francis (eds) *A Feminist Critique of Education: 15 Years of Gender Education*, London: Routledge, pp 189-97.

Ramamurthy, A. (2006) 'The politics of Britain's Asian youth movement', *Race & Class*, 48 (2): 38-60.

Randall, V. (1987) *Women & Politics: An International Perspective*, Basingstoke: Macmillan.

Rawlinson, G. (1992) 'Mobilising the unemployed: the National Unemployed Workers' Movement in the West of Scotland', in R. Duncan and A. McIvor (eds) *Militant Workers: Labour and Class Conflict on the Clyde, 1900-1950: Essays in Honour of Harry McShane 1891-1988*, Edinburgh: John Donald.

Rayside, D. (2001) 'The structuring of sexual minority activists opportunities in the political mainstream: Britain, Canada, and the United States', in M. Blasius (ed) *Sexual Identities, Queer Politics*, Princeton, NJ: Princeton University Press, pp 23-55.

Regan, T. (2004) *The Case for Animal Rights*, Berkeley, CA: University of California Press.

Reiss, M. (2005) 'Forgotten pioneers of the national protest march: the National League of the Blind's marches to London, 1926 & 1936', *Labour History Review*, 70 (2): 133-65.

Report of the Committee on Homosexual Offences and Prostitution (Wolfenden Report) (1957), London: HMSO.

Report of the Royal Commission on National Health Insurance (1926), London: HMSO.

Rex, J. (1979) 'Black militancy and class conflict', in R. Miles and A. Phizacklea (eds) *Racism and Political Action in Britain*, London: RKP, pp 72-92.

Richards, A. (2002) *Mobilizing the Powerless: Collective Protest Action of the Unemployed in the Interwar Period*, Estudio Working Paper 2002/175, Madrid: Instituto Juan March de Edtudios e Investigaciones.

Richardson, D. (2000) 'Constructing sexual citizenship: theorising sexual rights', *Critical Social Policy* 20 (1), 105-35.

Ridge, T. and Wright, S. (eds) (2008) *Understanding Inequality, Poverty and Wealth*, Bristol: The Policy Press.

Robbins, G. (2002) 'Taking stock – regeneration programmes and social housing', *Local Economy*, 17 (4): 151-64.

Romalis, S. (1985) 'Struggle between providers and recipients', in E. Lewin and V. Olesen (eds) *Women, Health & Healing: Towards a New Perspective*, London: Tavistock, pp 174-208.

Rootes, C. (1992) 'The new politics and the new movements: accounting for British exceptionalism', *European Journal of Political Research*, 22: 171-92.

Rootes, C. (ed) (2003) *Environmental Protest in Western Europe*, Oxford: Oxford University Press.

Rootes, C. (2008) *1968 and the Environmental Movement in Europe*, Draft Version, accessed online at www.kent.ac.uk/sspssr/research/papers/rootes-1968-and-env-movements.pdf

Rose, H. (1990) 'Activists, gender and the community health movement', *Health Promotion International*, 5 (3): 209-18.

Rowell, A. (1996) *Green Backlash*, London: Routledge.

Ruane, S. (2004) 'UK anti-privatisation politics', in M.J. Todd and G. Taylor (eds) *Democracy and Participation: Popular Protest and New Social Movements*, London: Merlin Press, pp 158-75.

Ruane, S. (2007) 'Acts of distrust? Support workers' experiences in PFI hospital schemes', in G. Mooney and A. Law (eds) *New Labour/Hard Labour? Restructuring and Resistance Inside the Welfare Industry*, Bristol: The Policy Press.

Runciman, W.G. (1966) *Relative Deprivation and Social Justice: A Study of Attitudes to Social Inequality in Twentieth Century Britain*, London: Routledge & Kegan Paul.

Ryan, L. (2006) 'Rethinking social movement theories in the twenty-first century', Sociology, 40: 169-76.

SACTRA (Standing Advisory Committee for Trunk Road Assessment) (1994) *Trunk Roads and the Generation of Traffic*, London: Department for Transport.

Sadler, R. (2006) 'Roads to ruin', *The Guardian*, 13 December, www.guardian.co.uk/society/2006/dec/13/guardiansocietysupplement3

Sahlins, P. (2006) 'Civil unrest in the French suburbs, November 2005', *SSRC: Riots in France*, http://riotsfrance.ssrc.org/

Sales, R. (2002) 'The deserving and the undeserving? Refugees, asylum seekers and welfare in Britain', *Critical Social Policy*, 22 (3): 456-78.

Salter, B. and Tapper, T. (1981) *Education, Politics and the State: The Theory and Practice of Educational Change*, London: Grant McIntyre.

Sartre, J.P. (2004) *Critique of Dialectical Reason*, London: Verso.

Sassen, S. (2004) 'Local actors in global politics', *Current Sociology*, 52 (4): 649-70.

Saville, J. (1957-58) 'The welfare state: an historical approach', *The New Reasoner*, 3: 5-25.

Saville, J. (1987) *1848: The British State and the Chartist Movement*, Cambridge: Cambridge University Press.

Saville, J. (1990) *1848: The British State and the Chartist Movement*, Cambridge: Cambridge University Press.

Scarman, Rt. Hon. Lord (1981) *The Brixton Disorder 10-12 April, 1981 (the Scarman Report)*, London: HMSO.

Scott, A. (1990) *Ideology and the New Social Movements*, London: Unwin Hyman.

Scott, J.C. (1977) *Moral Economy of the Peasant: Rebellion and Subsistence in South East Asia*, New Haven and London: Yale University Press.

Scott, J.C. (1985) *Weapons of the Weak: Everyday Forms of Peasant Resistance*, New Haven and London: Yale University Press.

Scott, J.C. (1990) *Domination and the Arts of Resistance: Hidden Transcripts*, New Haven and London: Yale University Press.

Scrambler, G. and Kelleher, D. (2006) 'New social and health movements: issues of representation and change', *Critical Public Health*, 16 (3): 219-31.

Shakespeare, T. (1993) 'Disabled people's self-organisation: a new social movement?', *Disability & Society*, 8 (3): 249-64.

Sharp, I. (1998) 'Gender issues in the prevention of and treatment of coronary heart disease', in L. Doyal (ed) *Women and Health Services*, Buckingham: Open University Press, pp 100-12.

Shaver, S. (1994) 'Body rights, social rights and the liberal welfare state', *Critical Social Policy*, 13: 66-93.

Sherdian, T. (1997) Research interview, 18 January.

Simon, B. (1974) *Education and the Labour Movement 1870-1920*, London: Lawrence & Wishart.

Simon, B. (1997) 'A seismic change: process and interpretation', in R. Pring and Walford, G. (eds) *Affirming the Comprehensive Ideal*, London: Falmer Press, pp 13-28.

Sivanandan, A. (1982) *A Different Hunger: Writings on Black Resistance*, London: Pluto Press.

Sivanandan, A. (2006) 'Race, terror and civil society', *Race & Class*, 47 (3): 1-8.

Sked, A. and Cook, C. (1988) *Post-War Britain: A Political History*, London: Penguin.

Skelton, C. and Francis, B. (eds) (2005) *A Feminist Critique of Education: 15 Years of Gender Education*, London: Routledge.

Sklair, L. (2001) *The Transnational Capitalist Class*, Oxford: Blackwell.

Smelser, N. (1962) Theory of Collective Behaviour, New York, NY: The Free Press.

Smelser, N.J. (1988) (ed) *Handbook of Sociology*, Newbury Park : Sage.

Smith, A.M. (1994) *New Right Discourse on Race and Sexuality: Britain 1968-1990*, Cambridge: Cambridge University Press.

Smith, M. (2001) *An Ethics of Place: Radical Ecology, Postmodernity and Social Theory*, New York, NY: SUNY Press.

Smith, M. (2007) 'Framing same-sex marriage in Canada and the United States: Goodridge, Halperin and the national boundaries of political discourse', *Social and Legal Studies*, 16 (1): 5-26.

Smith, N. (2000) 'Global Seattle', *Society and Space*, 18: 1-5.

Smout, T.C. (ed) (2001) *Nature, Landscape and People since the Second World War*, Edinburgh: Tuckwell Press.

Snow, D. and Benford, R.D. (1992) 'Master frames and cycles of protest', in A.D. Morris and C.M. Mueller (eds) *Frontiers in Social Movement Theory*, New Haven, CT: Yale University Press, pp 133-55.

Snow, D.A., Rochford, E.B., Worden, S.K. and Benford, R.D. (1986) 'Frame alignment processes, micromobilization and movement participation', *American Sociological Review*, 51: 464-81.

Socialist Medical Association (1933) *A Socialized Medical Service*, London: SMA.

Somerville, J. (1997) 'Social movement theory, women and the question of interests', *Sociology*, 31 (4): 673-95.

SRC (Strathclyde Regional Council) (1988) *M77 Ayr Road Motorway: Report of the Public Local Inquiry*, Volume 1, official document.

St Clair, J. (1999) 'Seattle diary: it's a gas, gas, gas', *New Left Review*, 238: 81-98.

Stacey, M. (1985) 'Women and health: the United States and the United Kingdom compared', in E. Lewin and V. Olesen (eds) *Women, Health & Healing: Towards a New Perspective*, London: Tavistock, pp 270-303.

Stachura, P.D. (1986) 'The social and welfare implications of youth unemployment in Weimar Germany', in P.D. Stachura (ed) *Unemployment and the Great Depression in Weimar Germany*, London: Palgrave Macmillan.

Stevenson, J. and Cook, C. (1994) *Britain in Depression: Society and Politics, 1929-39*, London: Longmans.

Stewart, J. (1999) *The Battle for Health: A Political History of the Socialist Medical Association, 1930-51*, Aldershot: Ashgate.

Susser, I. (2006) 'Global visions and grassroots movements: an anthropological perspective', *International Journal of Urban and Regional Research*, 30 (1): 212-8.

Tarrow, S. (1989) *Democracy and Disorder*, Oxford: Oxford University Press.

Tarrow, S. (1994) *Power in Movement: Social Movements and Contentious Politics*, New York, NY: Cambridge University Press.

Tatchell, P. (1992) 'Equal rights for all: strategies for lesbian and gay equality in Britain', in K. Plummer (ed) *Modern Homosexualities: Fragments of Lesbian and Gay Experience*, London: Routledge, pp 237-47.

Taverne, D. (2005) *The March of Unreason: Science, Democracy and the New Fundamentalism*, Oxford: Oxford University Press.

Thane, P. (1982) *The Foundations of the Welfare State*, London: Longman.

Thomas, H. (1998) 'Reproductive health needs across the life span', in L. Doyal (ed) *Women and Health Services*, Buckingham: Open University Press, pp 39-53.

Thompson, B. (1994) *Softcore: Moral Crusades against Pornography in Britain and America*, London: Cassell.

Thompson, D. (1958) 'The welfare state', *The New Reasoner*, 4: 125-30.

Thompson, D. (1984) *The Chartists: Popular Politics in the Industrial Revolution*, London: Pantheon.

Thompson, E.P. (1970) *The Making of the English Working Class*, Harmondsworth: Penguin.

Thompson, E.P. (1991) *Customs in Common*, London: Merlin Press.

Tilly, C. (1978) *From Mobilisation to Revolution*, New York, NY: McGraw Hill.

Tilly, C. (1986) The Contentious French, Cambridge: Harvard University Press.

Tilly, C. (1995) *European Revolutions, 1492-1992*, London: Wiley-Blackwell.

Tilly, C. (2004) *Social Movements: 1768-2004*, Boulder, CO: Paradigm Publishers.

Timmins, N. (1995) *The Five Giants: A Biography of the Welfare State*, London: HarperCollins.

Tomlinson, S. (2005*) Education in a Post-Welfare Society*, London: Open University Press.

Touraine, A. (1974) *The Post-Industrial Society: Tomorrow's Social History, Classes, Conflicts and Culture in the Programmed Society*, London: Wildwood House.

Touraine, A. (1977) *The Self-Production of Society*, Chicago, IL: University of Chicago Press.

Turner, B.S. (1993) *Citizenship and Social Theory*, London: Sage.

UN-Habitat (2003) *The Challenge of Slums: Global Report on Human Settlements 2003*, Nairobi: UN-Habitat.

UN-Habitat (2006) *State of the World's Cities 2006/7: The Millennium Development Goals and Urban Sustainability: 30 years of Shaping the Habitat Agenda*, London: Earthscan.

United Nations (1987) *Our Common Future: Report of the World Commission on Environment and Development (Brundtlan Report)*, Oxford: Oxford University Press.

United Nations (1992) *Report of the United Nations Conference on Environment and Development*, New York, NY: United Nations, www.nssd.net/references/KeyDocs/IIEDa7.htm

Valocchi, S. (1990) 'The unemployed workers movement of the 1930s: a reexamination of the Piven and Cloward thesis', *Social Problems*, 37 (2): 191-205.

Wahlstrom, M. and Peterson, A. (2006) 'Between the state and the market: expanding the concept of "political opportunity structure"', Acta Sociologica, 49: 363-77.

Waites, M. (2003) 'Equality at last? Homosexuality, heterosexuality and the age of consent in the United Kingdom', *Sociology*, 37 (4): 637-55.

Waites, M. (2005) 'The fixity of sexual identities in the public sphere: biomedical knowledge, liberalism and the heterosexual/homosexual binary in late modernity', *Sexualities*, 8 (5): 539-69.

Walby, S. (1994) *Theorising Patriarchy*, Cambridge: Blackwell.

Wall, D. (1999) *Earth First! and the Anti-Roads Movement*, London: Routledge.

Ward, S.V. (1988) *The Geography of Interwar Britain: The State and Uneven Development*, London: Routledge.

Warnock, M. (1977) *Schools for Thought*, London: Faber.

Wasoff, F. and Cunningham-Burley, S. (2005) 'Perspectives on social policies and families', in L. McKie and S. Cunningham-Burley (eds) *Families in Society: Boundaries and Relationships*, Bristol: The Policy Press, pp 261-70.

Wasoff, F. and Dey (2000) *Family Policy*, Eastbourne: Gildredge Press.

Wasoff, F. and Hill, M. (2002) 'Family policy in Scotland', *Social Policy and Society*, 1 (3): 171-82.

Watt, P. (2008) '"Underclass" and "ordinary people" discourses: representing/re-presenting council tenants in a housing campaign', *Critical Discourse Studies*, 5 (4): 345-57.

Webber, F. (2001) 'The Human Rights Act: a weapon against racism', *Race & Class*, 43 (2): 77-94.

Webster, C. (2002) *The National Health Service: A Political History*, Oxford: Oxford University Press.

Wedderburn, D. (1965) 'Facts and theories of the welfare state', *The Socialist Register*, London: Merlin Press.

Weeks, J. (1989) *Sex, Politics & Society: The Regulation of Sexuality since 1800*, London: Longman.

White, R.G. (2001) 'The rise of the environmental movement 1970-1990', in T.C. Smout (ed) *Nature, Landscape and People since the Second World War*, Edinburgh: Tuckwell Press, pp 44-51.

Whitehead, M. (1991) 'The health divide', in P. Townsend, M. Whitehead and N. Davidson (eds) *Inequalities in Health*, Harmondsworth: Penguin, pp 219-437.

Whitehouse, M. (1985) *Mightier than the Sword*, Eastbourne: Kingsway.

Widgery, D. (1986) *Beating Time*, London: Chatto and Windus.

Wilkinson, E. (1939) *The Town that was Murdered: The Life-Story of Jarrow*, London: Victor Gollancz.

Wilkinson, R. and Pickett, K. (2009) *The Spirit Level*, London: Allen Lane.

Williams, F. (1989) *Social Policy: A Critical Introduction*, Oxford: Blackwell.

Williams, F. (1992) 'Somewhere over the rainbow: universality and diversity in social policy', in N. Manning and R. Page (eds) *Social Policy Review 4*, Canterbury: Social Policy Association, pp 200-19.

Williams, F. (2002) 'The presence of feminism in the future of welfare', *Economy and Society*, 31 (4): 502-19.

Williams, R. (1989) *Resources of Hope*, London Verso.

World Bank (2008) *World Bank Development Report 2008: Agriculture for Development*, Washington, DC: World Bank.

Worley, C. (2005) 'It's not about race, it's about the community: New Labour and community cohesion', *Critical Social Policy*, 25 (4): 483-96.

Yeates, N. (2002) 'The "anti-globalisation" movement and its implications for social policy', in R. Sykes, C. Bochel and N. Ellison (eds) *Social Policy Review 14*, Bristol: The Policy Press, pp 127-50.

Yeates, N. (2008a) Global inequality, poverty and wealth', in T. Ridge and S. Wright (eds) *Understanding Inequality, Poverty and Wealth*, Bristol: The Policy Press, pp 81-101.

Yeates, N. (2008b) 'The idea of global social policy', in N. Yeates (ed) *Understanding Global Social Policy*, Bristol: The Policy Press, pp 1-24.

Yeates, N. (ed) (2008c) *Understanding Global Social Policy*, Bristol: The Policy Press.

Young, I.M. (2008) 'Structural injustice and the politics of difference', in G. Craig, T. Burchardt and D. Gordon (eds) *Social Justice and Public Policy: Seeking Fairness in Diverse Societies*, Bristol: The Policy Press, pp 77-104.

Young, S.C. (2000) *The Emergence of Ecological Modernisation: Integrating the Environment and the Economy*, London: Routledge.

Zald, M.N. (1991) 'The continuing vitality of resource mobilisation theory: response to Herbert Kitschelt's critique', in D. Rucht (ed) *Research on Social Movements: The State of the Art in Western Europe and the USA*, Campus Verlag: Westview Press, pp 348-54.

Zald, M.N. (1992) 'Looking forward to look back – reflections on the past and future of the resource mobilisation research program', in A.D. Morris and C.M. Mueller (eds) *Frontiers in Social Movement Theory*, New Haven, CT, and London: Yale University Press, pp 326-48.

Zinn, H. (2001) *A People's History of the United States, 1492-Present*, New York, NY: Perennial Classics.

Zolberg, A.R. (1972) 'Moments of madness', *Politics and Society*, 2: 183-207.

Index

Page references for notes are followed by n